T0135811

# Data Compression for Computational Fluid Dynamics on Irregular Grids

Inaugural-Dissertation

zur

Erlangung des Doktorgrades

der Mathematisch-Naturwissenschaftlichen Fakultät

der Universität zu Köln

vorgelegt von

Matthias Rettenmeier

aus Heidelberg

Köln

2012

Berichterstatter:  Prof. Dr. Ulrich Trottenberg

Prof. Dr. Caren Tischendorf

Tag der mündlichen Prüfung: 05.04.2012

Bibliografische Information der Deutschen Nationalbibliothek

Die Deutsche Nationalbibliothek verzeichnet diese Publikation in der
Deutschen Nationalbibliografie; detaillierte bibliografische Daten sind
im Internet über http://dnb.d-nb.de abrufbar.

ISBN 978-3-8325-3241-3

Logos Verlag Berlin GmbH
Comeniushof, Gubener Str. 47,
10243 Berlin
Tel.: +49 (0)30 42 85 10 90
Fax: +49 (0)30 42 85 10 92
INTERNET: http://www.logos-verlag.de

# Zusammenfassung

In der vorliegenden Arbeit werden zwei Methoden zur Kompression von numerischen Daten auf unregelmäßigen Gittern vorgestellt. Sie zeichnen sich dadurch aus, dass sie sich für Daten auf Gittern, die aus Zellen verschiedenen Typs bestehen, eignen. Derartige Gitter werden häufig im Bereich der numerischen Strömungsmechanik verwendet. Beide Methoden basieren auf demselben verlustbehafteten Kompressionsschema und unterscheiden sich in den Dekorrelationstechniken. Während eine der Methoden auf einer Vorhersage beruht, führt die andere eine Transformation zur Dekorrelation durch. Beide Methoden werden anhand von Simulationsdaten und der numerischen Strömungsmechanik ausgewertet und verglichen. Für die Evaluierung sind vor allem Kompressionsfaktor und Kompressionsgeschwindigkeit von Bedeutung. Es wurden mit beiden Methoden gute Kompressionsfaktoren erzielt, wobei mit dem Vorhersageverfahren ein wesentlich höherer Datendurchsatz erreicht wurde.

# Abstract

Two methods are presented for the compression of numerical data on irregular volumetric grids. They have the feature to be applicable to data on grids with non-unique cell types, as they are often used for computational fluid dynamics (CFD) simulations. Both methods are based on the same general lossy compression scheme and differ from each other in the decorrelation techniques that are applied. One of the two follows a prediction scheme, while the other is based on a transformation method. Both methods are evaluated on the basis of CFD data and compared in regard to compression and performance measures. It is shown that both methods yield good compression results, while the prediction-based method achieves a significantly higher data throughput.

# Contents

**1  Introduction**                                                       **1**

  1.1  Outline . . . . . . . . . . . . . . . . . . . . . . . . . . . . . . . . . .   4

**2  Data Compression**                                                   **7**

  2.1  Computational Fluid Dynamics . . . . . . . . . . . . . . . . . . . . .   7

     2.1.1  Grids . . . . . . . . . . . . . . . . . . . . . . . . . . . . . . .  13

        2.1.1.1  Terminology . . . . . . . . . . . . . . . . . . . . . . .  14

        2.1.1.2  Grid Representations . . . . . . . . . . . . . . . . . .  16

     2.1.2  File Content . . . . . . . . . . . . . . . . . . . . . . . . . . .  17

  2.2  Main Concepts of Data Compression . . . . . . . . . . . . . . . . . .  18

     2.2.1  Encoding . . . . . . . . . . . . . . . . . . . . . . . . . . . . .  18

     2.2.2  Preprocessing . . . . . . . . . . . . . . . . . . . . . . . . . .  20

     2.2.3  Quantization . . . . . . . . . . . . . . . . . . . . . . . . . . .  21

  2.3  Compression Approach for CFD . . . . . . . . . . . . . . . . . . . .  22

  2.4  Measures . . . . . . . . . . . . . . . . . . . . . . . . . . . . . . . . .  25

  2.5  Related Work . . . . . . . . . . . . . . . . . . . . . . . . . . . . . . .  26

**3  Tree Predictor**                                                     **33**

  3.1  Graphs . . . . . . . . . . . . . . . . . . . . . . . . . . . . . . . . . .  34

  3.2  Spanning Tree Predictor . . . . . . . . . . . . . . . . . . . . . . . . .  36

  3.3  Optimization . . . . . . . . . . . . . . . . . . . . . . . . . . . . . . .  38

     3.3.1  Distance-based Optimization . . . . . . . . . . . . . . . . . .  39

     3.3.2  Gradient-based Optimization . . . . . . . . . . . . . . . . . .  40

     3.3.3  Dynamics-based Optimization . . . . . . . . . . . . . . . . . .  42

     3.3.4  Optimization for Transient Solutions . . . . . . . . . . . . . .  44

     3.3.5  Storing Trees . . . . . . . . . . . . . . . . . . . . . . . . . . .  46

**4 Wavelet Compression** **49**

4.1 Multiresolution Analysis and Wavelets . . . . . . . . . . . . . . . . . . . . 50

4.2 The Lifting Scheme . . . . . . . . . . . . . . . . . . . . . . . . . . . . . . 55

4.3 The Transformation . . . . . . . . . . . . . . . . . . . . . . . . . . . . . . 58

    4.3.1 Algebraic Multigrid . . . . . . . . . . . . . . . . . . . . . . . . . . 60

    4.3.2 Operators . . . . . . . . . . . . . . . . . . . . . . . . . . . . . . . . 64

    4.3.3 Splitting . . . . . . . . . . . . . . . . . . . . . . . . . . . . . . . . . 65

    4.3.4 Prediction . . . . . . . . . . . . . . . . . . . . . . . . . . . . . . . . 67

    4.3.5 Update . . . . . . . . . . . . . . . . . . . . . . . . . . . . . . . . . 68

    4.3.6 Remarks . . . . . . . . . . . . . . . . . . . . . . . . . . . . . . . . . 70

        4.3.6.1 Operators and Interpolation . . . . . . . . . . . . . . . . 70

        4.3.6.2 Lossless Compression . . . . . . . . . . . . . . . . . . . . 71

**5 Evaluation** **73**

5.1 Simple Compressor . . . . . . . . . . . . . . . . . . . . . . . . . . . . . . 75

    5.1.1 Performance and Memory Requirements . . . . . . . . . . . . . . . 76

5.2 Tree Compressor . . . . . . . . . . . . . . . . . . . . . . . . . . . . . . . . 76

    5.2.1 Optimized Tree Compressor . . . . . . . . . . . . . . . . . . . . . . 78

    5.2.2 Weighting for Time Series . . . . . . . . . . . . . . . . . . . . . . . 85

    5.2.3 Performance and Memory Requirements . . . . . . . . . . . . . . . 86

5.3 Wavelet Compression . . . . . . . . . . . . . . . . . . . . . . . . . . . . . 89

    5.3.1 Performance and Memory Requirements . . . . . . . . . . . . . . . 92

**6 Discussion** **95**

**7 Summary and Conclusions** **103**

**Bibliography** **105**

**A Appendix** **111**

A.1 Test Cases . . . . . . . . . . . . . . . . . . . . . . . . . . . . . . . . . . . 112

A.2 Compression Factors Simple Compressor . . . . . . . . . . . . . . . . . . 121

A.3 Compression Factors Tree Predictor . . . . . . . . . . . . . . . . . . . . . 123

A.3.1   Unweighted Approach . . . . . . . . . . . . . . . . . . . . . 123

A.3.2   Distance-based Optimization . . . . . . . . . . . . . . . . . . 125

A.3.3   Gradient Optimization . . . . . . . . . . . . . . . . . . . . . . 127

A.3.4   Full Weighting . . . . . . . . . . . . . . . . . . . . . . . . . . 144

A.3.5   Motion of Flow Weighting . . . . . . . . . . . . . . . . . . . . 146

A.3.6   Motion of Flow Weighting Orthogonal . . . . . . . . . . . . . 148

A.4   Compression Factors Wavelet Compression . . . . . . . . . . . . . . 150

A.4.1   Graph Laplace Operator . . . . . . . . . . . . . . . . . . . . . 150

A.4.2   Distance-based Operator . . . . . . . . . . . . . . . . . . . . . 163

# 1  Introduction

In 2005 the Airbus A380 made its maiden flight. It replaced the Boing 747 after more than 30 years as the largest passenger airliner in the world. The decision to build the A380 was made in the early 1990s, when studies by Airbus revealed the need for an aircraft that had greater passenger capacity, longer reach, less fuel consumption and would be less noisy than the Boing 747. To achieve these goals while meeting the requirements to operate within todays airport infrastructures several design challenges had to be met. This meant the airplane had to take-off/land on existing runways, had to fit in an envelope of 80 m x 80 m x 80 ft and had to use existing supporting ground structure. When Airbus started the development on the A380 in the mid-1990s, it was already clear that it would require significant innovations in almost all areas of design to build an airliner that satisfies those needs. To achieve such innovations in the given time frame for developement, the reduction of development time through more efficient processes became the evolving strategy of the aerodynamics group. They found the key to get there in cutting back on wind tunnel experiments and complementing those by an increased use of *computational fluid dynamics* (CFD) simulations [21].

Projects like the above emphasize the importance that computer simulation has reached and, suggest that such developments can benefit from computer-aided engineering. Rather than only learning from real-life experiments to improve a product during development, the use of computer simulations helps to understand and optimize the product prior to the experimental process. Simulating multiple configurations, designs and situations can be done in significantly less time and at lower cost than the corresponding experiments. For example, simulations of airflows around differently shaped airplanes can be done much more economically than building a new airplane model for every design change. Thus, it has often been tried to minimize the number of experiments. In some cases simulations are accurate enough, so that experiments are only used to validate simulation results. Nevertheless, there are still many uncertainties that disqualify computer simulation as being the sole technique for design verification. Especially in the field of fluid dynamics it is far from reaching such status and even remains questionable if it ever will. For example, flow turbulences, in particular for flows with high Reynolds numbers, are still not understood well enough to be simulated with reliable results. Still the experimental process cannot be completely replaced. However, fundamental design decisions can be made upon simulation results prior to experiments allowing a faster and more optimal development. This is a reason why industry has embraced this technology so rapidly.

Computer simulations use mathematical models that are derived from physical laws that can be described by partial differential equations (PDEs). Depending on the complexity of the model more or less physical variables and relations are taken into account. To simulate the model one must discretize and linearize the PDEs and solve the resulting system of linear equations. The complexity of the resulting system of linear equations depends on the intricacy of the model and the granularity of the discretization. In today's simulations these equation systems usually have millions of unknowns and thus require a considerable amount of computing power to be solved.

In the context of CFD the complexity of the model strongly depends on the purpose of the simulation and the computer resources available. In general, simulations require a considerable amount of time and computing power. Therefore, models have to be carefully selected in respect to the problem and the time necessary for their simulation. For example, for flows for which friction can be neglected one would select a model based on the Euler equations. They are a simplification of the much more complex and otherwise used Navier-Stokes equations. On the other hand, if the flows also involve other phenomena like turbulence or chemical reactions, the calculations can become extremely time-consuming. This also has to do with the fact that the discretization granularity often has to be very fine to simulate some of these phenomena correctly. In general, the trend goes towards finer discretization to achieve higher accuracy. However, this can only be accomplished as long as computer systems have enough computing power and memory resources.

While computing power and memory are factors for the simulation itself, storage and data transfer become an obstacle for handling solution data. Today, the amount of solution data generated by a single simulation can often reach sizes of tens of gigabytes (GB), and in some cases even hundreds of GBs or terabytes (TB). Although the capacity of hard disk drives has exponentially grown from about 3 GB in 1995 to 3 TB in 2010, storage limitations still remain a field of concern when archiving solution data of series of simulations. It is not uncommon to host computer clusters or supercomputers and large storage systems in data centers in an effort to meet requirements for computational power and storage. As a result, large amounts of data have to be transmitted via computer networks to the workstation of the engineer for review and post-processing analysis. This is a time-consuming and expensive task. Data compression seems to be the solution to this problem. Yet, there have been hardly any serious approaches to compress result files from CFD simulations.

Today, data compression is used in a broad variety of applications. Most commonly, it is applied in the field of multimedia. The digitalization of photos, videos and music pieces helped data compression to achieve a breakthrough. Consequently, nearly every video or image file is stored in a compressed file format. For distribution of digital content it has even become vital to use compressed formats. Especially Internet content has profited from data compression, turning the Internet into a distribution channel for medial content. Presumably the Internet could only have developed into such a media platform because of data compression. This is true for other distribution channels as well. The DVD or BluRay standards also incorporate compression techniques necessary to fit the data on the optical discs and to enable a fluent playback.

The situation is somewhat different for result files from numerical simulations. Data compression for simulation results does not receive the same attention. The number of numerical simulations has gained significantly in recent years, producing tremendous amounts of data. Yet only general-purpose compression tools are used in many simulation disciplines. One exception is a compression tool for data from structural mechanics simulations developed at the Fraunhofer Institute for Algorithms and Scientific Computing (SCAI). It is specialized on data resulting from crash and noise vibration harshness simulations. Since notable compression can be achieved with this tool, it is a way for companies to save money and time.

Despite the advantages, companies are only cautiously implementing data compression into their standard work flows. Potential data corruption and proprietary formats weigh heavily against possible savings. For CFD data compression might be more than just a way of saving money. Aeroacoustic simulations require a very high time step resolution to resolve the frequencies. For reasons of stability and accuracy the geometric resolution of the grid must also be very high. All in all, it leads to extremely high resolution simulations which generate extremely large result data. Result files can reach multiple terabytes. Thus, data compression may also become of vital importance in this field of research.

Several challenges have to be addressed when looking at techniques suitable for compressing CFD data. First, CFD data is often stored on three-dimensional volumetric grids used to discretize the 3D domain through which the flow passes. Since data compression development focuses mainly on multimedia applications, only very few compression algorithms compatible with these grids have been developed. Multimedia applications use 3D surface grids for 3D visualization instead. Several compression algorithms are known for these grids. In the case of structured 3D volumetric grids standard image compression algorithms can often be extended to fit the 3D data. Thus, there are numerous algorithms for structured grids available. This is not the case for unstructured volumetric grids. However, they are often used for CFD, because they can be created more easily by automatic grid generators. More detail on related work will be given in Section 2.5. Secondly, simulated physical variables comprise physical phenomena such as shocks, turbulences or chemical reactions. These often become apparent by locally strongly differentiating values, a characteristic that is not easily compressed and does not correspond to the often used concept of eliminating local correlations between neighboring values. High deviations bring about requirements for high quantization resolutions in order to be resolved accurately enough to meet the precision demanded by the user. Third, compression algorithms have to be memory-efficient to cope with the data packages resulting from simulations.

To meet these challenges two lossy compression algorithms for the compression of solution data on single-resolution irregular grids are presented. They are connectivity-/grid-based and specially designed for grids with cells of a non-uniform type. This differentiates them from most other algorithms for numerical data on grids. Although both algorithms share this attribute, they follow two different approaches to achieve good compression. In both cases a uniform quantization is performed prior to the compression core which is accountable for the generated loss, and an entropy encoder is applied for encoding.

The first algorithm uses a tree-based prediction scheme. Thereby prediction trees are used to describe the traversal order in which the prediction is carried out. At the same time they provide a mechanism to control the prediction, which can be exploited for optimizing the traversal order and thus achieving higher compression. Several possibilities for the optimization as well as their benefit are discussed herein. The tree predictor combined with the possibility of optimizing the tree creation process are a unique feature of this algorithm. Similar to other prediction schemes it achieves fast performance while maintaining a small memory footprint. Also, the optimization yielded improved compression factors making it a strong contender for application in industry.

As a second approach a wavelet-based transform is introduced. The algorithm is based on the lifting scheme, which provides a technique to create more generic wavelets. To be suitable for the above mentioned irregular grids, suitable splitting and filtering operations were required. For that, techniques derived from the multilevel concept of algebraic multigrid solvers were carried over and adapted to fit the compression scheme. In this process interpolation is used to decorrelate the data at 'fine'-levels, and a smoothing restriction operation is used to carry the values to a 'coarser' level. The same procedure is repeated there until a coarsest level is reached. While it achieves high compression factors, high memory consumption and slow performance are the drawbacks of this method.

The evaluation of the compression algorithms has shown that satisfactory compression factors can be achieved, as both methods improve upon standard compression schemes. Comparing the two, the wavelet compression generally achieves better compression factors. For certain optimization approaches this advantage can be significantly reduced by optimization of the tree predictor, but cannot be matched consistently. The advantage in terms of compression factor comes at the cost of more expansive calculations and memory requirements. Especially with extremely large result data, this becomes a vital point to be considered.

## 1.1   Outline

This thesis is split up into 6 chapters. A short overview of standard approaches to data compression is given in Chapter 2. All utilities for the compression are pointed out and some are described in greater detail. In particular, the idea that leads to the presented schemes is outlined. After the general introduction into data compression related work is listed and described. The last section of this chapter describes the CFD data that is compressed and the general scheme utilized for compression. At its core lies the compression mechanism for which two different techniques are proposed in this thesis. Details of the compression algorithms are given in Chapter 3 and 4.

Chapter 3 introduces the tree predictor. In addition to the general functionality the concept of optimization is brought forward. Various possibilities to enhance the prediction are outlined. Chapter 4 then describes the wavelet compression approach. There, a short introduction to the concept of wavelets and of the lifting scheme is given. It is shown how these concepts are carried over to an irregular setting.

Chapter 5 comprises the evaluation of both methods and of a standard compression scheme that is used as reference. Based upon these results the two schemes are compared and discussed in Chapter 6. Finally, a conclusion is drawn in Chapter 7.

# 2 Data Compression

Currently, data compression is utilized in a great variety of applications and devices. It is employed when storing digital movies on DVDs or BluRays, taking pictures with digital cameras and transmitting speech across telecommunication networks. In addition, data generated in scientific and industrial research is being compressed more often. For most applications specially designed compression algorithms are employed. They are based on different techniques to acquire the most compact representation of given data. Despite their diversity they often share similar basic principles. The main concepts and fundamental ideas for the compression of numerical data will be described in this chapter. This includes some important insights from information theory and the explanation for the basic setup of the compression schemes introduced in this thesis. Some of their components as well as measures used to evaluate them are presented as well. State-of-the-art approaches relevant to the compression of CFD data are given at the end of the chapter.

Before the focus of this chapter is directed towards data compression, the origin of the data that is to be compressed and the motivation of compressing it is described first. The following section contains a brief introduction to CFD in which the basics of fluid dynamics and components of CFD simulation are outlined. The basic approach for data compression in the context of CFD is highlighted and relevant components of CFD simulation are detailed. Descriptions of CFD are based on textbooks [3, 25].

## 2.1 Computational Fluid Dynamics

It is known from fluid dynamics that all fluid flows are governed by three fundamental physical principles: mass conservation, Newton's second law, and energy conservation. Their mathematical description is formulated in the continuity, momentum and energy equations, also referred to as the Navier-Stokes equations (Fig. 2.2). In this mathematical model of flow the fact that fluids consist of discrete molecules is neglected and are instead assumed to be continuous. This simplification makes it possible to simulate flows in that these equations are solved by using numerical methods. This is the subject of CFD.

To establish the Navier-Stokes equations a suitable model of the flow has to be found to which the physical principles can be applied. Mathematical equations that reflect the physical principles need to be extracted from this application. This leads to the Navier-Stokes equations. While these equations have been known for decades, they are extremely complicated, because they form a system of nonlinear partial differential equations. The nonlinearity of the equations reflects the existence of turbulence and shocks and is the reason for the possibility of multiple solutions. The equations become even more complex if other phenomena such as mass diffusion or combustion are also considered. As mathematical model essentially four possibilities can be used for this purpose, they are shown in Figure 2.1.

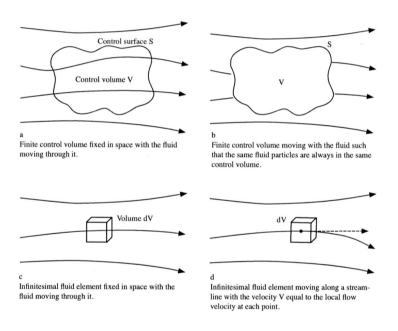

**Figure 2.1:** Different models of flow (modified from [3])

The first two models are based on the idea of observing a control volume to which the fundamental physical principles are applied. As a result, mathematical equations in integral form are obtained. If needed, these can be manipulated in order to obtain differential equations. There are two forms for these equations: a conservation and a non-conservation form. If the control volume is assumed to be fixed with the flow passing through the volume, the resulting equations are in conservation form. Otherwise, if the control volume moves with the flow, the equations are in non-conservation form. Both forms are mathematically equivalent, however, one or the other form is more convenient depending on the numerical method used to solve the equations. The second pair of models is based on the idea of an infinitesimal small fluid element. For these models partial differential equations are obtained directly. Again, depending on a fixed or moving perception, they are either in conservation or non-conservation form. All resulting systems of equations are equivalent independent of the choice of model.

Viscous flows are flows for which friction, thermal conduction, and/or mass diffusion are relevant. Following model c in Figure 2.1 and neglecting mass diffusion one obtains the following equations:

**Continuity equation:**

$$\frac{\partial \rho}{\partial t} + \nabla \cdot (\rho \mathbf{V}) = 0$$

**Momentum equations:**

$$\frac{\partial (\rho u)}{\partial t} + \nabla \cdot (\rho u \mathbf{V}) = -\frac{\partial p}{\partial x} + \frac{\partial \tau_{xx}}{\partial x} + \frac{\partial \tau_{yx}}{\partial y} + \frac{\partial \tau_{zx}}{\partial z} + \rho f_x$$

$$\frac{\partial (\rho v)}{\partial t} + \nabla \cdot (\rho v \mathbf{V}) = -\frac{\partial p}{\partial y} + \frac{\partial \tau_{xy}}{\partial x} + \frac{\partial \tau_{yy}}{\partial y} + \frac{\partial \tau_{zy}}{\partial z} + \rho f_y$$

$$\frac{\partial (\rho w)}{\partial t} + \nabla \cdot (\rho w \mathbf{V}) = -\frac{\partial p}{\partial z} + \frac{\partial \tau_{xz}}{\partial x} + \frac{\partial \tau_{yz}}{\partial y} + \frac{\partial \tau_{zz}}{\partial z} + \rho f_z$$

**Energy equation:**

$$\frac{\partial}{\partial t}\left[\rho\left(e + \frac{V^2}{2}\right)\right] + \nabla\left[\rho\left(e + \frac{V^2}{2}\right)\mathbf{V}\right] = \rho \dot{q}$$

$$+ \frac{\partial}{\partial x}\left(k\frac{\partial T}{\partial x}\right) + \frac{\partial}{\partial y}\left(k\frac{\partial T}{\partial y}\right) + \frac{\partial}{\partial z}\left(k\frac{\partial T}{\partial z}\right)$$

$$- \frac{\partial (up)}{\partial x} - \frac{\partial (vp)}{\partial y} - \frac{\partial (wp)}{\partial z}$$

$$+ \frac{\partial (u\tau_{xx})}{\partial x} + \frac{\partial (u\tau_{yx})}{\partial y} + \frac{\partial (u\tau_{zx})}{\partial z}$$

$$+ \frac{\partial (v\tau_{xy})}{\partial x} + \frac{\partial (v\tau_{yy})}{\partial y} + \frac{\partial (v\tau_{zy})}{\partial z}$$

$$+ \frac{\partial (w\tau_{xz})}{\partial x} + \frac{\partial (w\tau_{yz})}{\partial y} + \frac{\partial (w\tau_{zz})}{\partial z}$$

$$+ \rho \mathbf{f} \cdot \mathbf{V}$$

**Figure 2.2:** Conservation form of the Navier-Stokes equations [3]

In the equations above $\rho$ denotes density, $\mathbf{V}$ velocity, and $u$, $v$, $w$ the velocity components. The body forces that directly act on the volumetric mass of the fluid element are denoted by $\mathbf{f}$ with $f_x$ as its $x$ component. Surface forces that act directly on the surface of the fluid element are pressure $p$ and viscous forces. For the viscous forces, the normal stresses are denoted by $\tau_{xx}$ in the $x$ direction, where the shear stresses are denoted by $\tau_{xy}$ for the $xy$-plane. In the energy equation $\left(e + \frac{V^2}{2}\right)$ is the total energy, consisting of the internal energy $e$ and the kinetic energy $\frac{V^2}{2}$. Further, $\dot{q}$ denotes the heat flux, $\frac{\partial T}{\partial x}$ are local temperature gradients, and $k$ represents the thermal conductivity.

While the five equations above are the basis for the simulation of viscous flows, they count for six unknown variables: $\rho$, $p$, $u$, $v$, $w$, $e$. Consequently, additional physical relations or constants have to be known, as the system of differential equations is underdetermined. One possibility is to introduce a thermodynamical state, as it is often reasonable to assume a perfect gas. The equation of state for a perfect gas is

$$p = \rho R T$$

where $R$ denotes the specific gas constant. Since the temperature $T$ is another unknown that is introduced, a thermodynamical relation between state variables has to be specified as well. This relation would be $e = c_\nu T$ for a calorically perfect gas, where $c_\nu$ is the specific heat at constant volume [3].

Together with the definition of a domain in which the flow shall be simulated, the above equations and relations are the basis of a numerical simulation of a viscous flow. As mentioned before, these equations are the result of a model that neglects mass diffusion and thus, they cannot be used for chemically reacting fluids. Conservation equations for other constituents have to be taken into consideration for these fluids, too.

Another important aspect to consider for a CFD simulation has not been mentioned yet: Should a time-dependent or a steady state model be utilized as mathematical model? The choice is obvious for time-dependent problems with a transient flow. For steady state problems one can either work with a time-independent model or employ a so-called pseudo-unsteady model. The latter uses an unsteady formulation and follows the numerical solution in time until a steady state is reached.

The calculation of a numerical solution requires the discretization of the continuous model. This involves the discretization of the spatial domain and of the model equations. The discretization of the domain is accomplished by creating grids that define a tessellation of the domain. This process is one of the major parts of numerical simulation as the outcome and accuracy of the simulation strongly depends on the properties and quality of the grid. Consequently, for complicated domains grid generation can be very time-consuming. At designated data points on the grid the numerical values of the variable are approximated. Obviously, the quality of the approximation is directly related to the size of the grid. The closer the points on the grid lie by each other the better the continuum can be approximated. Grids employed for numerical simulations are treated in more detail in Section 2.1.1. Once the grid is obtained the continuous mathematical equations are transformed into discrete algebraic equations of the mesh-related unknowns. The most widely spread discretization method in CFD today is the finite volume method (FVM) [25]. Among other reasons, the ease of implementing it for arbitrary grids is one of its

**Figure 2.3:** Example of a flow around a flap

appealing features. Other methods are the finite difference method (FDM) and finite element method (FEM). The FDM is essentially only applicable to structured grids which limits the area of application. The FEM is extensively used in structural mechanics but not widely used in CFD. A distinction between the FVM and the other two methods is that it is based on cell-averaged values. The data points are associated with the cells of the mesh. In both other cases the space is discretized as local function values at mesh points, a property that also influences the compression scheme.

If the discretization method is selected and the numerical scheme is defined, the resulting algebraic system can be solved. For this purpose a numerical solver has to be selected. The choice of solver is strongly related to the problem at hand. In Chapter 4 algebraic multigrid (AMG) is briefly introduced. AMG is a class of algorithms suitable for numerically solving systems of linear equations and can also be applied in the context of CFD. For more detail on AMG and other solvers used in the context of CFD the reader is referred to [25, 65].

The solution of the algebraic equations yields a set of discrete values for each solution variable that approximates the solution of the PDEs over the domain. For grid sizes used in today's simulations this equates to millions of values for each variable. The obtained results are then analyzed in a final step, the graphic post-processing. It is used to interpret the physical properties of the obtained simulation results. The visualization of results of a transient simulation is shown in Figure 2.3. Such visualizations are made possible by powerful workstations.

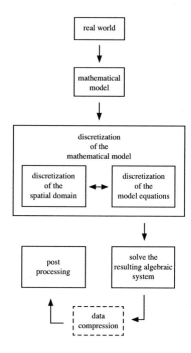

**Figure 2.4:** Components of a CFD simulation process, including a possible data compression step

Because of a large amount of result data generated by these simulations, it is suggestive to apply data compression in addition to the above mentioned components of a CFD simulation system. Prior to performing the post-processing the data can be compressed to reduce the data volume and to enable easier data handling (see Fig. 2.4). While the descriptions above outlines the necessary steps for CFD simulations, the individual numerical methods that are applied are of less concern to data compression. The most important aspect of numerical simulations in regard to data compression methods is the type of grid used. While the method employed to discretize the mathematical equations has some impact on the compression technique, this only concerns the location of the data points on the grid. Nevertheless, the structure of the grid determines which compression methods can be applied. Irregular grids are often used in the context of CFD, since they can be created more easily for complicated domains.

The compression methods presented here are specially designed for these grids and thus for practical use in the CFD context. Because of the importance of the grids in regard to the compression scheme, the following subsection is dedicated to grids. Various types of grids as well as the terminology used for their description are given.

## 2.1.1 Grids

Various types of grids are utilized depending on the simulation. Here, a short overview of grid types will be given with the intention to classify the examined compression schemes. This will be limited to the 3D case, since most CFD data results from simulations on 3D domains.

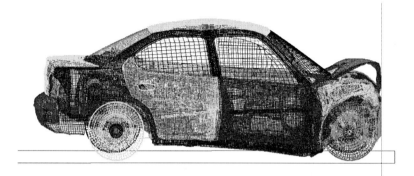

**Figure 2.5:** Unstructured, irregular grid around a car as used in car crash simulations (model data from [64])

Grids suitable for 3D domains are either surface or volumetric grids. Surface grids are used to represent 3D objects by modeling their 2D surface. Usually, the surfaces are tessellated by polygons of different shapes forming *unstructured, irregular surface grids*. The grid around a car shown in Figure 2.5 is an example thereof. It is taken from a crash simulation for which such grids are commonly used. In contrast to surface grids, volumetric grids model the entire volume of a 3D domain and are therefore used for CFD. Fluid flows are simulated on domains surrounding objects and lying in-between boundaries. The boundaries of volumetric grids describe the objects. Examples for volumetric grids are *Cartesian grids* and *boundary-fitted grids* which belong to the category of *regular grids*. While regular grids are numerically convenient, they are difficult to generate for complicated domains. Some relief can be found by employing *block-structured grids*. Instead of using one connected grid for the entire domain, the domain is divided into multiple parts for which a regular grid is created. Despite this possibility, generating high-density grids for 3D simulations can become very complex. In contrast thereto, irregular grids can be produced more easily by automatic grid generators and thus have been preferably implemented into many software packages. While some irregular grids consist of a unique cell type, for example tetrahedral grids, they are often composed of polygonal cells of arbitrary shape (Fig. 2.6). This poses a difficulty for most data compression methods. Regular grids on the other hand are more convenient in terms of data compression. Their regular structure can be exploited to achieve stronger compression factors. Nevertheless, this will not be done explicitly by the compression algorithms described herein. They are designed for irregular grids, and therefore do not exploit any regularity even when applied to regular grids. Two

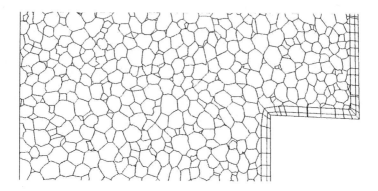

**Figure 2.6:** 2D slice of an unstructured grid with polyhedral cells

more variations of volumetric grids shall be mentioned here. First, moving grids used in transient simulations in which the domain changes over time. For example, such grids are necessary to model moving or deforming objects. There are two ways by which such time variations can be described. Sometimes assigning time-dependent coordinates is sufficient to model the alteration of the domain. If this is insufficient structural modifications have to be applied to the grid in order to mimic the behavior. Secondly, *self-adaptive grids* are utilized to automatically perform local refinements of the grid during the solution process. Thereby the spatial resolution of the discretization is increased depending on the behavior of the solution in an effort to locally enhance the accuracy of the solution. Automatic local refinement of the grid is an efficient alternative when trying to avoid inaccurate solutions compared to using overall finer grids. While both variations will not pose an immediate difficulty to the compression methods discussed here, some aspects might have to be considered. Particularly in the context of temporal compression time-varying grids can in some respects pose a problem. For disciplines such as aerodynamics and aeroacoustics for which data compression is particularly of interest, such grids do not seem to be used extensivly. For that reason only single-resolution meshes will be treated here. The concept of multiresolution grids is interesting for data compression as the hierarchy can be utilized by compression methods. For the complicated domains of CFD problems no natural hierarchy is given and it is difficult to create geometry-based hierarchical grids. The wavelet-based compression scheme that will be introduced in Chapter 4 uses techniques derived from AMG to create a hierarchy based on algebraic relations which can be exploited for compression.

### 2.1.1.1 Terminology

Two sets of information are required to fully define unstructured irregular volumetric grids. First, some spacing information has to be given in the form of coordinates, usually referred to as geometry. Secondly, information on how the grid is held together, which is called the topology of the grid, has to be provided. In order to describe the grids' topology the following elements are used:

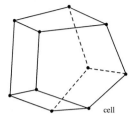 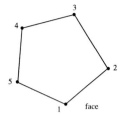

**Figure 2.7:** Cells and faces

### Vertices

Vertices represent locations in 3D space which are uniquely identified by their vertex ID. A coordinate vector is assigned to every vertex to locate its position.

### Faces

Faces are defined by ordered lists of vertices which are referred to by their vertex IDs. Two subsequent vertices in the order are connected by an edge. In addition, the direction of the face normal is defined, and often the faces are required to be convex. However, they usually don't have to be coplanar. There are two types of faces in a grid: inner and boundary faces. While inner faces connect two adjacent cells, boundary faces lie alongside the boundary of the domain. Each face is assigned a unique ID.

### Cells

Cells are specified by a list of faces which together form a polyhedron. Cells are usually required to be convex and their union has to cover the complete domain.

Several ways exist to fully describe the topology of a grid. The two most relevant formats for grid representations will be detailed in the following. Their layout is designed to serve two purposes. One the one hand, redundancy within the provided topology specification is avoided to be as storage-efficient as possible. On the other hand, designated information on the topology is explicitly given. For example, the connectivities between vertices of a cell could be given directly by the specific format, whereas adjacencies between cells would not be provided. They could still be determined by matching vertices of different faces, however, the reconstruction would be costly. Therefore, layouts are chosen according to the arrangement of data points during discretization. Data points can be assigned to vertices, faces or cells, and different data points can be used for different variables. In the context of CFD so-called *staggered grids* are often used, on which variables like pressure, temperature and others are placed on cells, while fluxes such as mass and heat fluxes are

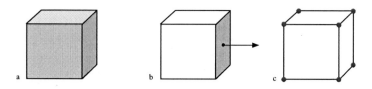

**Figure 2.8:** Illustration of data point locations on a 3D volumetric grid: (a) variable values are stored for the entire cell, (b) values are store on faces and (c) data points are located at the vertices of the grid.

assigned to faces. Adjacencies between cells have to be provided in that case. Illustrations of different data point locations are shown in Figure 2.8.

### 2.1.1.2   Grid Representations

#### *Face-based Representation*

In this representation the topology of the grid is described by its inner faces. Boundary faces are defined separately. Two lists of the same order are given, where the index induces the face IDs. In the first one every face is fully characterized by the number of vertices it consists of as well as by their IDs. The second one lists pairs of cell IDs. While the index in the list identifies the face, the pair identifies the cells that are connected by it. Thereby the topology of the grid is fully described.

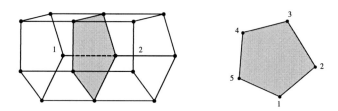

**Figure 2.9:** Face-based topology

#### *Connectivity-based Grid Representation*

Connectivity-based grid representations provide fast access to vertex connectivities. Every cell is defined by an ordered list of vertex IDs. The occurrence in the order determines the connectivities to other vertices in the cell. For each cell type this is predefined in the specifications of the file format. Usually lists of cell definitions are provided for every cell type separately. Examples of such allocations are illustrated in Figure 2.10. The reconstruction of the connectivities of all cells yields the complete set of vertex connectivities. Opposed to them, cell connectivities are only given implicitly and have to be identified by matching vertices of different cells.

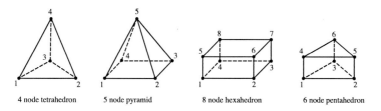

| 4 node tetrahedron | 5 node pyramid | 8 node hexahedron | 6 node pentahedron |

**Figure 2.10:** Vertex connectivities of cells of various types

## 2.1.2 File Content

CFD files consist of two main components: the grid and the solution variables. A grid is composed of two parts as described in the last section: its geometry and topology. Two formats in which grid topology can be stored were shown. The geometry is simply stored as a vector of vertex coordinates for each node in a floating point format. Both parts represent the geometry at a single state. This information is sufficient to represent the grid for steady state simulations. In the transient case there are three scenarios to store the grid information. If the geometry is steady, its topology and geometry has to be stored only once, analog to the steady state case. For simulations with moving grids, the movement can either only affect the geometry, or both geometry and topology. For transient geometry the vector of coordinates is simply stored for every time step, while the topology is stored only once. If the entire grid is affected, both parts have to be stored for every time step. This can cause the files to become extremely large.

Variables, such as pressure, density and velocity, are defined per vertex, face or element, which depends on the type of variable and on the discretization method. For each variable the solution values are usually stored in vectors of floating point values in either single or double precision. The length of the vectors is dependent on the variable type, as the number of vertex, faces and elements are different. In addition to the storage location, variables can either be scalars, vectors, tensors or complex-valued. For the last three types multiple values are stored for each data point. The order in which they appear and the way they are stored into the file is file format-specific. Potentially any variable used for the simulation can be stored, and it is up to the user to select the desired ones. In the case of steady state simulations only the final iteration is usually stored. For transient simulations a set of solution variables is stored for each time step. The frequency in which the variable are written to the output is also user-determined.

## 2.2   Main Concepts of Data Compression

Compression algorithms fall into two major categories: lossy and lossless compression. As stated by their names, lossless compression preserves all of the original data identically, whereas lossy compression does not. This disadvantage of lossy compression can be compensated in many applications by the significantly higher compression it can achieve. Furthermore, concepts like perceptive compression aim to bring the generated loss into a form that it is not or only barely noticeable by the user. For example, it is commonly applied to image and video compression. If the viewer cannot perceive every detail of the visualization, the original accuracy is no longer required. Details can be reduced or neglected in order to achieve higher compression. Perceptive compression is used in well-known standards such as JPEG, MPEG and MP3. Similar concepts can also be applied to scientific data. While the perception of the user is not a convenient measure to control the loss generated by a compression method designed for scientific applications, the accuracy of the approximation is a reasonable criterium and used instead. Reconstructed values after decompression then approximate the originals with the user-given precision. Often, the floating point precision used during simulation and with which the values are dumped to solution files is not required for post-processing analysis. It can therefore be reduced in favor of higher compression and is generally governed by the usage of the data.

Opposed to generic tools used for lossless compression such as gzip, bzip, bzip2, lossy compression requires an understanding of how the data is stored. Therefore, data formats in use have to be interpreted and data values have to be identified in order to be processed correctly. The interpretation of data formats is yet only a technical aspect which will not be discussed here any further. It will be assumed that the data has been read from the specific files and that data values are associated with data points on a grid.

Special purpose compression methods are commonly composed of two phases. The first phase consists of components which interpret data, identify relations and structures and use them to decorrelate the data. Procedures applied in this so-called preprocessing phase are usually based on mathematical methods and will make up the core of this thesis. The importance of decorrelating data will become evident when analyzing the second phase, the encoding phase. A more compact representation of the preprocessed data is formed during encoding, an essential part of data compression methods. Here, the preprocessing phase will be separated into decorrelation and quantization phases.

Since the reason for using a preprocessing phase is motivated by the limitations of encoding, this introduction will begin with a short description of the theory behind it. For more detailed descriptions the reader is referred to [48, 67].

### 2.2.1   Encoding

The term encoding is understood as entropy encoding or more precisely as

**Definition 2.1** *Let $\mathcal{X}$ and $\mathcal{Y}$ denote two alphabets. An **encoding** c is defined as a transformation*

$$c : \mathcal{X} \longrightarrow \mathcal{Y},$$

which assigns a **code word** $c(x) \in \mathcal{Y}$ to every value $x \in \mathcal{X}$. The set of code words are referred to as the **code**. If the mapping is injective, a unique inverse

$$c^{-1} : c(\mathcal{X}) \longrightarrow \mathcal{X},$$

the **decoding**, exists.

Concerning digital data, code words are a concatenation of many distinct binary values. The **length** $l(c(x))$ of a single code word is defined by the number of bits required for its binary representation. A compression is achieved when the binary representation of the original values can be transformed into a code word stream of shorter length. The goal is to find the shortest possible encoding. As one would expect, there is a limit for codes that are uniquely decodable. The limit can be described under certain constraints by using the entropy. This was first informally stated by Shannon's source coding theorem in [55].

**Definition 2.2** *[67] Let X denote a discrete random variable that takes values in a finite alphabet $\mathcal{X}$ and assume that $p(x)$ is the probability of $X = x$ for $x \in X$. Then the entropy of X is defined by*

$$H(X) := \sum_{x \in \mathcal{X}} p(x) \log_2 \frac{1}{p(x)}.$$

*In the case of $p(x) = 0$, $p(x) \log_2 \frac{1}{p(x)}$ will be defined as 0.*

The entropy quantifies the expected amount of the information contained in a message of values from a finite alphabet. It is noted that values are assumed to appear randomly, and thus no correlations within the message are known. The meaning of the entropy becomes evident when setting it in relation to the expected code word length of a code. This is possible for prefix codes.

**Definition 2.3** *[67] The **expected length** of a code c for a discrete random variable X is defined as*

$$E[l(c(X))] := \sum_{x \in \mathcal{X}} p(x) l(c(x)).$$

Prefix codes are codes that only consist of code words that are not prefix of any other code word. They have the important property of being uniquely decodable and hold the advantage of easily identifiable code words, a property which becomes useful when code words are stored consecutively as a stream. Since it is shown in [13] that every uniquely decodable code can be transformed into a prefix code without changing the code word length $l(x)$, $x \in \mathcal{X}$, there is no good reason to use codes other than prefix codes. For such codes the following theorems can be proven.

**Theorem 2.1** *[67] For any prefix code for a message that is encoded as a sequence of independent and identically distributed random values $x \in \mathcal{X}$,*

$$E[l(c(X))] \geq H(X).$$

**Theorem 2.2** *[67] For a message that is encoded as a sequence of independent and according to $\{p(x) : x \in \mathcal{X}\}$ distributed random variables $x \in \mathcal{X}$, there exists a prefix code $c$ that achieves*

$$\mathbf{E}[l(c(X))] < H(X) + 1.$$

Especially the statement of Theorem 2.1 is of great relevance, since it shows the limit of lossless entropy encoding. The second theorem shows that codes relatively close to the optimum exist. Altogether, they state that under the above assumptions a prefix code for a message with the entropy $H(X)$ exists, such that

$$H(X) \leq \mathbf{E}[l(c(X))] < H(X) + 1.$$

It is known that arithmetic and Huffman codes can be used to achieve optimal and near optimal results as shown in [44, 47]. In other words, there is no room for further improving the compression strength of entropy encoding. However, these results are based on the very broad assumption that one compresses identically distributed random variables. In general, this is not the case in the application of data compression. Virtually any type of data contains coherences between its values, regardless if it is image, text or numerical data derived from computer simulations. This can be exploited in an effort to reduce the entropy. Thus, a preprocessing step is applied in advance.

### 2.2.2   Preprocessing

Preprocessing is a very general term and can stand for a variety of approaches. They all share the common purpose of eliminating redundancy or of lowering the entropy. Here, preprocessing is understood to eliminate correlations from the data fields in order to lower the entropy. The motivation behind this idea can be illustrated by the following example.

**Example 2.2.1** *Assuming a message $m = (0, 1, ..., 15) \in \mathbb{N}^{16}$ of 16 values in increasing order is given. This message has the entropy*

$$\sum_{i=1}^{16} p(x_i) \log_2 \left( \frac{1}{p(x_i)} \right) = 4$$

*where $p(x_i) = \frac{1}{16}$ for $i = 1, .., 16$ denotes the relative frequency of all values $x_i$ in the message m. Consequently, optimal entropy encoding would result in a compressed stream of $16 \cdot 4 = 64$ bits. In a compression algorithm the order in which the values appear can be taken into account, and correlations between adjacent values can be removed. A preprocessing step can be utilized to transform the message m into a message $\tilde{m}$ of which the values indicate the increase over their predecessor:*

$$\tilde{m} = (0, 1, 1, ..., 1) \in \mathbb{N}^{16}.$$

*Since the original message can be easily reconstructed with the reverse transformation, no information is lost by this operation. Nevertheless, the entropy of $\widetilde{m}$ is only*

$$\frac{1}{16} \log_2(16) + \sum_{i=2}^{16} \frac{15}{16} \log_2 \left(\frac{16}{15}\right) \approx 1.5594.$$

*As a result of such a preprocessing, encoding the altered message $\widetilde{m}$ can be compressed to 25 bits only.*

As shown in the example, preprocessing can be used to reduce the entropy such that the data can be encoded more efficiently, and overall a higher compression can be achieved. While this looks very simple and efficient in the example above, there are two difficulties. First, one has to establish methods to identify and remove correlations from the data. For this to be profitable preprocessing methods have to be adjusted to the specific type and origin of data. Usually certain properties of the data are assumed on which the methods are then based on. The second difficulty arises when floating point data is to be compressed. While this approach works well for integer data, it is almost ineffective when applied to floating point values. The reason for that is that removing correlations from floating point values by differencing schemes does not lead to a clustering at a few values. Laxly speaking, the number of different floating point values remains roughly the same even if the range of values is reduced significantly. That poses the problem that the probability of matching values is extremely small. The entropy takes its maximum when every value in a message is unique.

**Theorem 2.3** *[67] If $X$ is a discrete random variable that takes values in a finite alphabet $\mathcal{X}$, then*

$$0 \leq H(X) \leq \log_2 \mathcal{X}.$$

*Furthermore, $H(X) = 0$ if and only if $p(x) = 1$ for some $x \in \mathcal{X}$, and $H(X) = \log_2(|\mathcal{X}|)$ if and only if $p(x) = \frac{1}{|X|}$ for all $x \in \mathcal{X}$.*

For integer values this relation is different. Since $\mathbb{Z}$ is closed in respect to addition and subtraction, the errors of a differencing scheme that is applied to integer values remain in $\mathbb{Z}$. Hence, if the resulting error values are small, the intended clustering is achieved since every closed interval in $\mathbb{Z}$ is finite. Presumably, a message with lower entropy is obtained when error values are small.

To efficiently compress floating point values quantization can be incorporated into the compression scheme. While therewith the described problem of compressing floating point values can be circumvented, a loss is introduced to the compression scheme.

### 2.2.3 Quantization

Quantization is a projection of a possibly infinite and continuous spectrum of values to a discrete set of values. For example, rounding real numbers to the nearest integer is a form of quantization. Functions used for quantization are in general not injective and therefore have no inverse. Quantization still consists of two operations. During compression a projection to a finite set of values is applied. A reverse transformation is used when decompressing the quantized data. The reversal cannot identically restore the values because the inverse of the projection does not exist. Thus, information is lost in the process leaving an error after reconstruction. The compression becomes lossy.

The generated loss or error of lossy compression is a characteristic by which the quality of the compression can be evaluated. Since the loss is taken in anticipation for higher compression, the quality of the compression becomes an important measure to compare lossy compression schemes. Depending on the application and requirements for the quality, various criteria for the judgment can be utilized.

## 2.3   Compression Approach for CFD

As described above CFD data consists of two major parts: grid data and variable data. In general both parts take up enough storage so that neither part should be left uncompressed by a compression tool built for practical use. Especially for result data obtained from steady state simulations the grid data usually cannot be left uncompressed if satisfactory compression results are aimed-at. More so this the case, if the grid data exceeds the variable data. This ratio between grid and variable data can be entirely different for results of transient simulations. For example, if constant grids are used much more variable data is generated as it has to be stored for multiple time steps, whereas the constant grid has to be stored only once. If the number of time steps is large enough, the grid data only accounts for a small fraction of the entire results. In some cases it can then even be irrelevant to compression. During development of a specialized compression tool these nexuses must be considered. While the content varies between simulations, example files from industry have indicated that variable data makes up the larger data volume. In other applications this is different, which can be noted from the composition of compression methods that will be provided in Section 2.5. Most compression techniques described there are designed to compress grid connectivity data. Those supporting the compression of variable data achieve this as a by-product of their grid compression technique. Grid compression is usually very assimilated to a certain type of grid and in many cases also limited to one. This in general does not include irregular grids with arbitrary or mixed cell types. Thus, they are often not suitable for the compression of CFD data on irregular grids. In addition, these methods might only achieve suboptimal compression for variable data as they are specialized for compressing grid data.

It is evident that grid compression is relevant for the data at hand. The representation above indicates, however, that little research has been dedicated to the compression of variable data. At the same time industry examples have shown that it accounts for the larger amount of result data. Therefore, the compression of variable data has been chosen as the subject of this research with the intention to establish independent and more efficient methods for compressing it. More precisely, they are designed to compress variable data stored on single-resolution irregular grids with non-unique cell types. This is the most general form of non-adaptive grids and thus especially suitable for the complex grids used in CFD applications, but also usable in many other applications.

Although transient simulations usually generate the most variable data, the research is not dedicated to temporal compression techniques. The presented methods are designed for static data, but can be easily combined with temporal compression schemes to enhance the overall compression for transient solution data. In [38] a variety of temporal compression schemes were analyzed and could be combined with the proposed methods. Additional methods are mentioned in 2.5. Also, it is common practice to reduce the overall data volume by not storing every time step of a transient simulation. This leads to less correlation between time steps and thus to a less effective temporal compression. While this does not mean that it should not be applied to transient data, the efficiency of compression methods for static data becomes more relevant.

The data to be compressed is assumed to be derived from CFD results as floating point values of either single or double precision. The complete compression scheme is illustrated in Figure 2.11.

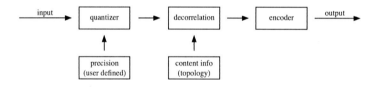

**Figure 2.11:** The general setup of the compression scheme used here consists of the three phases quantization, decorrelation and encoding

For the reasons mentioned above a quantization is used at first to map the floating point values to integer values. Of course, this step is only required if the data consists of floating point values and can be simply dropped from the compression setup otherwise. The utilized quantization is a uniform quantization. Uniform quantization means that the interval boundaries are uniformly spaced across a defined range. For this thesis the range was defined as the maximal range from the origin present in the data vectors of a variable and divided into $M$ intervals. For values $x_i$, $i = 1, \ldots, N$ of a variable vector, and their absolute maximum

$$x_{\max} = \max_i(|x_i|),$$

the step size of a $M$-Level quantization is given by

$$\Delta = \frac{x_{\max}}{M}.$$

Thus, the range $[-x_{\max}, x_{\max}]$ covering all $x_i$ is divided into $2M$ intervals. For an input value $x$ the corresponding quantization is then given by

$$Q(x_i) = \left[\frac{x_i}{\Delta}\right].$$

Here, $[\cdot]$ denotes rounding to the nearest integer value. Since the rounding cannot be undone, no inverse exists and for reconstruction only

$$\tilde{Q}^{-1}(y_i) = y_i \cdot \Delta$$

is applied, where $y_i = Q(x_i)$. If rounding to the next integer is used, the resulting absolute error is

$$d_\infty \leq \frac{\Delta}{2}.$$

The direct relation between the absolute error and the step size is a nice attribute of the uniform quantization. Instead of dividing the range of the variable values into a given number of intervals, a precision can be used to directly control the quantization. From the perspective of the user this is a much more tangible quantity to control. However, this only applies to the absolute error and is also one of the greatest weaknesses of uniform quantization. Since only the absolute error is controlled and the intervals are uniformly spread, variations smaller than the error are neglected. Furthermore, the same step size is applied to all data instead of adapting to the data.

After quantization, the variable data is processed by the compression core. It is provided with context information such as geometric and topological data of the grid as well as other data vectors from within the file. As pointed out before, the purpose is to lower the entropy of the present data. This part of the compression setup is subject to the research of this thesis. The two methods applied here are described in detail in Chapters 3 and 4.

While the above describes the origin of the data and the algorithmic setup of the compression scheme, for the mathematical model, however, the following will be considered here. It is assumed that the data values are values of a discrete function

$$f|_X : X \to \mathbb{R}, \quad X \subset \mathbb{R}^n$$

that approximates unknown continuous function $f : \mathbb{R}^n \to \mathbb{R}$ at discrete values $X = \{\mathbf{x}_1, \ldots, \mathbf{x}_N\}$. Here, $n \geq 1$ is the dimensionality of the Euclidean space $\mathbb{R}^n$. In addition it will be assumed that $f$ is a smooth function such that $f \in C^m(\mathbb{R})$ with $m \geq 1$.

In the context of CFD $f$ is a function describing a physical entity such as temperature, pressure or density. It is somewhat reasonable to assume that the functions are smooth so that nearby data points share similar values, or in other words, that the derivatives are small. If this is the case, estimates can be calculated by using neighboring data points in order to eliminate locally shared similarities. This is indicated by the Tayler expansion.

At last, the preprocessed data is encoded by means of an encoder based on the Rice code. Information about the Rice code can be found in [20] and a more detailed description of the utilized encoder can be found in [45]. Other encoders could be employed for this step as well. It is the preference of the author to use a rice encoder, as it has shown to be efficient when applied to simulation data.

For decompression the illustrated steps are performed in reverse order with their analog counterparts.

## 2.4 Measures

Three aspects are usually considered for the evaluation of compression algorithms. They are compression strength, speed of the algorithm, and quality of the reconstructed values after lossy compression. When seeking an optimum with all three aspects to acquire the best compression algorithm, one has to find a trade-off between them.

Compression strength is the most obvious of these aspects. It is commonly measured by the *compression factor* that is defined as

$$\text{compression factor} = \frac{\text{size of original stream}}{\text{size of compressed stream}}.$$

Alternatively, the inverse function, the *compression ratio*, can be used. In some cases the *compression rate* is used as comparison between algorithms. It is the average number of bits required to represent a single value instead of giving a relation between the size of the original and the compressed stream:

$$\text{compression rate} = \frac{\text{size of compressed stream in bits}}{\text{number of values}}.$$

Compression speed becomes an important gauge, when compression and/or decompression time is critical for the application. Often, compression as well as decompression speed are measured. They are calculated in regard to the size of the original or the decompressed data, respectively:

$$\text{de-/compression speed} = \frac{\text{size of original}}{\text{processing time of de-/compression}}.$$

In the case of lossy compression, quality loss, the third important aspect has to be taken into consideration. The acceptance of a loss may help to significantly raise the compression factor, however, it must be guaranteed that quality expectations of the user are met. In the data compression realm several measures are utilized for an objective quality comparison (see [48, 50]). For the compression of scientific data, such as data from numerical simulations, a tolerable limit for the compression error is usually given. This requires the maximum error

$$d_\infty = \|\mathbf{x} - \mathbf{y}\|_\infty$$

to be within the given limit. Here, $\mathbf{x}$ and $\mathbf{y}$ denotes the vector of source values and the corresponding vector of reconstructed values. The expression is formulated by using the $l_\infty$ norm $\|\mathbf{x}\|_\infty := \max_{i=1,\dots,n} |x_i|$, with $\mathbf{x} = (x_1, \dots, x_n)^T \in \mathbb{R}^n$ .

## 2.5   Related Work

As mentioned at the beginning of this chapter, reducing or eliminating redundancy is an essential part of data compression. For doing so, several types of correlations can be exploited in result files derived from CFD simulations. Models used for fluid flow simulations describe temporal, spatial and dynamics-based coherences. These correlations can also be found in the result data and can be used to achieve compression. In general, it is of advantage to exploit as many correlations as possible to reach the highest possible compression.

While exploitation of dynamics-based correlations is restricted to CFD data (or maybe other scientific data), temporal and spatial correlations can be utilized in a much wider spectrum of data types. Thus, they are used far more often in the realm of data compression. In fact, no compression scheme using dynamics-based correlations for the compression of data from numerical simulations even seems to exists.

***Temporal compression*** is applied in a wide variety of domains, such as video, audio, 3D animation and dynamics simulation. Although sequenced data could simply be compressed frame by frame with a suitable static compression method, it is often expedient to also exploit time correlations between time instances. As shown in Section 5.2.2, this is also the case for transient CFD simulations.

Since sequences describe a one-dimensional procedure, many of the ideas behind temporal compression can be shared among compression schemes specialized for different fields of application. Related work is therefore found in a variety of data compression fields.

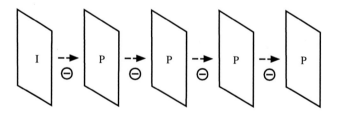

**Figure 2.12:** Constant extrapolation

The simplest methods used for sequence compression are based on prediction. In general, prediction consists of two parts: the determination of a sequential order in which the data is processed, and a mathematical predictor which calculates an estimate for the value to be predicted. For use in compression schemes the estimates are then subtracted from the originals, creating decorrelated residuals which are processed further or encoded directly. In the case of temporal compression a sequential order is given by the time series. Hence, it can directly be used by the predictor. One of the commonly applied predictors for time decorrelation is constant extrapolation used in [11, 27, 42] and illustrated in Figure 2.12. A more sophisticated predictor, a Lagrange extrapolation, is used by Engelson et al. [19]. While prediction techniques lead to good results, the methods mentioned above have the disadvantage of making it a possible time-consuming task to decompress selected single frames. Since the prediction is aligned with the time sequence by using preceding data and requiring it for decompression, dependencies to prior time steps exist. Only the initial time step is without prediction and therefore independent from any other. As long as decompression is performed in the same order as the compression, no problems arise. However, in order to decompress an arbitrary time step, possibly all prior time steps have to be decompressed as well. This can lead to weak performance and long access times. A commonly applied workaround is to divide the sequence into short blocks of frames. The problem is then restricted to a single block. Yet this comes at the price of more unpredicted time steps, which in return leads to lower compression.

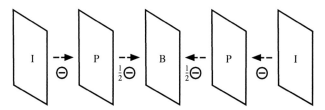

**Figure 2.13:** Difference scheme similar to the one utilized in MPEG. I-frames remain without prediction, P-frames are predicted from one direction, while a bidirectional prediction is used for B-frames.

Since arbitrary access is crucial in the field of video playback, blocking is commonly applied during video compression. To compensate the negative effect of unpredicted frames on the compression factor, standards like MPEG [48] take advantage of unpredicted time steps by using them for more sophisticated predictors. This is realized by using a mixture of forward and reverse extrapolation as well as bidirectional interpolation as shown in Figure 2.13. Similar to the MPEG approach, the unpredicted time steps can also be used in combination with hierarchical interpolation. This leads to another very efficient scheme for temporal compression. An overview of several temporal compression techniques is given in [38]. Its emphasis is on the comparison of different techniques in respect to random access performance.

Besides predictive compression schemes transformation methods known from image and video compression, such as the *discrete cosine transformation* (DCT) and the *discrete wavelet transformation* (DWT), can also be applied to time sequences. Both perform a basis transformation into a frequency domain. While the transformation itself has decorrelating properties, usually frequency coefficients are quantized or eliminated to achieve a stronger but lossy compression. There are versions of both transformations suitable for lossless compression of integer values, which only make use of the decorrelation properties of the transformation itself. While those versions could also be used in lossy compression schemes after a quantization step, it is often more reasonable to perform the quantization in the frequency domain. By this way frequency coefficients can be quantized at different levels to yield lower visual losses. For image compression, coefficients of higher frequencies are neglected, because it is assumed that high frequencies are less important to the appearance of an image. As shown in [52], this attribute can also be useful for time sequences of simulation data. In that case it is not the appearance of the data when visualized that makes it attractive, but the error behavior when data is used for post-processing analysis. Undesired staircase effects are not present and therefore interfere to a lesser extent with post-processing analysis. Examples for DWT-based compression can be found in [54] and [43].

Instead of using frequency-based transformations, Alexa and Müller proposed to use *principal component analysis* (PCA)-based transformations [1]. They suggested to describe time-coherent mesh geometry in terms of its principal components and their influence over time. Compression is achieved by discarding all but the first few most relevant components. This idea is expanded further in [49] in which PCA is not only applied to time series. Instead, a clustered PCA used for all values from several time steps is introduced, thereby not only exploiting time-coherence but also spatial correlations.

Apart from the approaches above some more specialized methods for time-varying meshes exist. They are designed for 3D graphics and do not entirely serve the purpose of compressing CFD data. However, some of the basic ideas might as well be used for compression of CFD data fields. They include a vertex-wise motion prediction proposed in [68]. There the prediction of the motion vector of each vertex is based on the motion vectors of neighboring vertices. Other methods are affine motion matching techniques proposed in [5] and [40]. Both works use the calculation of affine transformations to predict time-varying mesh geometry.

All of the compression schemes above require meshes with time-consistent topology. Since this is the case for most time-sequenced data, they can usually be applied. It should also be noted that all methods are targeted at mesh geometry or its variable data. None of the methods above compresses time-varying mesh connectivities or data on meshes with time-varying topology.

Many of the techniques to exploit temporal correlations mentioned above can easily be combined with algorithms exploiting other coherences, such as spatial correlations. This can usually be done by simply applying them one after another. Although temporal correlations are often high enough to achieve reasonable compression, it is crucial to also exploit other correlations in an effort to maximize compression. In [27] and [34] temporal and spatial compression is combined in a single algorithm. Stronger compression is achieved by exploiting both types of correlations.

**Spatial compression** is more diversified than temporal compression. The use of different grids in the computer environment to model space or objects in space are accountable for grid-assimilated compression schemes. Algorithms suitable for regular Cartesian grids are closest related to those used for temporal compression. They most often make use of the regularity as well as the lexicographical order given by the grid. Again, predictors can be designed to adopt the given order. One simple yet very effective predictor for data on multidimensional Cartesian grids has been introduced by Ibarria et al. [26]. Many other techniques can be acquired directly from image compression. This is a straightforward process especially for 2D data. However, many ideas from image compression are not unique to 2D data. They are often only dependent on the regularity of the grid. For example, DCT and DWT can be easily applied to higher dimension data fields. An application of image compression algorithms to CFD data on Cartesian grids is shown in [51].

Although these approaches give fairly good results, they are limited to regular grids. CFD software packages increasingly use unstructured, irregular grids. The trend towards unstructured grids is a result of automatic grid generation which has become very popular. It simplifies the process substantially, especially when complicated 2D and 3D domains are used. Multiple aspects of irregular grid representation have been and still are subject to data compression research.

Standard representations of irregular grids combine coordinate values and connectivity data. Connectivity data can vary between different grid types and representations. In all cases it consists of incidence and adjacency information on how the grid is held together. For CFD data, this includes face-vertex, cell-face incidences as well as cell adjacencies. While coordinates and scalar vertex data are often present in both structured and unstructured cases, the connectivity data is only required for unstructured grids. Both parts require a significant amount of storage space and are therefore subject to mesh compression algorithms. In addition, simulation result files not only include solution values in form of vertex data, but might as well contain face or cell data. All data must be compressed in order to achieve a satisfactory compression.

Most research is dedicated to connectivity data of polygonal surface meshes. This is probably due to the popularity of 3D meshes in the entertainment industry. In 3D computer graphics mostly surface meshes are used and their connectivity representation requires much of the storage necessary for 3D models. Compression schemes such as the *Face Fixer* [29], the *Edge Breaker* [46], the *Angle Analyzer* [39] and the *Topological Surgery* [63] are designed specifically for connectivity compression. They also include options to use them for compression of scalar vertex data. Methods such as the parallelogram predictor were introduced in these proposals. In [37] Kronrod and Gotsman introduced a method that optimizes the traversal order of the connectivity compression to improve the compression of geometric vertex data.

In the context of numerical simulations, surface meshes are mostly used in structural mechanics, such as car crash simulations. Full 3D CFD simulations are performed on volumetric meshes. This makes the mentioned algorithms useless for compression of CFD files. Some of the incorporated ideas and techniques are the foundation of algorithms suitable for 3D volumetric meshes.

The first effort to compress volumetric meshes was made by Szymczak and Rossignac with their *Grow & Fold* algorithm [62] which is designed for connectivity data of tetrahedral meshes. It is a generalization of the *Topological Surgery* [63] and also contains ideas of the *Edge Breaker* algorithm. Two data strings are created by the *Grow & Fold* algorithm

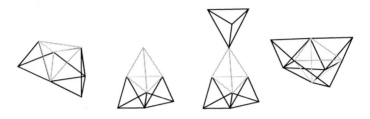

**Figure 2.14:** The different possibilities which exist for adding a new tetrahedron

during compression. The first string stores a tetrahedral spanning tree. It is created by starting at an arbitrary tetrahedron and growing by successively attaching unvisited tetrahedrons to external faces. This is continued until all tetrahedrons are covered. Since the tree obviously does not contain all connectivity information, a second string is created additionally. It stores the information required to uncover incident relations absent from the tree. This method is only intended for connectivity compression.

Differently, the generalization of the *Cut Border Machine* [24] for compression of tetrahedral meshes also inherits vertex data compression. This was a novelty for volumetric grids at the time of its proposal. Similar to the *Grow & Fold* algorithm, the *Cut Border Machine* also starts at an arbitrary tetrahedron and spreads through the grid by consecutively adding tetrahedrons to the already conquered part of the mesh. Only a few possibilities exist for the integration of a new tetrahedron (see Figure 2.14). The string of integration operations are encoded by using Huffman codes. During the process of encoding the connectivity, vertices can be compressed by applying a simple prediction. Whenever a tetrahedron is attached by adding a vertex, a linear approximation can be used to estimate the data values assigned to the newly added vertex. The difference between the approximation and the originals is then encoded. A quantization is usually carried out prior to the prediction when floating point values are compressed.

An approach similar to the *Grow & Fold* and the *Cut Border Machine* is proposed in [10]. Chen et al. use a constrained minimal spanning tree to more efficiently traverse the tetrahedrons. A flipping operation extended to work with tetrahedrons is used to predict vertex data. Other approaches to volumetric grids include works on hexahedral meshes, such as described in [28, 41].

All mentioned work on volumetric and surface meshes designed for connectivity data relies on meshes with consistent cell types. Their consistency is exploited to efficiently encode possible building operations, performed by the algorithm's traversal through the mesh. This cannot be accomplished in the same form on arbitrary polyhedral meshes limiting the application possibilities. For example, auto-generated meshes usually consist of a mixture of tetrahedrons, hexahedrons and other polyhedrons. Nevertheless, no compression method for connectivity data of arbitrary polyhedral meshes seems to exist.

A few transformation methods for geometric data of 3D meshes or other data fields over irregular grids have been proposed. These methods can also be applied to data on arbitrary volume meshes, since they solely depend on the connectivity graph of the mesh. From that the graph Laplacian operator can be formed. Based on its spectral properties a few transformation schemes suitable for compression were introduced. Karni and Gotsman determined the eigenvectors from the graph Laplacian to expand the data vectors in that basis [32]. The coefficients of the high frequencies are dropped from the gained representation. The guiding principle hereby is that low frequency modes can represent smooth shapes very well. As a consequence, the error is solely produced by high frequency modes. The downside of this approach is that the basis has to be calculated for every mesh connectivity. The complexity of the required computation renders this approach unusable for larger models. In an effort to overcome this problem Karni and Gotsman proposed a similar method based on fixed spectral basis functions [33]. In contrast, Sorkine et al. proposed a different Laplacian-based method which produces an error mostly consisting of low frequency modes [57]. The application of the graph Laplacian operator yields the forward transform of the method. Since the graph Lapacian is singular, at least one anchor point is set for every connected component of the grid to ensure reversibility. With the anchor points an over-determined system of linear equations can be solved to reconstruct the original values. In addition to the transformation a quantization is performed in the frequency domain. In that case, anchors are set in such a way that the error after reconstruction is reduced.

The benefits of these methods are the good properties of the visual appearance after decompression, however, computational costs are very high compared to prediction-based methods. These transformation methods require solving a least squares problem for decompression. For models with millions of cells or vertices, the decompression is too time-consuming for practical use in industry.

So far, only compression techniques for single-resolution meshes were outlined. Due to the steady growing models multiresolution or adaptive meshes have become more popular. Visualizing very large 3D models is a computational intensive task that can be accelerated by using adaptive meshes. Only the necessary detail is visualized at first and more added when required. In the field of numerical simulation adaptive grids are also used to increase accuracy locally. In the context of adaptive grids interpolation methods are often applied. While interpolation has been present in the realm of data compression for a long time [6], it is not applied as frequently as predictive methods. Many interpolation methods exist, such as reported in [2, 12, 31, 35, 36, 66].

***Dynamics-based compression*** is as far as the author is concerned not used for any compression scheme. The reason might be in part that it has to be specifically designed for a certain application, such as CFD.

# 3 Tree Predictor

In this chapter a prediction-based algorithm for lossless compression of integer-valued data is presented. Its design is targeted at the compression of data sets over unstructured single-resolution grids with mixed cell types as they are commonly found in CFD data. In contrast to comparable algorithms listed in Section 2.5, it is therefore not restricted to grids with a unique cell type. This is a noteworthy feature of the presented algorithm, particularly, because the uniformity of cell types is a property of grids which is often exploited for the layout of predictors. Since CFD data usually consists of floating point values, a uniform quantization is applied prior to this predictor as described in Section 2.3.

Prediction methods are based on two components: a sequential order in which data values are processed, and a predictor which is used to calculate estimates for the values to be compressed by only using values that have already been processed. Then the estimates are subtracted from the original values with the intention to obtain a set of differences that has lower entropy, so it can be encoded more efficiently compared to the original values. For this process to be reversible, the original values have to be reconstructed identically from the set of differences. This is achieved by following a suitable traversal order and by only using already processed values for the prediction. During decompression the original values can then be recovered from the differences by using the same traversal order and prediction, only this time the estimates are added to the differences. That way, the values needed for the calculation of the identical estimates are already decompressed.

Prediction-based compression schemes are often applied to data on regular grids, where they achieve good compression while showing fast performances [45]. However, these methods rely heavily on the regularity of the grid and cannot be simply extended to work on irregular grids. Canonical orders given on regular grids do not exist in the irregular case. In addition, regular structures that are exploited for second- and higher-order predictors are absent from grids with mixed cell types. Many of the known prediction techniques cannot be applied to CFD data.

For the presented algorithm connectivity graphs of grids are utilized. They are used to represent the connectivity relations between data points on grids. Traversal orders are determined by identifying spanning trees of those graphs and by using the hierarchical order they induce. The prediction is carried out following a parent-child predictor that is independent of any shape or form of the grid elements. Thus, it can be applied to irregular grids with mixed cell types.

As an alternative to improving the approximation by a more sophisticated predictor, an optimization of the traversal order can be employed to improve the approximation accuracy. Since multiple spanning trees exist for every graph in general, a better suitable tree can be determined to achieve higher compression factors. For this purpose, weighted graphs are introduced and minimal spanning trees are determined. Although it is possible to determine optimal trees for each dataset, there are limitations to using them for the optimization. Further details of the optimization possibilities as well as its limitations will be discussed in Section 3.3.

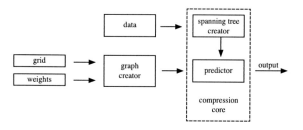

**Figure 3.1:** Outline of the components of the presented algorithm

The algorithm can be outlined as illustrated in Figure 3.1. While the setup of the graph and possibly its weights are essential for the algorithm, it can be seen as a separate task. Once the graph is set up, no additional information is required for executing the algorithm. Following the graph creation process only the information provided by the graph and the data to be compressed are processed by the compression core. It consists of two components. One is the determination of a spanning tree. The other is carrying out the prediction of the data values on the nodes of the graph or on those of the tree, respectively. The compression core remains the same for every graph, hence the graphs become a powerful mechanism to control the behavior of the algorithm. Similarly to the graph creation, the prediction tree has to be determined only once before it can be utilized for predicting multiple datasets.

## 3.1 Graphs

As described above, graphs are the basis of the algorithm. They are expected to contain all information necessary to enable a good compression. Undirected graphs are referred to when speaking of graphs.

**Definition 3.1** *An **undirected graph** is an ordered pair $G = (V, E)$, where $V$ is a set of nodes and $E \subseteq V \times V$ a set of edges. A graph is weighted if each edge has a numerical value assigned to it. The set of edges is then $E \subseteq V \times V \times W$, where $W$ is the set of weights.*

Based on these graphs a differential encoding between data values associated with adjacent nodes is performed by the predictor. They have to reflect the coherences between data points so that the prediction is useful for decorrelation. For this purpose multiple edges between nodes as well as loops, edges connecting a node with itself, are of no relevance. Consequently, only simple and weighted simple graphs are considered for this purpose.

**Definition 3.2** *A **simple graph** is an undirected graph with no more than one edge between any two different vertices and without any loops.*

Weighted graphs are used whenever an optimization of the traversal order is intended. The optimization is carried out on behalf of the weights assigned to the edges of the graph. This will be described in Section 3.3 in more detail. For more background on graph theory, the reader is referred to [18].

**Figure 3.2:** Various graphs resulting from diverse connectivity information: (a) node connectivity, (b) cell connectivity or (c) face connectivity

Though there are many ways to set up input graphs, the most obvious approach is to use the connectivity information given by the grid. In this case, the nodes of the graph correspond to the data points on the grid, whereas edges represent connectivities between them. There are various graphs that can be created depending on the connectivities that are considered. For example, under the assumption that data points are located at the cell centers, a graph based on direct face-based connectivities can be created as shown in Figure 3.2 b. The nodes of the graph correspond to the data points at the cell centers. Two nodes are connected by an edge if the associated data points lie in cells that share a common face. Other possibilities such as vertex-based connectivities, where two cells are considered neighbors as soon as they share a common vertex, are also reasonable. Sometimes grids are composed of multiple parts with no connectivities between them. In this case each component has to be treated separately. Connected grids are assumed for simplicity.

As described in Section 2.1.1, variables stored in CFD data may be vertex, face or cell data and hence, separate graphs need to be created for the different types as illustrated in Figure 3.2. Only relevant data points are considered for each graph.

## 3.2    Spanning Tree Predictor

The traversal order is an important component of prediction-based algorithms. The difficulty to find a traversal order on irregular grids emerges from the fact that no meaningful ordering of cells, faces and vertices exists. This is no different when using graphs to represent this information, as realized in the present case. While the intention is to find a good approximation for (almost) all data values and to store as little extra information as possible, reversibility of the prediction scheme has to be guaranteed. This is achieved by performing the prediction in a traversal order and by only using values that have already been processed. The identical order can be followed during decompression to restore the original values. Then, the same estimates can be calculated from the already decompressed prior values. Adding them to the stored approximation errors yields the reconstructed values.

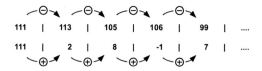

**Figure 3.3:** Prediction and differencing applied to a series of values yield the estimation errors. When using the same predictor and prediction order, the original values can be reconstructed from these errors by simply adding the predicted value.

The goal is to find a traversal order which covers all data points and allows a prediction of every value. Due to the precondition of maintaining reversibility, at least one initial value remains without prediction. A solution to this problem could be finding a path that visits every node of the graph exactly once, a so-called Hamilton path. However, determining its existence is a NP-complete problem [53], and therefore impractical for the intended purpose. A simpler solution is achieved by taking advantage of the parent-child relation present in a spanning tree of the graph.

**Definition 3.3** *A **tree** $T(V,E)$ is a connected graph that contains no cycles. Nodes of $T$ which are of degree 1 are called leaves.*

Assuming that a simple graph $G(V, E)$ created as described above is given, then a spanning tree $T(V, E')$ with $E' \subseteq E$ can be found. The fact of constructing a spanning tree opposed to any other tree ensures that every node in $V$ is covered and hence every data point on the grid. In contrast to $G(V, E)$, $T(V, E')$ is cycle-free and therefore can be used to establish a hierarchical order by appointing one of its nodes as root. The root node becomes the highest ranked node in the hierarchy and is, by definition, the only node without a parent. Though this hierarchy cannot be employed as traversal order for every prediction method, it can be used in combination with constant extrapolation as predictor, for example. A value of a node can be predicted by the value of its parent node. This leads to the following prediction algorithm.

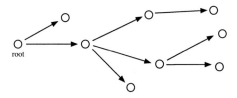

**Figure 3.4:** Parent-child hierarchy as implied by a tree (left to right)

Starting at the tree's root node, the associated value is used to predict the values of all of its child nodes. After predicting them, the same parent-child prediction is carried out for every one of them as parent nodes. This process is carried out recursively until all leaves of $T(V, E')$ are reached. In other words, the algorithm describes a recursion that follows through a tree from its root to its leaves, predicting all values along the way. Solely the value of the root node is not predicted. All predictions only utilize values from processed nodes, thus ensuring the existence of an inverse operation.

If $P(v_i)$ denotes the parent of $v_i$, the prediction leads to the following difference scheme

$$D(v_i) = \begin{cases} f(v_i), & \text{if } v_i \text{ is the root node} \\ f(v_i) - f(P(v_i)), & \text{otherwise} \end{cases}.$$

Here, the values at the data points are denoted as $f(v)$.

A possible way to determine such a tree is to follow a greedy strategy. Starting at an arbitrary node $v \in V$, a child node $v'$ is selected and marked as visited. The edge $(v, v')$ is added to the set of edges $E'$ of the tree $T(V, E')$. This process is recursively applied to node $v'$, where only unmarked adjacent nodes are considered. Whenever no such nodes are available, the process is repeated for the previous node until no more nodes are left unmarked. This strategy follows the principles of a depth first selection in trees. Surely, it could also be done in a breadth first manner, for which all edges to unvisited neighbors are added to the tree before moving on to the next node. In any case, a spanning tree that fulfills the desired purpose is created. Once a tree is determined, it can be used to compress any dataset associated with these data points of the grid.

By design, the graphs on which the prediction scheme is based reflect the connectivities of the grid, in that their nodes are associated with the data points on the grid and their edges indicate a connection between them. A subset of these edges is selected as prediction path during the spanning tree creation. Since multiple spanning trees exist in general, it could be possible to improve the prediction by selecting the best suiting one. This, however, requires a measure for the prediction quality of a tree. Weights are assigned to the edges of the graph for this purpose, each weight measuring the quality of the prediction along the particular edge it is assigned to. Within the compression core this weighting is considered for the creation of optimized spanning trees. Thereby, it is crucial to choose weights that

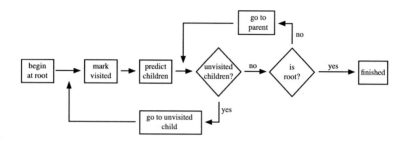

**Figure 3.5:** Outline of the tree predictor algorithm. Starting at a designated root node, the prediction is carried out in a depth first manner.

represent appropriate measures leading to a more accurate approximation and an overall stronger compression. The weights are assumed to reflect correlations, in that smaller weights mark edges along which the prediction is expected to be more accurate. The optimization searches for the tree with the overall cheapest edges, the minimal spanning tree. For the determination of the minimal spanning tree the Kruskal or Prim algorithm can be employed. The Kruskal algorithm can be shown to run in $O(|E| \log |E|)$ runtime, while the Prim algorithm has been shown to run in $O(|E|+|V| log |V|)$. Here, the cardinality of sets is denoted by $| \cdot |$. In the following section the possibility of optimizing the tree creation process is described in more detail.

## 3.3 Optimization

As with every part of the prediction algorithm, the optimization has to be implemented in such a way that the reversibility of the prediction algorithm is maintained. Hence, it must be ensured that the weights can be reconstructed during decompression to be able to create the same optimized prediction trees. Alternatively, it is also possible to store the optimized trees together with the compressed data. The generated overhead is however significant, meaning that optimization benefits can in general only be achieved if multiple data sets are compressed by using the same tree. In the case that one tree is used for the compression of multiple data sets, the optimization is only useful if it leads to an overall better compression. The following three scenarios show cases in which the optimization is beneficial:

*Scenario 1*: It is not necessary to store the optimized trees, because they can be reconstructed identically during decompression. In addition, the optimization yields a stronger compression.

*Scenario 2*: Optimized trees have to be stored with the compressed data to maintain reversibility, however, an overall stronger compression is still achieved.

*Scenario 3*: A few trees that are used for compression are stored with the compressed data to speed up the decompression. Since the tree is stored anyway, an optimization is performed to achieve the best possible compression under the given circumstances.

The last scenario describes a special case, since it primarily results from a design decision driven by performance optimization for the decompression. This is different from the other two which are both a result of the specific choice of weights. It has to be evaluated which of the two scenarios describes a more efficient compression. While no tree has to be stored in the first scenario, weights can be chosen more freely in the second one. Essentially, the question has to be answered if it is possible to store trees and still benefit from optimization, even when compared to the proceedings from Scenario 1, or from an unoptimized prediction.

The best prediction tree might be obtained when using the data set one wants to compress also for optimization. Differences between adjacent values can be used as weights for the graph. While this could be a general approach to compress any data stored on a grid, it requires the prediction tree to be stored with the compressed data. The generated overhead might render the optimization useless. In the context of CFD all data sets stored in CFD files contain function values of various physical variables. Since these variables are results of the same simulation, there are correlations between them. This gives some reason to use a single optimized tree for multiple data sets to obtain higher compression factors for each data set, while keeping the overhead for storing the tree as small as possible. The idea to incorporate variable data into the optimization has the benefit that besides the geometric correlations, physical correlations are also exploited.

In the following three subsections different types of weights are introduced. Weights will be denoted as $w_{ij}$, $i, j \in \mathbb{N}$, where the indices indicate to which edge they are assigned to. An edge can then be written as the triple $e_{ij} = (v_i, v_j, w_{ij})$, with $v_k \in V$, $k \in \{1, \ldots, |V|\}$ and $w_{ij} \in \mathbb{R}$, $w_{ij} \geq 0$. It is assumed that smaller weights indicate stronger concurrence between the data points incident to the corresponding edge. From the data contained in CFD files several correlations can be derived for this purpose. This includes dynamics-based relations.

### 3.3.1 Distance-based Optimization

The idea behind distance-based optimization is to utilize Euclidean distances between data points as weights for the graph. This approach is driven by the assumption that less distant data points share a more similar value than those that are further apart. Since the graph already describes the connectivities between data points, this seems to be a natural choice. As a result, an algorithm is obtained, which is solely based on connectivity and geometric information provided by the grid. If $\mathbf{x}_i$ denotes the coordinate vector of the data point associated with the node $v_i \in V$, the weights are calculated as

$$w_{ij} := \|\mathbf{x}_i - \mathbf{x}_j\|_2, \quad \mathbf{x}_i, \mathbf{x}_j \in \mathbb{R}^3.$$

Although this approach seems natural, it might only be usable for vertex data. Unless explicitly calculated at cell centers, scalar variables are usually assumed to be constant across an entire cell. The relevance of a distance measure between neighboring cells is then questionable. This also applies to face data. Nevertheless, for evaluation purposes data points are assumed to be located at cell centers to calculate distances. The coordinates of the centers are obtained as the average

$$\mathbf{x}_i = \frac{1}{|C_i|} \sum_{x_k \in C_i} \mathbf{x}_k,$$

where $C_i$ is the set of vertices $x_k$ that belong to the cell of $v_i$ and $|C_i|$ is its cardinality. The coordinates of $x_k$ are denoted by $\mathbf{x}_k$.

If a prediction tree is constructed by employing geometric weights and used for the compression of variable data, it does not need to be stored with the compressed data. However, it shall be noted that distances are calculated from the coordinates of vertices which might be altered by a lossy compression. Despite this possibility, the necessity of having to store the tree can still be avoided in some cases. For example, if the loss is caused by a quantization, the quantized coordinates can be used instead.

### 3.3.2  Gradient-based Optimization

This approach is derived from the idea to optimize the prediction tree by using the actual values of the data sets. It might seem very logical from the optimization point of view to use the values one wants to compress for the optimization. However, this obviously bares the disadvantage of having to additionally store the prediction tree, whenever datasets used for the optimization are also compressed with the resulting prediction scheme. As described for Scenario 2 at the beginning of this section, it has to be clarified if such an approach can be beneficial for the compression.

Suitable weights are obtained from data sets by calculating gradients between adjacent data points. If $f(v) \in \mathbb{R}^n$, $n \in \mathbb{N}$ denotes the value of a variable at the node $v \in V$ of $G(V, E)$, then the weights are calculated as the $l_1$-norm of the differences between the values at adjacent nodes $v_i$, $v_j$:

$$w_{ij} := \|f(v_i) - f(v_j)\|_1.$$

The reason for this choice of weights can be seen as a direct consequence of the predictor used. From the comparison between the weights and the error of the differential scheme the following result can be obtained.

**Lemma 3.3.1** *Corresponding to the tree predictor described in Section 3.2, for any spanning tree $T(V, E')$ of $G(V, E)$ with $v_r$ being its root node, one has*

$$\sum_{e_{ij} \in E'} w_{ij} = \sum_{v \in V \setminus v_r} \|D(v)\|_1.$$

**Proof** Since only edges of $T(V, E')$ are considered, it can be assumed without any loss of generality that the edges $e_{ij} = (v_i, v_j)$ are ordered such that $v_j$ is the parent of $v_i$, or $P(v_i) = v_j$. The equality can be easily obtained as follows:

$$
\begin{aligned}
\sum_{e_{ij} \in E'} w_{ij} &= \sum_{e_{ij} \in E'} \|f(v_i) - f(v_j)\|_1 = \sum_{e_{ij} \in E'} \|f(v_i) - f(P(v_i))\|_1 \\
&= \sum_{v \in V \setminus v_r} \|f(v) - f(P(v))\|_1 \\
&= \sum_{v \in V \setminus v_r} \|D(v)\|_1
\end{aligned}
$$

$\square$

Accordingly, the use of these weights leads to an optimization that minimizes the prediction error for the specific data set used for weighting. The optimal tree-based prediction can be obtained as shown by the following lemma.

**Lemma 3.3.2** *For a given data set $X$ and a simple graph $G(V, E)$ that is weighted by using the weights introduced above, a tree-based prediction with minimal*

$$\sum_{v \in V \setminus v_r} \|D(v)\|_1$$

*can be determined. Similarly, the prediction with the maximal error can be computed.*

**Proof** A minimal spanning tree $T(V, E')$ of the weighted graph $G(V, E)$ can be determined. No other spanning tree with smaller weights exists by definition. Therefore, $T(V, E')$ is the tree with minimal $\sum_{e_{ij} \in E'} w_{ij}$. The claims of this Lemma are proven by Lemma 3.3.1. The worst tree-based prediction is obtained analogously by negating the weights. $\square$

Regardless of the benefits that this sort of optimization might provide to the overall compression, it certainly is of value to the evaluation. If it is assumed that smaller values are compressed more efficiently, the best possible tree-based prediction can be determined for any data set as described by the previous lemma. Consequently, this can be carried out for each data set that is to be compressed, essentially resulting in an optimal prediction scheme. This is not useful for actual compression, since all prediction trees would have to be stored. Nevertheless, this can be used as reference for the evaluation of any other optimization, as it indicates a theoretical limit to all possible weightings. Analogously, the worst possible tree-based prediction can also be computed. Together, they show the range of the optimization effect and thereby allow a grading of other weightings.

In an effort to keep the overhead of stored prediction trees as low as possible, their number has to be limited. In general, there are two ways to achieve this. The same optimized trees can either be used for data sets from different variables or, in the case of transient solutions, for a series of time frames of the same variable. Of coarse, the combination of both can also be used to further reduce the overhead. In any case, the compression of multiple data sets has to benefit from the same optimization. Reference data sets have to be selected based on which the optimization is then performed. Such a selection process is impractical when multiple variables are compressed by using the same tree. It is liable that the selection has to be dependent on the specific type of simulation and the stored variables.

For optimizing a predictor that is applied to different variables, one can simply select a single data set of any variable as reference. While this seems to be an arbitrary procedure, there is some motivation behind it. In the case of CFD data every variable has a physical meaning to it. A small variance in the physical entity alongside an edge is indicated by a small weight. For example, when using the variable 'density' as reference, edges along which the density changes less are preferred during optimization. Depending on the simulation a small change in density can be interpreted as an indication for a similar behavior shared among various other variables. Then the selection of that particular variable as reference is reasonable. The various results will be discussed in more detail in Chapter 5. Opposed to using a single data set, it might be of advantage to generate the weights depending on multiple data sets. For example, let $X_1, \ldots, X_n, n \in \mathbb{N}$ denote a variety of data sets with $x^k$ being a value in $X_k$. The weights can then be calculated as

$$w_{ij} := \sum_{k=1}^{n} \left| x_i^k - x_j^k \right|.$$

Such an approach has the advantage that multiple data sets are considered during the optimization. In fact, if all variables are employed, the selection process becomes superfluous. This weighting method will be denoted as *full weighting*.

### 3.3.3 Dynamics-based Optimization

It was mentioned in the context of gradient-based optimization that the physical meaning of the variables might give reason to the selection of a particular reference data set. This thought can be expanded to what becomes the idea behind dynamics-based optimization introduced here. Conclusions on the correlations within the variable data can be made from the dynamics of the flow and integrated into the weighting. Opposed to the gradient-based approach, the weights are not limited to the differences between values of adjacent data points. Instead, weights are computed according to certain characteristics of the flow.

### Motion of Flow

The motion embodied in fluid flows is one of their prominent characteristics. Hence, it seems reasonable to assume correlations related to the motion paths of the flow. The following set of weights is designed to exploit this characteristic. The velocity magnitudes of the flow between adjacent data points are estimated and used for the weighting. Edges along which the flow has a greater velocity are either assigned larger or smaller weights. This corresponds to the assumption that a larger velocity in a certain direction indicates either less or more correlation in that same direction.

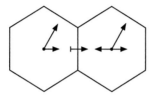

**Figure 3.6:** Estimate for the velocity across the face of two adjacent cells

In the case that velocity vectors are given for each node on the graph, the velocity along an edge will be estimated from the two nodes it connects. To calculate the direction to which the edge is aligned the coordinates of the data points associated with the nodes are used. For both nodes the velocity acting in this and respectively in the opposite direction is then determined by

$$V_{ij} := \left\langle \mathbf{V}_i \middle| \frac{\mathbf{x}_i - \mathbf{x}_j}{\|\mathbf{x}_i - \mathbf{x}_j\|_2} \right\rangle.$$

Here, $\mathbf{V}_i$ denotes the velocity vector and $\mathbf{x}_i$ the coordinate vector of $v_i$. The $\langle | \rangle$ represents the scalar product in $\mathbb{R}^n$. To acquire a fair weighting solely based on the velocity and its direction but independently of the distance between adjacent data points, the vector $\mathbf{x}_i - \mathbf{x}_j$ is normalized. The normalization can be applied without restriction, since every data point on the grid is unique and simple graphs are utilized, thus $\|\mathbf{x}_i - \mathbf{x}_j\|_2 > 0$ holds true for all $(v_i, v_j) \in E$. Eventually, the actual weights are calculated as either an average of $V_{ij}$ and $V_{ji}$:

$$w_{ij} := \frac{|V_{ij}| + |V_{ji}|}{2}$$

or as the inverse thereof

$$w_{ij} := \begin{cases} \dfrac{2}{|V_{ij}| + |V_{ji}|}, & \text{if } V_{ij} \wedge V_{ji} \neq 0 \\ \\ w_{\max}, & \text{otherwise.} \end{cases}$$

The inverse is required to adjust the weights to the assumption that higher velocities indicate higher correlations. In the case that $V_{ij} = V_{ji} = 0$, a maximal weight is set as

$$w_{\max} := \max_{\substack{ij \\ V_{ij} \wedge V_{ji} \neq 0}} \left( \frac{2}{|V_{ij}| + |V_{ji}|} \right).$$

According to how the weighting is performed in the context of the presented algorithm, the direction of the flow is only partially considered. That is due to the fact that the weights itself cannot indicate any direction, since only positive scalar values are allowed. In addition, the graph is not directed and therefore cannot hold any such information.

### 3.3.4   Optimization for Transient Solutions

In the transient case an even greater variety of optimization possibilities exists. As a proof of concept, only two conceptionally different approaches will be pursued here. The first can be applied independently of the temporal compression scheme, as it is designated to store the prediction trees in addition to the compressed data. Thus, data used for optimization can be freely chosen. It will be referred to as *free optimization*. The other one is dependent on a prediction-based temporal compression scheme. For each time step a new prediction tree is determined. The weights used for its optimization are derived from the approximation calculated by the temporal prediction scheme. No tree has to be stored with the compressed data, since it can be recreated from the estimates calculated for reversing the temporal prediction. It will be denoted as *shadow optimization*.

#### *Free Optimization*

Since the tree is stored with the compressed data, a multitude of possibilities to execute this optimization exists. Nevertheless, there are basically two decisions to be made. First, the time span for which a single tree is employed has to be determined, and secondly, a corresponding weighting has to be identified. Especially the second part may still involve a great variety of possibilities to consider. To limit this number only the full optimization will be considered here. It can either be applied to all variables of a time frame or to multiple time frames of each variable. In the first case, the middle frame of a fixed time span will be used as reference for evaluation purposes. These two possibilities are illustrated in Figure 3.7 and 3.8.

The disadvantage of this method is that trees have to be stored with the compressed file which influences the overall compression negatively. It would have to be evaluated if such an approach is viable. Nevertheless, there is also an advantage of such a procedure. Since the tree is stored with the compressed data, it does not have to be reconstructed during decompression and therefore enables a faster processing.

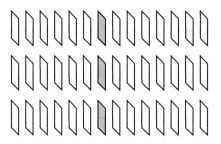

**Figure 3.7:** Multiple variables of one time step are selected for optimization.

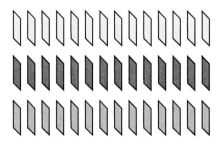

**Figure 3.8:** For each variable multiple time frames are selected for optimization.

### *Shadow Optimization*

In contrast to the free optimization described above this method does not allow many variations. It is mainly predefined by the applied temporal prediction scheme. The idea behind this approach is to circumvent the necessity to store the tree in addition to the compressed data. For every time step a new optimized prediction tree is determined. The estimates calculated by the temporal prediction are used as reference for the full weighting. Consequently, the quality of the optimization is dependent on the accuracy of the temporal prediction. Figure 3.9 illustrates which time frames are used for the optimization.

The disadvantage of this procedure is that the prediction trees have to be calculated for every time frame during compression and decompression. Since every optimization involves the determination of a minimal spanning tree, the compression and decompression speed may be reduced significantly.

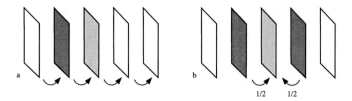

**Figure 3.9:** Time frame selected for optimization according to the temporal prediction scheme: constant extrapolation (a) and linear interpolation (b). Time frames marked with light gray are currently predicted, while time frames marked with dark gray are used in the weighting process.

### 3.3.5 Storing Trees

Provident formats or ways have to be utilized to keep the overhead of storing prediction trees at a minimum. These only have to contain enough information that the trees can be reconstructed from the data that is contained in the compressed files anyhow. Two possibilities are outlined in the following.

#### *Condensed Tree Format*

The unique IDs of the data points provided by the grid description are also used in this representation. These IDs associated with the nodes of the tree are stored in an order derived from a depth first traversal.

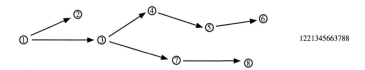

**Figure 3.10:** A possible order in which the tree is elapsed and the corresponding stream used to encode the prediction tree

Starting at the root node, the complete tree is elapsed in a depth first traversal as illustrated in Figure 3.10. The IDs of the nodes are stored consecutively in the stream. When a leaf is reached, the ID of the leaf node is added twice. Thus, every leaf is marked by a double appearance of the same ID. Before adding the ID of the next node in the traversal order to the stream, its parent node ID is added. This way the connection to the previous stripe can be reconstructed.

In the worst and unlikely case of a tree with all nodes connected to the root $3(n-1)$, $n = |V|$ IDs have to be stored. However, this should not be expected in general.

The advantage of this approach is that the tree can be easily reconstructed without any other connectivity data.

### Bit Mask Format

Since it can be assumed that the connectivities on which the graph is based are obtainable from the compressed file, storing (almost) any IDs can be avoided. In contrast to the previous format only a simple bit mask is stored. It is associated with a list of edges of the connectivity graph indicating the edges that are part of the tree. This requires that the edge list of the connectivity graph can be reconstructed in the identical order as during compression. In addition to this bit mask the ID of the root node has to be stored, so that the same hierarchy of nodes can be reconstructed.

While here no further connectivities are stored in addition to the compressed data, a complete reconstruction of the connectivity graph and the tree is required during decompression.

# 4 Wavelet Compression

An alternative compression approach to the previously introduced tree predictor is presented in this chapter. Likewise, it supports lossless data compression of integer-valued data over irregular grids with non-unique cell type. However, the compression strategy is substantially different, as it follows a lifting scheme that is used to calculate wavelet transforms.

Wavelet transforms constitute a time/space-frequency transformation that describes a multi-resolution decomposition. It has the distinct attribute to capture both location and frequency information of the original signal. Since most signals have time/space and frequency correlations, the essence of the signal can be captured efficiently. This property makes it particularly interesting for signal processing, such as data analysis, data filtering and data compression. For example, a discrete wavelet transformation is part of the image data compression standard JPEG 2000 [4]. The decorrelating properties [7] are used for lossless compression and are combined with a quantization of the frequency coefficients in the lossy case. For the latter, the essence of the image is usually captured in only a small set of coefficients. High frequency coefficients are quantized stronger or discarded, because they are assumed to have less impact on the visual appearance of an image, a form of perceptive compression. Here, a transform is presented that is used as a decorrelation step within the compression scheme introduced in Section 2.3. Consequently, the quantization is carried out prior to the lossless transformation.

The lifting scheme was introduced by Sweldens [60] as a tool to construct wavelets and wavelet transforms. In particular, it is the basis of the fast wavelet transform, an algorithm to efficiently compute wavelet transforms. Based on the lifting scheme, a method that can be used more generally as it is suitable for the irregular grids present in CFD is created. The presented transformation combines the procedure of the lifting scheme with techniques from algebraic multigrid (AMG) to achieve this purpose.

A short introduction to multiresolution analysis and wavelets is given in the following section. The lifting scheme is described in Section 4.2. Eventually, the proposed transformation is presented in Section 4.3.

## 4.1   Multiresolution Analysis and Wavelets

Multiresolution analysis provides a convenient framework for the description of wavelets. A multiresolution analysis is a sequence of successive approximation spaces $V_l \in L_2$ that can be used to construct a decomposition of $L_2$, where each of the spaces $V_l$ has a Riesz basis.

**Definition 4.1** *A sequence of $\varphi_i$ in a Hilbert space $(H, \langle \cdot \rangle)$ is called **Riesz basis** if positive constants $0 < A \leq B$ exist, such that*

$$A \sum_{i \in \mathbb{Z}} |c_i|^2 \leq \| \sum_{i \in \mathbb{Z}} c_i \varphi_i \|^2 \leq B \sum_{i \in \mathbb{Z}} |c_i|^2$$

*for all $(c_i)_{i \in \mathbb{Z}} \in \ell_2$ and $\overline{span(\varphi_i)} = H$.*

In the traditional sense a multiresolution analysis for $L_2(\mathbb{R})$ can be defined as follows.

**Definition 4.2** *A multiresolution analysis M of $L_2(\mathbb{R})$ is a sequence of nested closed linear subspaces $M = \{V_l \subset L_2(\mathbb{R}) | \ l \in \mathcal{L} \subset \mathbb{Z}\}$, so that:*

(1)   $V_l \subset V_{l+1}$

(2)   $\overline{\bigcup_{l \in \mathcal{L}} V_l} = L_2,$

(3)   $\bigcap_{l \in \mathcal{L}} V_l = \{0\},$

(4)   $f(x) \in V_l \Leftrightarrow f(2x) \in V_{l+1}$

(5)   $f(x) \in V_l \Leftrightarrow f(x - n2^{-l}) \in V_l, n \in \mathbb{Z}$

(6)   *for each $l \in \mathcal{L}$, $V_l$ has a Riesz basis given by functions $\{\varphi_{l,i} \mid i \in \mathcal{I}(l)\}$.*

As implied by conditions (4) and (5), one way to construct these subspaces is to form translates and dilates

$$\varphi_{l,i}(x) := 2^{l/2} \varphi(2^l x - i), \quad l, i \in \mathbb{Z}$$

of a function $\varphi \in L_2(\mathbb{R})$. Because of this relation functions $\varphi_{l,i}$ are referred to as *scaling functions*. Wavelet functions are defined as basis functions of spaces complementing the $V_l$ in $V_{l+1}$. Depending on the attributes one requires from the wavelet functions, various definitions are possible. For example, orthogonal wavelets can be defined as follows.

**Definition 4.3** *A set of functions $\{\psi_{l,j} \mid l \in \mathcal{L}, j \in \mathcal{J}(l)\}$, where $\mathcal{J}(l) := \mathcal{I}(l+1) \setminus \mathcal{I}(l)$ is a set of orthogonal wavelet functions if the two conditions apply:*

1)   *The space $W_l = \overline{span\{\psi_{l,j} \mid j \in \mathcal{J}(l)\}}$ is a complement of $V_l$ in $V_{l+1}$ and $W_l \perp V_l$.*

2)   *The set $\{\psi_{l,j} \mid l \in \mathcal{L}, j \in \mathcal{J}(l)\}$ is an orthonormal basis for $L_2$.*

Less restrictive definitions can be obtained by demanding only biorthogonality, a setting that is chosen for the generalized approach introduced with the lifting scheme. The above mentioned attribute that $\varphi_{l,i}$ are translates and dilates of each other is a property that cannot be maintained on irregular grids. Since it can be shown that the same relations apply to wavelets, they are inherently related to regular samplings and grids. More detailed descriptions of wavelets in the classical sense are found in [16, 30].

The lifting scheme provides a tool to construct so-called second generation wavelets that are not limited to the regular setting. Nevertheless, it can also be employed to construct wavelets in the classical sense, so-called first generation wavelets [17]. The following brief introduction is based on the generalized approach introduced together with the lifting scheme in [60].

Considering, $L_2 = L_2(\Omega, \Sigma, \mu)$, where $\Omega \subset \mathbb{R}^n$ is the spatial domain, $\Sigma$ is a $\sigma$-algebra and $\mu$ a non-atomic measure on $\Sigma$, one can define a multiresolution analysis as follows.

**Definition 4.4** *A multiresolution analysis $M$ of $L_2$ is a sequence of nested closed linear subspaces $M = \{V_l \subset L_2 | \ l \in \mathcal{L} \subset \mathbb{Z}\}$, so that:*

(1) $V_l \subset V_{l+1}$

(2) $\overline{\bigcup_{l \in \mathcal{L}} V_l} = L_2$,

(3) *for each $l \in \mathcal{L}$, $V_l$ has a Riesz basis given by functions $\{\varphi_{l,i} \ | \ i \in \mathcal{I}(l)\}$.*

*One can think of $\mathcal{I}(l)$ as a general index set, where it is assumed that $\mathcal{I}(l) \subset \mathcal{I}(l+1)$. There are two cases to consider:*

$\mathcal{L} = \mathbb{N}:$ *This means there is one coarsest level $V_0$. This is the case if $\mu(\Omega) < \infty$.*

$\mathcal{L} = \mathbb{Z}:$ *This is the bi-infinite setting in which typically $\mu(\Omega) = \infty$.*
    *Then it is also required that $\bigcap_{l \in \mathbb{Z}} V_l = \{0\}$.*

While the above definition of a multiresolution analysis is similar to that used in the regular setting, the scaling and translation attributes are dropped from the definition. Still, they are thought of as spaces of multiple resolutions, and functions $\varphi_{l,i}$ are still referred to as scaling functions. For a multiresolution to be of use projections $P_l$ onto $V_l$ that satisfy

$$\lim_{l \to \infty} \|f - P_l f\| = 0, \quad f \in L_2 \tag{4.1}$$

are necessary. Functions $f \in L_2$ can then be approximated by multiple resolutions. To define such a projection dual scaling functions are of relevance. A dual multiresolution analysis $\widetilde{M} = \{\widetilde{V}_l \ | \ l \in \mathcal{L}\}$ consists of spaces $\widetilde{V}_l$ with Riesz bases given by the dual functions $\widetilde{\varphi}_{l,i}$ of the $\varphi_{l,i}$. Scaling functions and dual scaling functions are biorthogonal in the sense that

$$\langle \varphi_{l,i}, \widetilde{\varphi}_{l,i'} \rangle = \delta_{i,i'} \quad \text{for } i, i' \in \mathcal{I}(l).$$

This property can be exploited for the definition of a projection $P_l$ onto $V_l$

$$P_l f := \sum_{l,i} \lambda_{l,i} \varphi_{l,i},$$

with coefficients $\lambda_{l,i} := \langle f, \widetilde{\varphi}_{l,i} \rangle$. If the projection is uniformly bounded the condition (4.1) is satisfied.

Identical to the first generation case, wavelets are defined as basis functions of the space $W_l$ complementing $V_l$ in $V_{l+1}$.

**Definition 4.5** *A set of functions $\{\psi_{l,j} \mid l \in \mathcal{L}, j \in \mathcal{J}(l)\}$, where $\mathcal{J}(l) := \mathcal{I}(l+1) \setminus \mathcal{I}(l)$ is a set of wavelet functions if the two conditions apply:*

1) *The space $W_l = \overline{\text{span}\{\psi_{l,j} \mid j \in \mathcal{J}(l)\}}$ is a complement of $V_l$ in $V_{l+1}$ and $W_l \perp \widetilde{V}_l$. Here $\widetilde{V}_l$ denotes the dual space of $V_l$.*

2) *If $\mathcal{L} = \mathbb{Z}$: The set $\{\psi_{l,j}/\|\psi_{l,j}\| \mid l \in \mathcal{L}, j \in \mathcal{J}(l)\}$ is a Riesz basis for $L_2$.*
   *If $\mathcal{L} = \mathbb{N}$: The set $\{\psi_{l,j}/\|\psi_{l,j}\| \mid l \in \mathcal{L}, j \in \mathcal{J}(l)\} \cup \{\varphi_{0,i}/\|\varphi_{0,i}\|\}$ is a Riesz basis for $L_2$.*

The dual wavelet basis is given by dual wavelets $\widetilde{\psi}_{l,j}$ that are biorthogonal to the wavelets

$$\langle \psi_{l,j}, \widetilde{\psi}_{l',j'} \rangle = \delta_{j,j'} \delta_{l,l'} \quad \text{for } j, j' \in \mathcal{J}(l), l \in \mathcal{L}.$$

The dual wavelets span $\widetilde{W}_l$ that complement $\widetilde{V}_l$ in $\widetilde{V}_{l+1}$ and $\widetilde{W}_l \perp V_l$. Since the wavelets constitute a Riesz basis, every $f \in L_2$ can be written as the expansion

$$f = \sum_{l,j} \gamma_{l,j} \psi_{l,j}.$$

It follows from the biorthogonality that the coefficients satisfy $\gamma_{l,j} = \langle f, \widetilde{\psi}_{l,j} \rangle$. This can be simply verified by inserting $f$ into $\langle \cdot, \widetilde{\psi}_{l,j} \rangle$ and exploiting the biorthogonality of the wavelets and their duals. These coherences and the refinement relations described in the following are used to construct the wavelet transform. The refinement relations are implied by the definitions of a multiresolution analysis and of wavelets. Every function $\varphi_{l,i}$ can be written as a linear combination of functions $\varphi_{l+1,i}$ of the next finer level $V_{l+1}$. Hence, some coefficients $\{h_{l,i,k} \mid k \in \mathcal{I}(l+1)\}$ exist, such that

$$\varphi_{l,i} = \sum_k h_{l,i,k} \varphi_{l+1,k}. \tag{4.2}$$

Similarly, a refinement relation is given for wavelets by

$$\psi_{l,j} = \sum_k g_{l,j,k} \varphi_{l+1,k}, \tag{4.3}$$

as $W_l \subset V_{l+1}$. The sets $\{h_{l,i,k} \mid k \in \mathcal{I}(l+1)\}$ and $\{g_{l,j,k} \mid k \in \mathcal{I}(l+1)\}$ are called filters. Analogous relations exist for the duals with filters $\widetilde{h}$ and $\widetilde{g}$. Here, only finite filters are taken into consideration.

**Definition 4.6** *A set of real numbers* $\{h_{l,i,k} \mid l \in \mathcal{L}, i \in \mathcal{I}(l), k \in \mathcal{I}(l+1)\}$ *is called a finite filter if the following conditions apply:*

1) *For each $l$ and $i$ only a finite number of coefficients $h_{l,i,k}$ are non zero, and thus the set*

$$\mathcal{K}(l,i) = \{k \in \mathcal{I}(l+1) \mid h_{l,i,k} \neq 0\}$$

*is finite.*

2) *For each $l$ and $k$ only a finite number of coefficients $h_{l,i,k}$ are non zero, and thus the set*

$$\mathcal{I}(l,k) = \{i \in \mathcal{I}(l) \mid h_{l,i,k} \neq 0\}$$

*is finite.*

3) *The cardinality of the sets $\mathcal{K}(l,i)$ and $\mathcal{I}(l,k)$ is uniformly bounded for all $l, i,$ and $k$.*

It is noted that filter coefficients are defined for each level and data point. Furthermore, a set of filters will be called biorthogonal if the following definition applies.

**Definition 4.7** *A set of filters* $\{h, \widetilde{h}, g, \widetilde{g}\}$ *is a set of biorthogonal filters if*

$$\sum_k g_{l,j,k} \widetilde{g}_{l,j',k} = \delta_{j,j'}$$

$$\sum_k h_{l,i,k} \widetilde{h}_{l,i',k} = \delta_{i,i'}$$

$$\sum_k h_{l,i,k} \widetilde{g}_{l,j,k} = 0$$

$$\sum_k g_{l,j,k} \widetilde{h}_{l,i,k} = 0$$

*is satisfied.*

So far, only the definitions and some attributes of scaling and wavelet functions were mentioned. The way to construct them remains to be shown. Without going into much detail, it shall be mentioned that scaling functions can be constructed by the cascade algorithm. As in the first generation case, often no analytical representation is known or exists for scaling functions. Instead, they are defined through an iterative process that is described by the cascade algorithm. One only needs a set of filters and a set of partitionings for the computation.

**Definition 4.8** *A set of measurable subsets* $\{S_{l,i} \in \Sigma \mid l \in \mathcal{L}, i \in \mathcal{I}(l)\}$ *is called a set of partitionings if*

1) $\forall l \in \mathcal{L} : \overline{\bigcup_{i \in \mathcal{I}(l)} S_{l,i}} = \Omega$ *and the union is disjoint,*
2) $\mathcal{I}(l) \subset \mathcal{I}(l+1)$,
3) $S_{l+1,i} \subset S_{l,i}$,
4) *For a fixed $i \in \mathcal{I}(l_0), \bigcap_{l>l_0} S_{l,i}$ is a set which contains 1 point.*

However, one obtains the desired scaling functions only if the cascade algorithm converges. Also, the outcome is dependent on the filters as well as the splitting. If the cascade algorithm converges for a set of biorthogonal filters and a set of splittings, then the resulting scaling functions, wavelets and their duals are biorthogonal in the sense that

$$\langle \widetilde{\varphi}_{l,i}, \varphi_{l,i'} \rangle = \delta_{i,i'}$$
$$\langle \widetilde{\psi}_{l,j}, \psi_{l,j'} \rangle = \delta_{j,j'}$$
$$\langle \widetilde{\varphi}_{l,i}, \varphi_{l,j} \rangle = 0$$
$$\langle \widetilde{\psi}_{l,j}, \varphi_{l,i} \rangle = 0.$$

The reader is referred to [60] for a description of the cascade algorithm. If feasible filters are found, wavelet coefficients $\{\gamma_{l,j} \mid j \in \mathcal{J}(l)\}$ can be calculated from a set of given coefficients $\{\lambda_{l,i} \mid i \in \mathcal{I}(l)\}$. The refinement relations of dual scaling functions and wavelets (4.3) show that the forward transform is given by the recursive calculation of

$$\lambda_{l,i} = \sum_{k \in \mathcal{K}(l,i)} \widetilde{h}_{l,i,k} \lambda_{l+1,i} \quad \text{and} \quad \gamma_{l,j} = \sum_{k \in \mathcal{K}(l,j)} \widetilde{g}_{l,j,k} \lambda_{l+1,i}.$$

This can be seen from the definition of $\lambda_{l,i}$, $\gamma_{l,j}$ and the refinement relation as

$$\lambda_{l,i} = \langle f, \widetilde{\varphi}_{l,i} \rangle$$
$$= \langle f, \sum_i \widetilde{h}_{l,i,k} \widetilde{\varphi}_{l+1,i} \rangle$$
$$= \sum_i \widetilde{h}_{l,i,k} \lambda_{l+1,i}.$$

The coherences are obtained analogously for coefficients $\gamma_{l,j}$. The inverse transform is a result of the recursive application of

$$\lambda_{l+1,i} = \sum_{i \in \mathcal{I}(l,k)} h_{l,i,k} \lambda_{l,i} + \sum_{j \in \mathcal{J}(l,k)} g_{l,j,k} \gamma_{l,i}.$$

While these relations may be used to calculate a wavelet transform, they have the disadvantage that one needs to know biorthogonal filters for every scale $l \in \mathcal{L}$. This also includes the filters $h$ and $g$ that are utilized for the reconstruction. With the lifting scheme an alternative approach to calculate wavelet transforms is introduced.

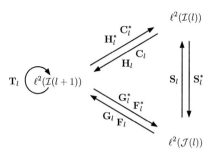

**Figure 4.1:** Schematic representation of operators used for the lifting scheme (modified from [60])

## 4.2 The Lifting Scheme

The lifting scheme is essentially a method to calculate a new set of biorthogonal filters from an 'old' set of filter coefficients. An operator notation is introduced for the description. Considering the sequence spaces $\ell^2(\mathcal{I}(l+1))$, $\ell^2(\mathcal{I}(l))$ and $\ell^2(\mathcal{J}(l))$. For $\boldsymbol{\xi}_{l+1} = \{\xi_{l+1,k} \mid k \in \mathcal{I}(l+1)\} \in \ell^2(\mathcal{I}(l+1))\}$ and likewise $\boldsymbol{\lambda} \in \ell^2(\mathcal{I}(l))$ and $\boldsymbol{\gamma} \in \ell^2(\mathcal{J}(l))$, two operators are defined as:

1)  $\mathbf{H}_l : \ell^2(\mathcal{I}(l+1)) \to \ell^2(\mathcal{I}(l))$, where $\boldsymbol{\lambda}_l = \mathbf{H}_l\boldsymbol{\xi}_{l+1}$ means

$$\lambda_{l,i} = \sum_{k\in\mathcal{I}(l+1)} h_{l,i,k}\xi_{l+1,k}.$$

2)  $\mathbf{G}_l : \ell^2(\mathcal{I}(l+1)) \to \ell^2(\mathcal{J}(l))$, where $\boldsymbol{\gamma}_l = \mathbf{G}_l\boldsymbol{\xi}_{l+1}$ means

$$\gamma_{l,j} = \sum_{k\in\mathcal{I}(l+1)} g_{l,j,k}\xi_{l+1,k}.$$

In Figure 4.1 a schematic representation of the operators used in this section is illustrated. By using the operator notation lifting is expressed in the following theorem.

**Theorem 4.1** *(Lifting). Take an initial set of biorthogonal filter operators $\{\mathbf{H}_l^{old}, \widetilde{\mathbf{H}}_l^{old}, \mathbf{G}_l^{old}, \widetilde{\mathbf{G}}_l^{old}\}$. Then a new set of biorthogonal filter operators $\{\mathbf{H}_l, \widetilde{\mathbf{H}}_l, \mathbf{G}_l, \widetilde{\mathbf{G}}_l\}$ can be found as*

$$\mathbf{H}_l = \mathbf{H}_l^{old}$$
$$\widetilde{\mathbf{H}}_l = \widetilde{\mathbf{H}}_l^{old} + \mathbf{S}_l\widetilde{\mathbf{G}}_l^{old}$$
$$\mathbf{G}_l = \mathbf{G}_l^{old} - \mathbf{S}_l^*\mathbf{H}_l^{old}$$
$$\widetilde{\mathbf{G}}_l = \widetilde{\mathbf{G}}_l^{old}.$$

where $\boldsymbol{S}_l$ is an operator from $\ell^2(\mathcal{J}(l))$ to $\ell^2(\mathcal{I}(l))$.

The advantage of employing lifting is that one can apply a trivial set of biorthogonal filters and use lifting to achieve the effect of a new and different set of filters with desired properties. The new set of filters is not calculated specifically, instead the old filters and a lifting step are applied. The desired properties of the new filter operators are held by the operator $\boldsymbol{S}_l$. Various possibilities of simple biorthogonal filter sets have been proposed to start the lifting scheme [60, 61].

One possible choice of trivial filter operators is introduced by Sweldens as the lazy wavelet transform. It essentially does nothing and can be described formally by two subsampling operators $\mathbf{C}_l$ (coarse) and $\mathbf{F}_l$ (fine):

$$\mathbf{C}_l : \ell^2(\mathcal{I}(l+1)) \rightarrow \ell^2(\mathcal{I}(l)), \text{where } \boldsymbol{\lambda} = \mathbf{C}_l\boldsymbol{\xi} \text{ means that } \lambda_i = \xi_i \text{ for } i \in \mathcal{I}(l).$$
$$\mathbf{F}_l : \ell^2(\mathcal{I}(l+1)) \rightarrow \ell^2(\mathcal{J}(l)), \text{where } \boldsymbol{\gamma} = \mathbf{F}_l\boldsymbol{\xi} \text{ means that } \gamma_j = \xi_j \text{ for } j \in \mathcal{J}(l).$$

Since these operators provide a trivial orthogonal splitting, any operator

$$\mathbf{W} : \ell^2(\mathcal{I}(l)) \rightarrow \ell^2(\mathcal{I}(l))$$

can be decomposed as

$$\mathbf{W} = \mathbf{W}_C\mathbf{C} + \mathbf{W}_F\mathbf{F}, \quad \text{with} \quad \mathbf{W}_C = \mathbf{W}\mathbf{C}^* \quad \text{and} \quad \mathbf{W}_F = \mathbf{W}\mathbf{F}^*. \qquad (4.4)$$

This property can be exploited in association with interpolating scaling functions.

**Definition 4.9** *[60] A set of scaling functions $\{\varphi_{l,i}|l,i\}$ is interpolating if a set of interpolation points $x_i$ exists, so that $\varphi_{l,i} = \delta_{i,i'}$ for $i, i' \in \mathcal{I}(l)$.*

For interpolating scaling functions the following condition is satisfied as stated in [60]:

$$\mathbf{H}_l^{\text{int}}\mathbf{C}^* = \mathbf{I}.$$

It follows from (4.4) that

$$\begin{aligned}
\mathbf{H}_l^{\text{int}} &= \mathbf{H}_l^{\text{int}}\mathbf{C}^*\mathbf{C} + \mathbf{H}_l^{\text{int}}\mathbf{F}^*\mathbf{F} \\
&= \mathbf{C} + \mathbf{H}_l^{\text{int}}\mathbf{F}^*\mathbf{F}.
\end{aligned}$$

Defining $\widetilde{\mathbf{S}}_l := \mathbf{H}_l^{\text{int}}\mathbf{F}^*$ yields $\mathbf{H}_l^{\text{int}} = \mathbf{C} + \widetilde{\mathbf{S}}_l\mathbf{F}$, which can be interpreted as the result of applying dual lifting to the lazy wavelet. The new set of biorthogonal filters can then be written as

$$\mathbf{H}_l = \mathbf{C}_l + \widetilde{\mathbf{S}}_l\mathbf{D}_l$$
$$\widetilde{\mathbf{H}}_l = \mathbf{C}_l$$
$$\mathbf{G}_l = \mathbf{F}_l$$
$$\widetilde{\mathbf{G}}_l = \mathbf{F}_l - \widetilde{\mathbf{S}}_l^*\mathbf{D}_l.$$

However, only $\mathbf{H}$ and $\widetilde{\mathbf{G}}$ are modified by lifting, and filters $\widetilde{\mathbf{H}}$ and $\mathbf{G}$ remain the trivial filter operators. Therefore, a regular lifting is applied in addition. The resulting filters can then be used to define a wavelet transform in which each iteration can be calculated as a lazy wavelet transform followed by a dual lifting and a regular lifting. With operators $\mathbf{S}_l$ and $\widetilde{\mathbf{S}}_l$ the transformation is fully controlled. The new filter coefficients are then obtained as

$$\mathbf{H}_l = \mathbf{C}_l + \widetilde{\mathbf{S}}_l\mathbf{F}_l,$$
$$\widetilde{\mathbf{H}}_l = (\mathbf{I} - \mathbf{S}_l\widetilde{\mathbf{S}}_l^*)\mathbf{C}_l + \mathbf{S}_l\mathbf{F}_l,$$
$$\mathbf{G}_l = -\mathbf{S}_l^*\mathbf{C}_l + (\mathbf{I} - \mathbf{S}_l^*\widetilde{\mathbf{S}}_l)\mathbf{F}_l,$$
$$\widetilde{\mathbf{G}}_l = -\widetilde{\mathbf{S}}_l^*\mathbf{C}_l + \mathbf{F}_l.$$

In Figure 4.2, a diagram of one iteration of the corresponding forward transform is illustrated. First, the lazy wavelet transform is carried out, which can essentially be interpreted as a splitting. Points are separated into coarse and fine points. Thereafter, the dual lifting and regular lifting are applied to obtain the coefficients of the coarser representation and the wavelet coefficients on the fine points. By construction, the wavelet coefficients hold the detail that is absent from the coarser approximation. Thus, the dual lifting can be regarded as a prediction and the regular lifting as an update process. Based on this idea a transformation is constructed in the following section.

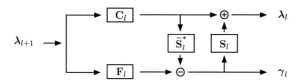

**Figure 4.2:** One iteration of the wavelet transform involves the application of the lazy wavelet transform using $C$ and $F$, followed by the dual and regular lifting (modified from [60]).

## 4.3   The Transformation

As mentioned in the brief description of the lifting scheme, wavelets are constructed by
using a set of partitionings and the cascade algorithm. For the current application no such
set is known, rather the tessellation of the domain is given by a single-resolution irregular
grid. The intention of the approach followed here is to construct a transformation from
single-resolution data to multiresolution data. It is based on the procedure of the lifting
scheme and combines it with techniques derived from AMG. Using the lifting scheme as
basis for the algorithm has mainly two advantages. First, the inverse is given directly
and thus, no additional operators have to be determined for the inverse transformation.
The second advantage is that finding suitable transformation operators can be confined to
the search for splitting, update and prediction functions. Feasible solutions are subject to
the condition that the properties of the resulting transformation have attributes similar
to those of classical transforms. Furthermore, they must be applicable to the highly
irregular grids found in CFD. To meet these requirements, the algorithmic procedure of
the lifting scheme is combined with grid simplification strategies for grid coarsening as well
as approximation methods that are derived from techniques of AMG.

It is assumed that the data to be compressed $(\lambda_i)_{i \in \mathcal{I}}$ belongs to some function $f \in L_2$ in
that

$$f = \sum_{i \in \mathcal{I}} \lambda_i \varphi_i.$$

Here, $\varphi_i$ are functions defined on some domain $\Omega$ in $\mathbb{R}^n$, and $\mathcal{I} \subset \mathbb{Z}$ is some index set. The
intention is to transform this single-resolution data into a multiresolution representation. A
transformation $\mathbf{T}$ mapping single scale data $\boldsymbol{\lambda} = (\lambda_i)_{i \in \mathcal{I}}$ to a multiresolution representation
$\boldsymbol{\gamma}$ is necessary for this purpose,

$$\mathbf{T}\boldsymbol{\lambda} = \boldsymbol{\gamma}.$$

For data compression and other signal processing applications the success of the resulting
method relies on the efficiency, the decorellating properties and the accuracy of this transformation. Its efficiency is a matter of the computational complexity that is relative to
the sparsity of the transformation matrix $\mathbf{T}$. Hence, to be of practical interest $\mathbf{T}$ and its
inverse $\mathbf{T}^{-1}$ should be sparse. The decorrelating properties of the transformation are essential to the application at hand. The overall compression factor is strongly dependent on
this property, since it is embedded into a compression scheme as a lossless method. While
the stability is not the main concern here, it is of particular importance if the transformation is used as a lossy compression scheme in which a quantization of the transformed
coefficients is performed. Then, it is important that the quantization does not lead to
any significant loss in the accuracy of the data once it is reconstructed. The stability of
multiscale transformations was treated by Dahmen in [14, 15]. For Dahmen a uniformly
bounded condition was of interest for these transformations, e.g.

$$\|\mathbf{T}\|, \|\mathbf{T}^{-1}\| = \mathcal{O}(1), \quad |\mathcal{I}| \to \infty$$

is of interest. Here, $\| \cdot \|$ denotes the operator norm induced by the underlying sequence or vector norm.

As mentioned before, the structure of $\mathbf{T}$ is aligned with the procedure of the lifting scheme. It is assumed that single-resolution data $\boldsymbol{\lambda}_{l+1}$ is given at some discretization level $l+1 \in \mathcal{L}$. Associated with that level, $\boldsymbol{\lambda}_{l+1}$ denotes a series of data values $\lambda_{l+1,i}, i \in \mathcal{I}(l+1)$. Two bounded linear operators

$$\widetilde{\mathbf{H}}_l \in L(\ell(\mathcal{I}(l+1)), \ell(\mathcal{I}(l))) \quad \text{and} \quad \widetilde{\mathbf{G}}_l \in L(\ell(\mathcal{I}(l+1)), \ell(\mathcal{J}(l)))$$

are applied at each level $l+1$. The application of these operators yields two series: $\boldsymbol{\lambda}_l$ is an approximation of $\boldsymbol{\lambda}_{l+1}$ and $\boldsymbol{\gamma}_l$ contains the detail absent from $\boldsymbol{\lambda}_l$. The complete transformation is obtained as follows. If one defines the values on the next coarser level by setting

$$\boldsymbol{\lambda}_l := \widetilde{\mathbf{H}}_l \boldsymbol{\lambda}_{l+1}, \quad \boldsymbol{\gamma}_l := \widetilde{\mathbf{G}}_l \boldsymbol{\lambda}_{l+1} \quad \text{for } l \in \mathcal{L},$$

the complete transformation is described by the following scheme:

$$
\begin{array}{ccccccc}
& \widetilde{\mathbf{H}}_l & & \widetilde{\mathbf{H}}_{l-1} & & \widetilde{\mathbf{H}}_{l-2} & \\
\boldsymbol{\lambda}_{l+1} & \rightarrow & \boldsymbol{\lambda}_l & \rightarrow & \boldsymbol{\lambda}_{l-1} & \rightarrow & \cdots \boldsymbol{\lambda}_0 \\
& \widetilde{\mathbf{G}}_l & & \widetilde{\mathbf{G}}_{l-1} & & \widetilde{\mathbf{G}}_{l-2} & \\
& \searrow & & \searrow & & \searrow & \\
& & \boldsymbol{\gamma}_l & & \boldsymbol{\gamma}_{l-1} & & \cdots \boldsymbol{\gamma}_0
\end{array}
.$$

At every level, the associated linear operator is applied to the approximation values recursively until a coarsest level is reached. Eventually, a multi-scale representation is obtained in the form of

$$\boldsymbol{\gamma}^{(l+1)} := (\boldsymbol{\lambda}_0, \boldsymbol{\gamma}_0, \boldsymbol{\gamma}_1, \dots, \boldsymbol{\gamma}_l).$$

The multiresolution data consists of an approximation set at the coarsest level as well as of detail sets that differentiates each level from the next coarser one.

Relaxing notation and denoting the identity operator by $\mathbf{I}$ regardless of its dimensionality, the transformation can be written as follows. Concatenating matrices $\mathbf{W}_l := (\widetilde{\mathbf{H}}_l, \widetilde{\mathbf{G}}_l)$ yields the transformation $\mathbf{T}$. By defining

$$\mathbf{T}_l := \begin{pmatrix} \mathbf{I} & 0 \\ 0 & \mathbf{W}_l \end{pmatrix}$$

the transformation can be written as

$$\mathbf{T}\boldsymbol{\lambda}_l = \boldsymbol{\gamma}^{(l)},$$

where

$$\mathbf{T} := \mathbf{T}_0 \dots \mathbf{T}_l.$$

Instead of creating these operators, a splitting is performed first that is then followed by a prediction and an update process according to the lifting scheme. The following representation uses a block-structured operator notation. It is assumed that data vectors are sorted such that fine and coarse points are grouped in blocks,

$$\lambda_l = (\lambda_l^F, \lambda_l^C)^T.$$

Here, $\lambda_l^F \in \mathbb{R}^m$ and $\lambda_l^C \in \mathbb{R}^n$, with $m := |\mathcal{J}(l)|$, $n := |\mathcal{I}(l)|$. Differently, the block notation can also be seen as the result of applying the splitting. The prediction operator is $\mathbf{P} \in \mathbb{R}^{(m \times n)}$, and $\mathbf{U} \in \mathbb{R}^{(n \times m)}$ is the update operator. The prediction process can be written with this notation as

$$\mathbf{W}_l^P := \left( \begin{array}{c|c} \mathbf{I} & -\mathbf{P} \\ \hline \mathbf{0} & \mathbf{I} \end{array} \right)$$

and the update as

$$\mathbf{W}_l^U := \left( \begin{array}{c|c} \mathbf{I} & \mathbf{0} \\ \hline \mathbf{U} & \mathbf{I} \end{array} \right),$$

respectively. Applying $\mathbf{W}_l^P$ and $\mathbf{W}_l^U$ in the order of the lifting scheme, one has

$$\mathbf{W}_l := \mathbf{W}_l^U \mathbf{W}_l^P = \left( \begin{array}{c|c} \mathbf{I} & -\mathbf{P} \\ \hline \mathbf{U} & \mathbf{I} - \mathbf{U}\mathbf{P} \end{array} \right).$$

Since the lifting scheme directly implies an inverse transform, one has

$$\mathbf{W}_l^{-1} = \left( \begin{array}{c|c} \mathbf{I} - \mathbf{P}\mathbf{U} & \mathbf{P} \\ \hline -\mathbf{U} & \mathbf{I} \end{array} \right).$$

While the above description outlines the structure of a multiresolution transformation, operators suitable for the underlying irregular grid have to be defined for each transformation step. In addition, it must be determined how attributes such as efficiency, decorrelation properties and accuracy can be added to the transformation. The techniques of AMG are consulted for this purpose.

AMG is a class of algorithms suitable for numerically solving systems of (sparse) linear equations obtained from discretization of differential equations. In particular, they are suitable for elliptic problems. In multigrid methods a multiresolution strategy is pursued to solve these problems. Although AMG has nothing to do with data compression, it comprises methods that can be used to complete the compression scheme due to its multiresolution background.

### 4.3.1 Algebraic Multigrid

One differentiates between geometric and algebraic multigrid methods. Geometric multigrid (GMG) relies on a hierarchy of grids of various resolutions. The hierarchy is obtained from coarsening the grid used for discretization. In contrast, AMG is solely based on the linear equations:

$$\mathbf{A}\mathbf{x} = \mathbf{b}, \quad \mathbf{A} \in \mathbb{R}^{n \times n}, \ \mathbf{x}, \mathbf{b} \in \mathbb{R}^n.$$

Although AMG is independent of any grid structure, the same multiresolution concept is applied. The grid coarsening of GMG translates to a reduction of the system of linear equations based on the algebraic coherences. The general idea behind both multigrid concepts is to accelerate the convergence of an iterative solver by performing a defect correction on a reduced system. For the above system of linear equations the error of an approximation $\mathbf{x}^r$ of the solution $\mathbf{x}$ is defined by

$$\mathbf{y}^r := \mathbf{x} - \mathbf{x}^r$$

and the defect by

$$\mathbf{d}^r := \mathbf{b} - \mathbf{A}\mathbf{x}^r.$$

These definitions can be used to rewrite the original equation to obtain the defect equation:

$$\mathbf{A}\mathbf{y}^r = \mathbf{d}^r.$$

Since this equation is equivalent to the original and no numerical benefit is achieved, a simplified form of this equation is utilized in the defect correction process of multigrid methods. The reduced system

$$\widehat{\mathbf{A}}\widehat{\mathbf{y}}^r = \widehat{\mathbf{d}}^r$$

yields the approximation $\widehat{\mathbf{y}}^r$ of the error that can be calculated significantly faster. Once the approximation of the error is determined, it can be used as correction term of $\mathbf{x}^r$. The equality $\mathbf{x} = \mathbf{x}^r + \mathbf{y}^r$ suggests that a new and improved approximation is obtained as

$$\mathbf{x}^{r+1} = \mathbf{x}^r + \widehat{\mathbf{y}}^r.$$

Altogether, this process implicates an iterative procedure that, if it converges, can be used to solve the system of linear equations. It also describes the iteration of which the convergence is meant to be accelerated by means of multigrid. The essential idea is the simplification of the defect equation to speed up the calculations for a defect correction. As indicated by the name and in the case of GMG, this is achieved by restricting the linear system to a coarser grid. Although AMG is strictly based on the algebraic equations and does not require any underlying grid structure, the simplification can still be thought of as a grid coarsening. Essentially, the grid coarsening of GMG corresponds to a reduction of the linear system. Coarsening strategies are required for this reduction.

While the description above shows how the coarse grid correction can be integrated into an iterative process, its motivation is derived from two principles: the smoothing principle and the coarse grid principle. The smoothing principle is a consequence of the behavior of classical iterative methods such as the Gauß-Seidel method. If these methods are applied appropriately to elliptic problems, it can be observed that the error of the approximation becomes smooth after a few iterations. While it does not necessarily become small, the smoothness is the attribute that is exploited in an interplay with the coarse grid principle. It follows the idea that a smooth error can be approximated well on a coarser level. The defect correction on a coarser or reduced system requires significantly less computational

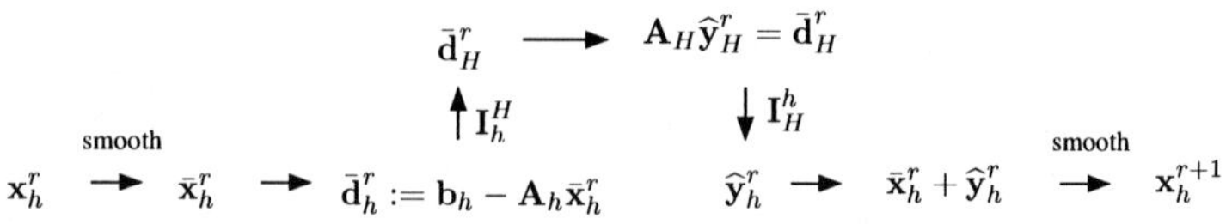

$$\bar{\mathbf{d}}_H^r \longrightarrow \mathbf{A}_H \widehat{\mathbf{y}}_H^r = \bar{\mathbf{d}}_H^r$$

$$\uparrow \mathbf{I}_h^H \qquad\qquad \downarrow \mathbf{I}_H^h$$

$$\text{smooth} \qquad\qquad\qquad\qquad\qquad\qquad \text{smooth}$$

$$\mathbf{x}_h^r \;\rightarrow\; \bar{\mathbf{x}}_h^r \;\rightarrow\; \bar{\mathbf{d}}_h^r := \mathbf{b}_h - \mathbf{A}_h \bar{\mathbf{x}}_h^r \qquad \widehat{\mathbf{y}}_h^r \;\rightarrow\; \bar{\mathbf{x}}_h^r + \widehat{\mathbf{y}}_h^r \;\rightarrow\; \mathbf{x}_h^{r+1}$$

**Figure 4.3:** A two-level grid correction scheme is shown. The restriction operator $\mathbf{I}_h^H$ is applied to the defect vector $\mathbf{d}_h^r$ to transfer it to the coarse level. Once the defect equation is solved at the coarse level, the correction $\widehat{\mathbf{y}}_H^r$ is interpolated back onto the fine level.

time, since far less equations and unknowns are present, and even more so if this is applied in an iterative procedure.

In Figure 4.3, the coarse grid correction is illustrated for a fine and a coarse level denoted by $\Omega_h$ and $\Omega_H$. Indices $h$ and $H$ mark vectors and operators on $\Omega_h$ and $\Omega_H$, respectively. This notation will be maintained throughout the rest of this chapter. After pre-smoothing, the defect is determined at the fine level by $\bar{\mathbf{d}}_h^r := \mathbf{b}_h - \mathbf{A}_h \bar{\mathbf{x}}_h^r$. The defect is then transferred to the coarse level by a restriction $\mathbf{I}_h^H$: $\bar{\mathbf{d}}_H^r = \mathbf{I}_h^H \bar{\mathbf{d}}_h^r$. At the coarse level, the defect equation $\mathbf{A}_H \widehat{\mathbf{y}}_H^r = \bar{\mathbf{d}}_H^r$ is solved. The operator $\mathbf{A}_H$ is obtained by using the Galerkin method as $\mathbf{A}_H = \mathbf{I}_h^H \mathbf{A}_h \mathbf{I}_H^h$. The correction $\widehat{\mathbf{y}}_h^r$ is transferred to the fine level by the interpolation operator $\mathbf{I}_H^h$. By using the correction $\widehat{\mathbf{y}}_h^r = \mathbf{I}_H^h \widehat{\mathbf{y}}_H^r$ the new approximation at the fine level is obtained by $\bar{\mathbf{x}}_h^{r+1} = \bar{\mathbf{x}}_h^r + \widehat{\mathbf{y}}_h^r$. Finally, a post-smoothing is applied to obtain $\mathbf{x}_h^{r+1}$.

The smoothing, the splitting and the coarse grid correction form the components of an AMG cycle. The complete two-level AMG cycle comprises the following steps that are performed in the order of their listing. The terminology used originated from the geometric multigrid, where coarse and fine points refer to points on a coarse and a fine grid, respectively.

### Pre-Smoothing
According to the smoothing principle several iterations of a classical solver, such as the Jacobi solver, are computed to acquire an approximation that shows a smooth error. Based on this approximation, the interplay with the coarse grid correction is performed.

### C/F-Splitting
A meaningful selection of variables or points has to be performed to find a reduced system. This is achieved by the C/F-Splitting. It divides the set of points into two disjoint subsets of coarse and fine points (C- and F-points). C-points compose the points of the reduced system.

### Restriction
The restriction is the process, during which the defect $\mathbf{d}_h^r$ is transferred to the coarse level. In the AMG context, for symmetric positive definite problems the restriction is usually

performed with the transpose of the interpolation. In that case a variational principle is
maintained. It states that the Galerkin-based coarse-grid corrections minimize the energy
norm of the error and, consequently, that divergence is impossible if the energy norm of
the smoother is smaller than 1 [65].

### Solving

Once the defect is restricted to the coarse level, the coarse defect equation $\mathbf{A}_H \widehat{\mathbf{y}}_H^r = \mathbf{d}_H^r$
has to be solved. As mentioned before, the operator $\mathbf{A}_H$ is obtained by means of the
Galerkin principle.

### Interpolation

After the coarse grid correction is performed, the correction term is interpolated back to
the fine grid.

### Post-Smoothing

As a final step of the AMG cycle a few iterations of a classical solver are applied again.

Solving the coarse defect equation directly is usually too computationally expensive, hence
the same two-level approach is applied again. This recursion is performed until a coarsest
level has been reached. At the coarsest level the defect equation is solved by applying a
direct solver. Since one cycle is equivalent to one iteration at the finest level, usually several
cycles have to be performed until the accuracy of the approximation is sufficient. There is
a great number of variations and adjustments to AMG depending on the characteristics of
the linear equations at hand. All in all, there are far too many facets to multigrid methods
to be covered in this short introduction. For that reason, the interested reader is referred
to [65, 58], where a detailed description of the multigrid approach is given. However, the
excerpts listed here are sufficient for the description of the transformation method.

Although solving linear equations is a totally different topic, the common multiresolution
background is obvious. This can be exploited in the search for a suitable splitting, prediction and update, in that the corresponding AMG techniques are utilized. Hence, the
C-/F-splitting, interpolation and restriction are incorporated into the three phases of the
lifting scheme. The smoothing and solving process of AMG are of no use in the present
context. While the similarities make the general proceedings clear, there are some details
that have to be considered when assembling this compression scheme by using AMG components. One important aspect arising from the decision to use AMG components is that
all methods are operator-dependent. However, no such operator is given in the context of
data compression and, consequently, it has to be defined.

For the reader unfamiliar with AMG, it is difficult at this stage to see the impact the
choice of the operator will have on the transformation. It is therefore not very useful to go
into detail at this point. The impact of the operator on this transformation scheme will
become apparent from the descriptions of the transformation introduced here. The choice

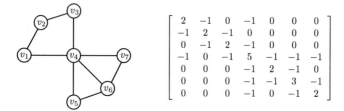

**Figure 4.4:** An unweighted graph and the corresponding Laplacian matrix

of the operator shall be uncovered to simplify the following descriptions. The author will elaborate more on this in Section 4.3.6.

The compression strategy followed in this thesis requires a lossless decorrelation. Consequently, the prediction phase becomes the focal point for designing a fitting transformation. As mentioned above, the prediction will be carried out by interpolation techniques used for AMG. The techniques of all components of AMG are closely tied to an operator and are meaningless without one. Although feasible operators can be expected to be sparse, the number of entries in the corresponding operator matrix will still be a multiple of the number of data points on the grid. Storing such an operator with the compressed data is ineffectual. Instead, it must be possible to determine the operator from the given data.

### 4.3.2  Operators

The definitions and descriptions in this section show that all components of AMG are operator-dependent. Since no operator is given in the context of data compression, a reasonable operator has to be created in order to establish a compression based on the AMG components. The data vector is decorrelated during the prediction phase of the algorithm and thus, the interpolation used for that is vital to achieve high compression factors. Consequently, the operators are chosen according to the resulting interpolation scheme.

#### *Graph Laplace Weighting*

It is also referred to as the Laplacian matrix that is used in graph theory as a matrix representation of a graph. An example is given in Figure 4.4. As in the case of the tree-based approach in Chapter 3, the connectivity between neighboring data points on the grid can be represented as graph $G(V, E)$. Its Laplacian matrix $\mathbf{A} = (a_{ij})_{n \times n}$ is defined as

$$
a_{ij} = \begin{cases} \deg(v_i) & \text{if } i = j \\ -1 & \text{if } i \neq j \text{ and } (v_i, v_j) \in E \\ 0 & \text{otherwise} \end{cases} ,
$$

where $\deg(v_i)$ is the degree of the node $v_i \in V$. It can be concluded from the inequality in Section 4.3.3 that all neighbors are considered strongly negative coupled if this matrix is used as operator.

**Distance-based Operator**

Similarly to the graph Laplace operator a distance-based operator $\mathbf{A} = (a_{ij})_{n \times n}$ can be defined as

$$a_{ij} = \begin{cases} \sum_{j \in S_i^C} w_{ij} & \text{if } i = j \\ -w_{ij} & \text{if } i \neq j \text{ and } (v_i, v_j) \in E \\ 0 & \text{otherwise} \end{cases} ,$$

where $d_{ij} = \|\mathbf{x}_i - \mathbf{x}_j\|_2$ is the Euclidean distance between two adjacent data points $i, j$, because unique coordinates are assumed for every data point $d_{ij} > 0$. Again, the row sum is constructed to be 0, and constant functions are interpolated exactly. It can also be seen that the graph Laplace weighting is the special case, where data points are equally spaced.

### 4.3.3 Splitting

In the process of transforming single-resolution data into a multiresolution representation various levels of detail have to be defined. Determining the next coarser level is the purpose of the splitting. At each resolution level, $\Omega_h$ is split into a set of approximation points $C$ and a set of detail points $F$. Points associated with the index set $C$ correspond to C-points, and points of $F$ will also be referred to as F-points. To be useful for the transformation, data points have to be selected so that a good approximation of the fine level is possible. Consequently, the selection has to spread throughout the entire domain while achieving a uniform coarsening. The Ruge-Stüben coarsening often used in AMG follows similar principles, however, the motivation is different. In the context of AMG an efficient interplay between smoothing and coarse grid correction is of particular importance. Since AMG is operator-based, the coarsening has to be determined upon algebraic coherences. Because of the desired interaction between smoothing and coarse grid correction, the splitting is adjusted to the selected smoothing process. The coarsening is performed in the direction in which the smooth error changes slowly. Strong negative couplings are used as indication for this relation and are the basis for the coarsening of AMG.

**Definition 4.10** [59] *Let $\mathcal{I} \subset \mathbb{N}$ denote an index set. For a matrix $\mathbf{A}$ with entries $a_{ij}$ $i, j \in \mathcal{I}$, $i$ is called strongly negative coupled to $j$ if*

$$-a_{ij} \geq \epsilon_{str} \max_{a_{ik} < 0} |a_{ik}| \quad \text{with fixed } 0 < \epsilon_{str} < 1.$$

Strong connectivity between F- and C-points usually leads to a better approximation of the smooth error by the interpolation, as elucidated in Section 4.3.4. For this purpose, strongly

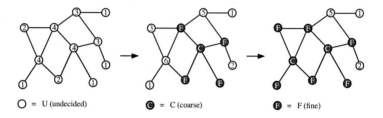

**Figure 4.5:** Progress of the C/F-splitting algorithm (modified from [59])

coupled points are favored when selecting C-points. Ideally, a maximal independent subset of strongly negative coupled points is determined. Finding a truly maximal independent subset is a NP-hard problem [23] and thus impractical. Instead, a heuristic described by the following algorithm is used. While searching for a maximal independent subset, one also avoids to obtain randomly distributed C/F-patches. Instead, a uniform distribution is intended. To achieve such a distribution neighborhood information is exploited in the process. For a point indexed by $i$ and its neighborhood $N_i = \{j \in \Omega \setminus \{i\} \mid a_{ij} \neq 0\}$, the following two sets are defined to describe the splitting process: a set of strongly negative coupled points

$$S_i = \{j \in N_i : i \text{ strongly negative coupled to } j\},$$

and its transpose

$$S_i^T = \{j \in \Omega : i \in S_j\}.$$

The procedure to determine a C/F-splitting is started by marking all points as undecided (U-points). As outlined in Figure 4.5, then all undecided neighbors are weighted with

$$\tau_i = \left|S_i^T \cap U\right| + 2\left|S_i^T \cap F\right| \quad (i \in U).$$

The undecided point with the largest weight $\tau_i$ is selected as coarse grid point, and all strongly negative coupled neighbors are marked as F-points. Then weights $\tau_i$ are updated before another C-point is selected. This procedure is performed until all undecided points are processed. The complete algorithm is outlined in Figure 4.6. Opposed to splittings utilized in the context of wavelet transforms on regular grids in 1D, this splitting does not necessarily separate the data samples into two subsets of the same size.

Two aspects of the C/F-splitting play an essential part for fast convergence of an AMG solver: a well approximated smooth error and small coarse-level operators. The size of the coarse-level operator strongly depends on the number of selected C-points. It is thus vital to limit their number, which has to be realized in respect to the quality of the interpolation. Although the wavelet transform should be efficient, limiting the number of C-points is of less concern. No intensive tasks, such as smoothing and solving procedures, are performed at each level. Instead, solely the C/F-splitting and the transfer operators

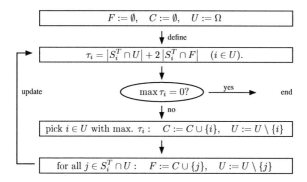

**Figure 4.6:** Algorithm of coarse grid selection heuristic (modified from [59])

have to be determined and applied. Furthermore, the transfer operators only have to be determined once and can then be reused to compress other data on the same grid. It is more important for the efficiency of the transformation that the transformation matrix remains sparse. Other coarsening strategies, such as aggressive coarsening that can be used to considerably reduce the number of C-points, would not contribute to the efficiency of the transformation.

The above described standard coarsening is based on direct couplings, in that F-points are required to have a certain number of strongly coupled C-points as direct neighbors. In contrast, aggressive coarsening does not require C-points in the direct neighborhood of F-points. While this is used to considerably reduce the number of C-points, and hence, to significantly speed up the coarse grid correction and consequently the entire multigrid cycle, it reduces the interpolation accuracy. The quality of the approximation is more important for the transformation, because no speed-up can be expected from stronger coarsening. This is further supported by the fact that the interpolation is the key component to achieve decorellation. For this reason the presented compression scheme only relies on standard coarsening. In respect to the graph Laplace operator every neighboring point is considered strongly coupled, as one can conclude from the inequality 4.10. Hence, initially all neighboring points are selected as supporting points for the interpolation. This may vary on coarser levels where the Galerkin operator is used.

### 4.3.4 Prediction

The prediction is the most important component of the transformation in respect to decorellation. While certain points are selected as approximation points during the splitting, the information or detail that is absent thereof has to be determined. It is acquired as the difference between the original data and the approximation obtained by an interpolation. Several different interpolation schemes are utilized in the context of AMG. Direct interpolation is used for the prediction at hand. This is interpolation based on direct neighbors and only includes C-points as supporting points that are strongly coupled $(S_i^C := C \cap S_i)$. In contrast, other interpolation strategies such as standard interpolation also incorporate strong F-point neighbors. However, this is unhelpful for the purpose of compression, since it is mandatory to only use C-points as supporting points to guarantee reversibility.

The direct interpolation approximates every $\lambda_i \in F$ by

$$\widetilde{\lambda}_i^F = \sum_{j \in S_i^C} w_{ij} \lambda_j^C,$$

where the weights $w_{ij}$ are defined as

$$w_{ij} = \begin{cases} -\alpha_i a_{ij}/a_{ii} & (j \in S_i^{C-}) \\ -\beta_i a_{ij}/a_{ii} & (j \in S_i^{C+}) \end{cases}$$

with

$$\alpha_i = \frac{\sum_{j \in N_i} a_{ij}^-}{\sum_{k \in S_i^C} a_{ik}^-} \quad \text{and} \quad \beta_i = \frac{\sum_{j \in N_i} a_{ij}^+}{\sum_{k \in S_i^C} a_{ik}^+}.$$

Here, $S_i^{C-}$ and $S_i^{C+}$ denote sets of strongly negative and strongly positive coupled points, and $a_{ij}^-$ and $a_{ij}^+$ denote negative and positive matrix entries. These weights are derived from the assumptions that an algebraic smooth error approximately satisfying

$$a_{ii}\lambda_i + \sum_{j \in N_i} a_{ij}\lambda_j \approx 0$$

is interpolated. It can be shown that the algebraic smooth error slowly varies in the direction of strong couplings and can therefore be essentially determined by a weighted average of merely the strongly coupled neighbors. In other words, weak connections only have a small impact on the smooth error and thus, the following can be assumed:

$$\frac{1}{\sum_{k \in S_i^C} a_{ik}} \sum_{k \in S_i^C} a_{ik}\lambda_i \approx \frac{1}{\sum_{j \in N_i} a_{ij}} \sum_{j \in N_i} a_{ij}\lambda_j.$$

This suggests selecting the weights as shown above. Smoothing however is not applied during compression and therefore, this explanation is meaningless here. Nevertheless, it is assumed that the values $\lambda_i$ are discrete values from smooth functions. Hence, the approximation still seems reasonable, at least, when using an operator with a row sum equal to zero. This requirement is fulfilled by the two operators presented in Section 4.3.2.

### 4.3.5  Update

As described above, the techniques used for the splitting and the prediction were directly derived from AMG. Likewise, the transpose of the interpolation that is normally used in the context of AMG as restriction could be employed for the update. However, utilizing the transpose of the interpolation can lead to individually scaled update values in the irregular case. Figure 4.7 illustrates how update coefficients are affected by irregular grid structures in comparison to regular ones.

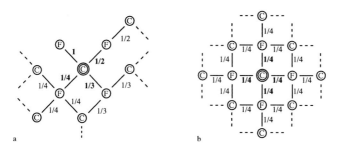

**Figure 4.7:** Weighting resulting from standard AMG restriction on regular and irregular grids

To eliminate this inequality, a scaled version of the restriction will be used for the update instead. The scaling is adapted to match the regular case of the linear wavelet transform [61]. The linear wavelet transform is built by utilizing the lifting scheme and uses a second order predictor for regular data samples on the real line. Thereby, an odd sample $\lambda_{l,2k+1}$ is predicted by the average of the neighboring sample on the left $\lambda_{l,2k}$ and right $\lambda_{l,2k+2}$:

$$\gamma_{l-1,k} = \lambda_{l,2k+1} - \frac{1}{2}\left(\lambda_{l,2k} + \lambda_{l,2k+2}\right).$$

The update is carried out in that every even sample is updated by

$$\lambda_{l-1,k} = \lambda_{l,2k} + \frac{1}{4}\left(\gamma_{l-1,2k-1} + \gamma_{l-1,2k+1}\right)$$

after the prediction. This procedure is also illustrated in Figure 4.8.

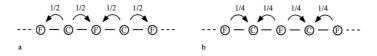

**Figure 4.8:** Prediction (a) and update (b) of the linear wavelet transform

Two attributes of the linear wavelet transform will be used to establish a generalized update operator. First, the coefficients used to calculate the update values sum up to $\frac{1}{2}$ for every even sample. Second, if one thinks of the linear wavelet transform in operator notation, the update operator can obviously be interpreted as the transpose of the prediction operator scaled by $\frac{1}{2}$. Similarly, two scaling factors are introduced, a global scaling factor $\alpha$ and a local scaling factor $\beta$. Local scaling is utilized to scale the update value for every C-point individually, to balance the row sum. Therefore, $\beta$ is set to

$$\beta_i = 1 \Big/ \sum_{\substack{j=1 \\ j \neq i}}^{r} p_{ij}^T,$$

where $p_{ij}^T$ are the entries of $\mathbf{P}^T$, the transpose of the prediction matrix $\mathbf{P}$. The scaled update $\mathbf{U}_s$ is defined in matrix notation as

$$\widetilde{\mathbf{U}}_s := \mathbf{B}\mathbf{P}^T,$$

where $\mathbf{B} = (b_{ij})_{(m \times m)}$ with

$$b_{ij} := \begin{cases} \beta_i, & \text{if } i = j, \\ 0, & \text{otherwise} \end{cases}$$

is the local scaling matrix.

While this scaling normalizes the weighting effect on each C-point, it does not lead to an update process that is conform with the regular case. Hence, the global linear scaling is used in addition. It is set to $\alpha = \frac{|C|}{|C|+|F|}$. For an even number of samples on the real line this ratio equals $\frac{1}{2}$ in the regular case. It then matches the factor used for the linear wavelet transform. The resulting update matrix introduced in Section 4.3 is then defined as

$$\mathbf{U} := \alpha \mathbf{B}\mathbf{P}^T.$$

### 4.3.6   Remarks

#### 4.3.6.1   Operators and Interpolation

As described in Section 4.3.4, the interpolation is constructed as

$$\lambda_i^F = \sum_{j \in S_i^C} w_{ij} \lambda_j^C, \qquad (\star)$$

with weights

$$w_{ij} = \begin{cases} -\alpha_i a_{ij}/a_{ii} & (j \in S_i^{C-}) \\ -\beta_i a_{ij}/a_{ii} & (j \in S_i^{C+}) \end{cases}$$

for positive and negative coupled coarse grid neighbors. In association with the two operators mentioned in Section 4.3.2 this interpolation complies with the following interpolation schemes on the finest level. This conformity is in general not maintained on the coarser levels as the Galerkin operator is used.

### Averaging

Employing the graph Laplace operator yields an interpolation based on simple averaging. Values on F-points $\lambda_i^F$ are approximated as average of their coarse neighbors $\lambda_j^C, j \in S_i^C$. If the cardinality of $S_i^C$ is denoted by $|S_i^C|$, the averaging can be formally written as

$$\lambda_i^F = \frac{1}{|S_i^C|} \sum_{j \in S_i^C} \lambda_j.$$

### Shepards Method

Euclidean distances are considered by the interpolation that results from utilizing the distance-based operator. Thereby, values that are further away are weighted less than closer ones. This method was originally introduced by Shepard [56] and, in a general form, can be formally written as

$$\lambda_i^F = \frac{1}{\sum_{j \in S_i^C} w_{ij}} \sum_{j \in S_i^C} w_{ij} \lambda_j^C,$$

where the weights are defined as

$$w_{ij} = \frac{1}{d_{ij}}, \quad i \neq j.$$

Here, $d_{ij} = \|\mathbf{x}_i - \mathbf{x}_j\|_2$ is the Euclidean distance between two adjacent data points $i, j$ and thus $d_{ij} > 0$, because unique coordinates are assumed for every data point.

#### 4.3.6.2   Lossless Compression

At the beginning of this chapter it was mentioned that the presented transformation is utilized as a lossless decorrelation technique and that a quantization is applied prior to the transform. Since this is the case, the transformation is actually performed as an integer transform. Prediction and update values are rounded in every lifting step to ensure a lossless transformation. Thereby the linearity of the transformation is lost.

# 5 Evaluation

In this chapter several properties of the two previously introduced compression schemes
will be examined. Files from a selection of CFD simulations are used as the basis for this
evaluation. They contain results from simulations of various physical phenomena and comprise solution data of multiple physical quantities. The number of solution vectors present
in the data is user-controlled and thus strongly dependent on the engineers' requirements
and settings. This can also be observed from the files used here. Only a selection of very
few physical variables such as 'velocity' and 'pressure' are found across all files. The file
content also varies in the number of data values, as the simulations were computed on
various grids. The smallest grid is composed of several hundred thousand cells, whereas
the largest includes more than 37 millions. The test cases are results of steady state simulations, however, an additional file containing the result of a transient simulation is used
for evaluating the optimization possibilities in the transient case. A short description of
the test cases as well as some basic statistics about the variable values stored in the files
are given in the appendix of this thesis (A.1).

The main intention of this thesis was to find compression schemes suitable for solution data
of variables. For their evaluation only the targeted data will be taken into consideration.
Additional data, such as file headers, problem descriptions and other contents present
in the files, is discarded. As most of these components are only small in size they can
also be disregarded in practice without greatly affecting the overall compression strength.
Differently, file parts that hold grid connectivities and coordinates must be considered.
Especially for steady state results the grid representation might make up large amounts
of the file. While these parts are not subject of this research, it shall be noted that the
presented methods may also be used to compress coordinate values of grids. The analysis
is carried out for three different quantization levels that are determined by the relative
precisions 0.001, 0.0001, 0.00001, respectively. These precisions are set relative to the
maximum of the absolute values of the entries in a data vector. In the case of time-varying

data, the maximum is determined across the entire time series. If $\{c_i\}_{i \in \{1,\ldots,N\}}$ denotes the scalar values of a data vector, the absolute precision $p$ is obtained as

$$p = \max_i(|c_i|) \cdot p_{rel}.$$

Here, $p_{rel}$ is the relative precision mentioned before. The resulting error of the uniform quantization equals $\frac{p}{2}$, which is due to rounding to the next integer. The spectrum of quantized values is covered by 10, 14 and 17 bits, respectively. Hence, the quantization is accountable for a substantial part of the compression in the case of double precision floating point values.

Floating point values are compressed by first, cutting off detail during the quantization, and then reducing the numerical value by decorrelation. The latter is performed by the compression methods evaluated here. The fact that not all data values are stored with 64-bit double precision has to be considered when comparing compression factors obtained for individual test cases. In the case of 64-bit values a stronger reduction is achieved by quantization, as the values are reduced to the same integer spectra. This problem can be circumvented by employing the entropy as measure. The difference between the entropy before and after preprocessing reveals to which extent the preprocessing contributes to the compression. Nevertheless, the value of data compression is best measured by the capability to reduce space requirements in practice, as indicated by the compression factor. Besides the reduction of space requirements, compression solutions applied in industry are also required to be performant and memory-efficient. Therefore, results on performance and memory efficiency are also evaluated for each method. This is of particular interest regarding examples with millions of cells for which memory efficiency and performance might become essential.

The outline of this chapter is structured as follows. First, a simple compressor scheme used as reference is introduced briefly. Then, the tree compressor is evaluated in Section 5.2. Hereby, the unweighted tree predictor and the effect of optimization will be studied. For the latter, the strategies mentioned before for constructing suitable weightings are evaluated. Next to the possible gains achieved for the data vectors, the overhead generated by additional information that has to be stored alongside the compressed data is also regarded. The effect of weighting on the compression of time-varying data fields is treated separately in Section 5.2.2. This is followed by some performance and memory measurements. These tests were performed on a 2.93 GHz 8-core Intel Xeon X5570 with 24 GB of RAM. At last, the wavelet compression is evaluated according to the same criteria in Section 5.3. Results for the two presented operators and a number of different coupling thresholds are listed. In the context of the performance and memory measurements the sparseness of a transfer matrix used during the transformation is evaluated. More detailed results that were obtained during the evaluation can be found in the appendix. Relevant results are summarized and displayed in this chapter, so that the reader is not required to go through the variety of result tables listed in the appendix. Variable names are abbreviated as follows:

**Table 5.1:** Variable names and their abbreviation

| Name | Abbreviation |
|---|---|
| Density | $\rho$ |
| Dissipation Rate | $\epsilon$ |
| Enthalpy | $H$ |
| Static Enthalpy | $H_s$ |
| Pressure | $P$ |
| Static Pressure | $P_s$ |
| Thermodynamic Pressure | $Pt$ |
| Turbulent Kinetic Energy | TKE |
| Turbulent Viscosity | TVis |
| Temperature | $T$ |
| Velocity Component U | $V_0$ |
| Velocity Component V | $V_1$ |
| Velocity Component W | $V_2$ |
| Mass Fraction Isocyanate | $w_{iso}$ |
| Mass Fraction Polyol | $w_{pol}$ |
| Molar Concentration Isocyanate | $c_{iso}$ |
| Molar Concentration Polyol | $c_{pol}$ |

## 5.1  Simple Compressor

In order to provide reference compression factors, a simple yet effective compression scheme is applied to the test data. The overall compression method uses the same general setup, in that a quantization, a preprocessing and an encoding phase are performed. Quantization and encoding are inherited from the introduced compression schemes, and only the preprocessing is replaced by a data stream prediction. In contrast to the tree-based approach, the prediction is carried out from one to the next storage location in the data vector and not to a geometrically close data point on the grid. The name 'simple compressor' is derived from the fact that no particular effort is put into this prediction method. Since no context data such as grid connectivities or geometry data is required during execution of this simple prediction, it can be applied to any data vector. At the same time the success of this approach is highly dependent on the order in which the data values are stored in the files. Table 5.2 shows the results that were obtained by applying this method to the solution data of the test case files.

It is noticeable that compression factors obtained for the 'Car Venting System' are substantially lower than those obtained for the other test cases. The reason for this behavior is the precision with which the data values were originally stored. While the integer spectra after quantization remain the same in all cases, 32-bit single precision is used only in the 'Car Venting System'. In other words, the quantization is not accountable for as much reduction as in the cases where 64-bit double precision values are quantized to the same integer spectrum. The impact of the compression is similar to those for the other cases, as supported by the results on the entropy shown in Table 5.3. Also, it is evident that the two 'Wind Tunnel' simulations are compressed stronger. This could result from the

**Table 5.2:** Compression factors obtained by applying the simple method to the individual test cases. The results for different precision levels are listed in separate columns.

|  | Compression factor | | |
|---|---|---|---|
|  | 1e-03 | 1e-04 | 1e-05 |
| Wind Tunnel I | 21.062 | 11.126 | 7.304 |
| Wind Tunnel II | 19.947 | 10.912 | 7.159 |
| Car Venting System | 7.693 | 4.997 | 3.633 |
| Mixing Chamber I | 15.874 | 9.079 | 6.198 |
| Mixing Chamber II | 12.333 | 7.758 | 5.559 |
| Mixing Pipe | 11.723 | 7.682 | 5.656 |

high resolution of the underlying grids or simply from a smoother behavior of the variable data. Considering the type of simulation, it is somewhat reasonable to assume a smoother behavior by the variables in the case of wind tunnel experiments than in the case of simulating a mixing process.

**Table 5.3:** Entropy results obtained before and after applying the simple method to the individual test cases. The results for different precision levels are listed in separate columns.

|  | Before | | | After | | |
|---|---|---|---|---|---|---|
|  | 1e-03 | 1e-04 | 1e-05 | 1e-03 | 1e-04 | 1e-05 |
| Wind Tunnel I | 7.702 | 10.839 | 14.060 | 3.054 | 5.595 | 8.478 |
| Wind Tunnel II | 7.506 | 10.712 | 13.985 | 3.306 | 6.211 | 9.342 |
| Car Venting System | 6.843 | 9.873 | 12.895 | 5.272 | 8.072 | 11.061 |
| Mixing Chamber I | 6.389 | 9.647 | 12.882 | 4.044 | 7.181 | 10.443 |
| Mixing Chamber II | 7.239 | 10.534 | 13.801 | 5.165 | 8.293 | 11.557 |
| Mixing Pipe | 7.104 | 9.985 | 12.625 | 5.303 | 8.150 | 10.918 |

### 5.1.1 Performance and Memory Requirements

All operations carried out by this method can be performed on the same memory location, and no additional context data, such as connectivity data, is required for processing. Consequently, the amount of memory consumed in the process is identical to the amount necessary to hold the data vector that is being compressed. Performance results are listed in Table 5.4. The data throughput measured at around 1 GB/s, independent of the test case.

## 5.2 Tree Compressor

The tree compressor scheme has many facets when considering all the optimization possibilities outlined in Chapter 3. To begin the evaluation, the compression factors obtained with the unoptimized version are listed in Table 5.5. Here, an arbitrary prediction tree was created from the connectivity graph. If the grid is not simply connected, a separate spanning tree is created for every component. For test cases where this occurred, only a

**Table 5.4:** Simple compressor for test cases using reference method

|                    | Run time (s) | Throughput (MB/s) |
| ------------------ | ------------ | ----------------- |
| Wind Tunnel I      | 0.155        | 974.47            |
| Wind Tunnel II     | 0.077        | 980.48            |
| Car Venting System | 0.002        | 998.88            |
| Mixing Chamber I   | 0.004        | 993.12            |
| Mixing Chamber II  | 0.007        | 991.01            |
| Mixing Pipe        | 0.001        | 996.37            |

few trees had to be created. Hence, no noticeable impact was caused, and so the number of prediction trees is not further regarded in this evaluation. As mentioned in the previous section, the lower compression factors listed for the 'Car Venting System' are due to the lower floating point precision used for most of the original values. In contrast, the comparably low compression factors for 'Mixing Chamber II' are a result of the inefficiently compressed 'Density' data vector (Table A.23). And again, the best compression factors were achieved for the wind tunnel results.

**Table 5.5:** Compression factors obtained by applying the unoptimized tree-based method to the test cases. The results for different precision levels are listed in separate columns.

|                    | Compression factor | | |
|                    | 1e-03 | 1e-04 | 1e-05 |
| ------------------ | ------ | ------ | ----- |
| Wind Tunnel I      | 25.277 | 12.512 | 7.842 |
| Wind Tunnel II     | 22.383 | 11.794 | 7.557 |
| Car Venting System | 9.136  | 5.661  | 4.007 |
| Mixing Chamber I   | 18.396 | 10.042 | 6.647 |
| Mixing Chamber II  | 14.084 | 8.521  | 5.955 |
| Mixing Pipe        | 13.062 | 8.288  | 5.986 |

As one would expect, less precise quantization resulted in stronger compression. This coherence can be anticipated simply because the quantization is then accountable for a larger entropy reduction. In addition, coarser quantized values can be predicted more accurately. This effect can be observed from the entropy results listed in Table 5.6. The reduction in entropy caused by the prediction is strongest for the lowest precision and becomes smaller with higher precision. At the same time, the entropy results clearly show that the stronger compression of the wind tunnel simulation files is related to the preprocessing, as a more distinct reduction of the entropy is achieved. While the entropy of the wind tunnel experiments directly after the quantization is higher than of that of the other files, it is also reduced furthest by the preprocessing. The comparison of the various methods in the discussion chapter will show if this is related to the predictor or to the data.

One should note, that the numbers listed in the tables are an average of the entropy values determined for every variable vector of the specific file. Despite being only the average,

they underline the previously listed compression results. Hence, encoding does not greatly
alter the effect of preprocessing.

**Table 5.6:** Entropy results before and after preprocessing obtained by using the unoptimized tree
predictor. The results for different precision levels are listed in separate columns.

|                    | Before |        |        | After  |        |        |
| ------------------ | ------ | ------ | ------ | ------ | ------ | ------ |
|                    | 1e-03  | 1e-04  | 1e-05  | 1e-03  | 1e-04  | 1e-05  |
| Wind Tunnel I      | 7.702  | 10.839 | 14.060 | 2.422  | 4.725  | 7.532  |
| Wind Tunnel II     | 7.506  | 10.712 | 13.985 | 2.825  | 5.632  | 8.714  |
| Car Venting System | 6.843  | 9.873  | 12.895 | 4.429  | 7.131  | 10.077 |
| Mixing Chamber I   | 6.389  | 9.647  | 12.882 | 3.537  | 6.621  | 9.886  |
| Mixing Chamber II  | 7.239  | 10.534 | 13.801 | 4.573  | 7.655  | 10.923 |
| Mixing Pipe        | 7.104  | 9.985  | 12.625 | 4.634  | 7.476  | 10.307 |

## 5.2.1 Optimized Tree Compressor

The evaluation of possible weightings feasible for optimizing the tree prediction involves
a great number of facets. Obviously, it has to be clarified if an optimization or weighting
can be implemented in such a way that it is beneficial for the compression. On the one
hand, this concerns possible gains in terms of a stronger compression. The effectiveness
has to be inspected in particular for cases that require additional information to be stored
alongside the compressed data to ensure reversibility. On the other hand, the feasibility
of implementing optimizations has to be examined. This mainly concerns the universality
of the optimization. For practical use it has to be considered that variables required for
an optimization might not be present in every file. Adapting the optimization to specific
files is in general not utilitarian.

The three general optimization approaches, geometry-based, gradient-based and dynamics-
based optimization will be subject to the following evaluation.

**Table 5.7:** Compression factors obtained by applying the tree compressor with distance-based
optimization to the test cases. Data that might be required during reconstruction is
not taken into consideration.

|                    | Compression factor |        |        |
| ------------------ | ------------------ | ------ | ------ |
|                    | 1e-03              | 1e-04  | 1e-05  |
| Wind Tunnel I      | 25.450             | 12.747 | 7.979  |
| Wind Tunnel II     | 22.664             | 12.111 | 7.768  |
| Car Venting System | 9.653              | 5.915  | 4.156  |
| Mixing Chamber I   | 19.932             | 10.696 | 6.952  |
| Mixing Chamber II  | 14.540             | 8.713  | 6.058  |
| Mixing Pipe        | 12.158             | 7.871  | 5.767  |

Geometry-based optimization has the advantage that the necessity to store the prediction
tree can usually be avoided. All files used in this thesis only contain cell variables. The
distances are calculated by using coordinate values that are stored on the vertices of the
grid. Even if the tree compressor would be utilized for the compression of the coordinate

values, a separate tree would be needed. If a lossy compression is considered, the reconstructed coordinate values can be used for the calculation of the weights instead. This way, the prediction tree can be reconstructed with the decompressed coordinate values. Despite this advantage and as already stated in the description of the geometry-based optimization, it is unclear whether such a distance-oriented optimization is useful. This is in particular the case if the discretization is adjusted to the smoothness of the functions or if cell centers are equally spaced. Also, the method only exploits topological and geometric information that does not reflect the behavior of the flow. These doubts are somewhat affirmed by the results listed in Table 5.7. It shows that compression factors obtained for most cases are only slightly improved over the basic version of the algorithm. Results for the 'Mixing Pipe' even show a noticeable reduction of the compression factor.

The unique idea brought forward in this thesis is to use variable data and physical relations for this purpose. In general, the idea of employing the data that is compressed for optimizations yields the problem that additional information or data has to be stored to ensure reversibility of the compression scheme. To keep the overhead as low as possible multiple data sets have to be compressed by using a single optimized tree. It is assumed that correlations within datasets are related across several different variables as they contain the information of the same physical process. On this conjecture, a single optimized tree can improve the compression of multiple variables. Several possibilities will be evaluated in the following. First, the steady state cases will be examined before a more detailed analysis is performed for a transient case in Section 5.2.2.

The potential of the optimization approach is uncovered when determining the theoretically optimal tree compressor. The latter is obtained by optimizing every data vector present in the file with itself by using the variable gradients. This way each vector is optimally predicted providing the upper limit for the compression factor which can possibly be obtained with this method. Additional information that would have to be stored to form a reversible process is left out of the equation. Table 5.8 shows the tremendously improved compression factors compared to previous results. However, it should be noted that in general such improvements cannot be achieved by using a single tree. While one tree might be a decent choice for the compression of a specific variable, it might not be a good choice for other variables of the simulation. In addition, it always has to be considered that an optimization usually requires some information to be stored for reversing the prediction. Especially in the case of multiple spanning trees this can reduce the benefit significantly, if not render the compression method useless. This thought will be revisited in more detail later.

Results for a single tree optimized by using variable gradients as weights are listed in the appendix (A.3.3). For the evaluation, every variable was used for the gradient weighting to determine the impact on the overall compression of the file. This applied at least to all test cases but 'Wind Tunnel I'. There, only a selection of variables was chosen to limit the number of experiments for this particular file. The results reveal that the variable employed as basis for the optimization is also compressed the strongest. While this is the natural behavior one expects from this approach, it also points out the hurdle of using this

**Table 5.8:** Theoretically optimal compression factors obtainable via the tree-based method. Each variable was compressed by using a tree that was optimized by employing the gradient weighting in combination with the variable itself.

| | Compression factor | | |
| --- | --- | --- | --- |
| | 1e-03 | 1e-04 | 1e-05 |
| Wind Tunnel I | 72.321 | 27.741 | 14.457 |
| Wind Tunnel II | 67.391 | 21.642 | 11.578 |
| Car Venting System | 13.997 | 7.565 | 4.947 |
| Mixing Chamber I | 28.851 | 16.848 | 9.286 |
| Mixing Chamber II | 27.933 | 13.097 | 7.979 |
| Mixing Pipe | 23.079 | 11.991 | 7.818 |

method. Optimizing for just any variable does not equally improve the overall compression. Compression factors for each file and for the medium precision are visualized as diagrams in Figures 5.1 to 5.6.

Although any choice of variable enhanced the compression strength, the diagrams illustrate that the effect of the optimization varies significantly. For example, a compression factor of 6.38 is achieved for the medium quantization level when using the turbulent viscosity data to optimize the compression of the 'Venting System'. In contrast, the use of the thermodynamic pressure data only leads to a compression factor of 5.86. A similar 10% increase in the compression factor was found for the wind tunnel experiments, when the velocity components instead of the pressure were employed as basis for the weighting. While these variations show that some variables are better suitable for the optimization than others, no candidate can be appointed as a good choice in general. Simulation type and user settings are the primary reasons for the varying file content that makes a generic selection so difficult. This can be illustrated with the mixing chamber simulations. While the same process was simulated, variables present in the two files differ. In the case of 'Mixing Chamber I', optimizing for the mass fraction and molar concentration data results in very similar compression factors. This observation is due to the direct relation of these quantities. Since only polyol and isocyanate are used in the mixing process and the sum of the mass fractions equals 1 by definition, the following relations apply. For the mass fraction of polyol $w_{pol}$ and of isocyanate $w_{iso}$ one has: $w_{pol} = 1 - w_{iso}$. Consequently, the differences calculated during the weight creation are identical for both variables. Similar relations apply to the molar concentrations, since they are directly related to the mass fractions. The molar concentration $c_i$ of a constituent can be converted to its mass fraction $w_i$ by $w_i = c_i \cdot \frac{M_i}{\rho}$. Here, $M_i$ is the molar mass of the constituent and $\rho$ its density. Although the density has its part in the conversion, these dependencies explain the similar results obtained for the optimization. Apparently, this implies that choosing one of the variables for optimization increases the compression of multiple variables to a similar or equal extent. Thus, the overall compression can be improved significantly, since more than one third of the values contained in the file is predicted by using an almost optimal tree. It becomes obvious from these perceptions that the problem of identifying variables, preferably for the optimization in respect to the specific simulation, remains unsolved.

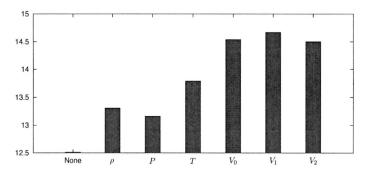

**Figure 5.1:** Impact of the gradient-based optimization for 'Wind Tunnel I'

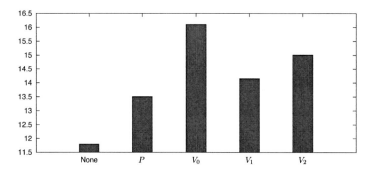

**Figure 5.2:** Impact of the gradient-based optimization for 'Wind Tunnel II'

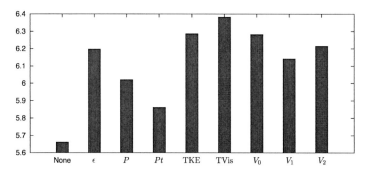

**Figure 5.3:** Impact of the gradient-based optimization for 'Venting System'

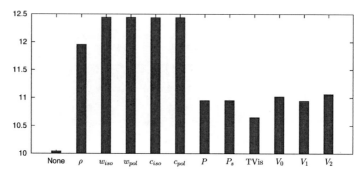

**Figure 5.4:** Impact of the gradient-based optimization for 'Mixing Chamber I'

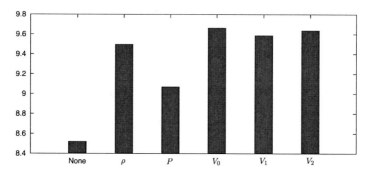

**Figure 5.5:** Impact of the gradient-based optimization for 'Mixing Chamber II'

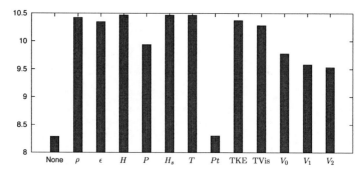

**Figure 5.6:** Impact of the gradient-based optimization for 'Mixing Pipe'

Alternatively, the dynamics-based approach could be employed. Instead of using gradients between neighboring data points, the optimization is based on the direction of the flow. While the actual direction cannot be considered in the weighting process because weights are expected to be positive numbers, their magnitude was used as indicator. Two principles were proposed: Large velocity magnitudes indicate either large correlation or they imply small correlations. The results obtained by applying these measures are shown in Table 5.9. Only for the 'Wind Tunnel' cases and the 'Mixing Pipe' example significant differences between the two approaches can be perceived from the listed numbers. There the weighting, based on the assumption that large velocities indicate higher correlations, yielded better compression factors. While the compression factors mostly improved when compared to the unweighted tree prediction, no general improvements were reached in comparison to the previously displayed results for the gradient weighting. For 'Wind Tunnel I' the dynamics-based optimization leads to significantly better compression factors than any of the shown gradient weightings. In contrast, the results for 'Mixing Chamber I' show that no improvement was achieved compared to the unweighted tree prediction. Hence, each variable used for the gradient led to better compression factors.

**Table 5.9:** Compression factors for test cases obtained by using the tree-based method with velocity-based optimization. Additional information which may be required for decompression is not taken into consideration.

|  | In-flow | | | Orthogonal | | |
|---|---|---|---|---|---|---|
|  | 1e-03 | 1e-04 | 1e-05 | 1e-03 | 1e-04 | 1e-05 |
| Wind Tunnel I | 30.284 | 14.865 | 9.123 | 28.565 | 14.465 | 8.969 |
| Wind Tunnel II | 29.178 | 14.407 | 8.742 | 26.000 | 13.779 | 8.616 |
| Car Venting System | 9.303 | 5.722 | 4.028 | 9.500 | 5.851 | 4.122 |
| Mixing Chamber I | 18.443 | 10.093 | 6.676 | 18.944 | 10.331 | 6.785 |
| Mixing Chamber II | 14.075 | 8.519 | 5.962 | 14.046 | 8.521 | 5.962 |
| Mixing Pipe | 17.291 | 9.989 | 6.852 | 12.434 | 8.026 | 5.842 |

Although the dynamics-based weighting has the advantage that selection of employed variables is set, they might not be present in every file. Consequently, it is not truly a universal method. In the context of the gradient-based approach another form of weighting was introduced and proposed as solution to the problem of selecting suitable weights: the full weighting (3.3.2). On the one hand, no selection process has to be carried out to determine which variables are present and which should be used. On the other hand, every variable that is compressed is considered in the optimization process, what might be advantageous for the compression. The results of this attempt are listed in Table 5.10. Again, these results do not include the overhead for the information that is required to recreate the exact tree during decompression.

Compared with the previously listed optimization results a distinct gain in the compression factor can be observed with the exception of the 'Car Venting System' case. The compression factors for that particular case are similar to those obtained for other optimizations. The results listed for the theoretically optimal tree prediction show that room for improvement is very limited for this case. For all other cases the compression factors

**Table 5.10:** Compression factors obtained with the tree-based method and by optimization based on full weighting. Additional information which may be required for decompression is not taken into consideration.

| | Compression factor | | |
|---|---|---|---|
| | 1e-03 | 1e-04 | 1e-05 |
| Wind Tunnel I | 34.588 | 16.345 | 9.730 |
| Wind Tunnel II | 38.718 | 17.121 | 9.864 |
| Car Venting System | 9.878 | 6.020 | 4.227 |
| Mixing Chamber I | 25.396 | 12.253 | 7.583 |
| Mixing Chamber II | 18.422 | 10.006 | 6.651 |
| Mixing Pipe | 17.869 | 10.267 | 7.002 |

exceed those obtained with the gradient weighting or are close to those obtained for the best suiting variable.

As already mentioned multiple times, the requirement of having to store a prediction tree alongside the compressed data can substantially affect the achievable compression. So far, this overhead was left out of the equation to enable a better comparison between the optimization methods. Nevertheless, in order to evaluate the optimization it is essential to determine the compression factors in regard to the overhead generated by storing the tree. These compression factors were evaluated for both tree-encoding techniques that were introduced in Section 3.3.5. The adjusted results for the full weighting are listed in the table below. The significant impact on the compression becomes immediately obvious from the obtained numbers. The comparison of the two tree-encoding techniques indicates that the condensed-tree method is less efficient. The difference is so large in most cases, that it cannot be considered a reasonable choice for storing this information. It becomes evident from the results that the benefit of the optimization is lost when using the tree-encoding techniques. While the bit mask encoding requires a more computationally involving reconstruction of the tree, an optimization can be beneficial even when having to store this information. Clearly, the bit mask encoding turns out to be more memory-efficient than the condensed-tree encoding.

**Table 5.11:** Compression factors obtained by optimization based on the full weighting and regarding the information required to reconstruct the tree during decompression. Results for both tree storage formats are displayed here.

| | Condensed tree | | | Bit mask | | |
|---|---|---|---|---|---|---|
| | 1e-03 | 1e-04 | 1e-05 | 1e-03 | 1e-04 | 1e-05 |
| Wind Tunnel I | 24.029 | 14.005 | 9.055 | 32.079 | 15.762 | 9.520 |
| Wind Tunnel II | 11.516 | 9.850 | 7.343 | 26.639 | 14.261 | 8.843 |
| Car Venting System | 7.260 | 5.008 | 3.712 | 9.059 | 5.706 | 4.069 |
| Mixing Chamber I | 15.051 | 9.269 | 6.333 | 20.452 | 10.973 | 7.072 |
| Mixing Chamber II | 8.727 | 6.340 | 4.813 | 13.217 | 8.243 | 5.823 |
| Mixing Pipe | 13.748 | 8.771 | 6.275 | 16.733 | 9.881 | 6.821 |

The explanation for the strong impact is straightforward. In principle, there are three factors accountable for the extent of this effect. First of all, the number of variables that are compressed by utilizing the same tree is a key factor. If only a few variables are compressed, the overhead of the tree is very large relative to the total amount of data. This is due to that fact that the number of nodes of the tree only depends on the number of data points. Its relative size becomes small with an increasing number of variables, as evident from the results of the two wind tunnel experiments. While the simulations are quite similar, 'Wind Tunnel I' contains 21 variables compared to the 4 variables stored in 'Wind Tunnel II'. A similar effect can be observed for coarse quantization levels for which a strong compression is achieved. Again, the space that is required to store the tree relative to the size of the compressed data becomes larger as the size of the compressed data shrinks. The third aspect is the size of the connectivity graph. While it does not have an impact on the size of the encoded tree when using the condensed format, it strongly affects the size of the bit mask. This effect was observed for 'Mixing Chamber I' and 'Mixing Chamber II'. It can be seen in the file description that there are more than six times as many faces as cells. This ratio is doubled compared to the wind tunnel files, and thus the bit mask vector becomes much longer. Consequently, the bit mask encoding requires comparably more space.

## 5.2.2 Weighting for Time Series

The optimization of the compression for transient solutions involves several different aspects. In comparison to the steady state case the overhead problem is of less concern, since enough data sets are present within the files. Nevertheless, it must be considered when establishing a strategy for the optimization over time. It was mentioned in Section 3.3.2 that in the transient case the optimization can be carried out for multiple time steps of each variable or for multiple variables of each time step and, of course, the combination of both. Based on the overhead caused by storing the information to reconstruct the prediction tree, the combination of both seems to be the most reasonable choice. The first possibility might also be profitable if enough time steps are present in the file. Optimizing for multiple variables can be expected to yield a similar outcome as in the steady state case. Concerning the other two possibilities, it has to be determined if an optimization remains profitable for larger numbers of time steps. If the benefit is limited, the time series should be separated into blocks of frames. The compression would then be optimized for each block separately. As this creates more overhead, the number of frames per block has to be large enough. In this case optimizing for a combination of variables and time steps has the advantage that a large number of data sets are involved. As a result, the number of time steps per block can be reduced. At the same time, the results for the steady state have shown that considerably varying compression factors were obtained for the individual variables. This finding might indicate that optimizing for the same variable but for multiple time steps leads to better results.

To limit the number of experiments information retrieved from the steady state case are utilized, in that only the most promising and practical methods will be selected for evaluation. This selection involves two optimization methods. One is using the full weighting for all variables for one of the two middle time frames of the example. This approach will be referred to as 'Tree Middle'. The other one is to create an optimized tree for each variable that is optimized by utilizing full weighting over all time steps. The method is denoted 'Tree Variable'. In addition to these two methods, the shadow optimization was also evaluated. The prediction tree was optimized by using the gradient weighting determined for the specific variable of the preceding time step. This method is referred to as 'Tree Shadow'. For reference, the simple method as well as the unoptimized tree method were also evaluated. The results are provided in Table 5.12.

**Table 5.12:** Compression factors obtained for the transient test case 'Fire Simulation' by using the different methods

|  | Compression factor | | |
|---|---|---|---|
|  | 1e-03 | 1e-04 | 1e-05 |
| Reference | 17.136 | 9.604 | 6.494 |
| Tree | 20.342 | 10.743 | 7.017 |
| Tree Middle | 22.370 | 11.597 | 7.391 |
| Tree Variable | 23.069 | 12.039 | 7.599 |
| Tree Shadow | 24.147 | 12.619 | 7.872 |

The shadow optimization utilizes information of the preceding time frame and hence, temporal correlations are exploited. It also bares the advantage that the optimized trees can be reconstructed during decompression without any further information. The benefit of this method can be derived from the compression factors. The drawback of this strategy is that a new tree has to be determined for every variable and time step. Also, the results listed in the following section reveal that the tree creation process is very time-consuming. Therefore, the shadow optimization exhibits significantly lower performance than the other methods. An alternative approach for the compression of transient solutions is to simply combine tree predictor with known temporal compression techniques. Results obtained when combining the methods from above with a simple time-differencing scheme are listed in Table 5.13.

All compression methods except 'Tree Shadow' gain from the temporal decorellation. The reason why the shadow optimization performs worse is a consequence of using a different tree for each time step. When the same tree is employed for the prediction of each time step of a variable, the combination with constant extrapolation yields a 2-dimensional prediction as illustrated in Figure 5.7. This predictor is of higher order than the tree prediction carried out in space, and thus higher compression factors can be expected. This coherence is lost when utilizing the shadow optimization.

Compression factors obtained for 'Tree Variable' only exceeded those of 'Tree Middle' in the case of the highest precision. This is an example that the use of multiple optimizations does not pay off because of the data volume required for storing the prediction trees.

### 5.2.3    Performance and Memory Requirements

The tree compressor scheme was introduced as a two-part process consisting of a 'spanning tree creator' and a 'predictor'. For the steady state cases above only a single tree was

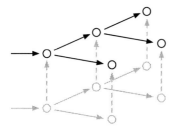 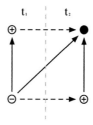

**Figure 5.7:** Paralellogram prediction as a result of using the same prediction tree for consecutive time frames. Two values from the previous and one of the current time step are utilized to form the prediction.

**Table 5.13:** Compression factors obtained for the transient test case 'Fire Simulation' by using the different methods in combination with constant extrapolation for decorellation between time steps

|  | Compression factor | | |
| --- | --- | --- | --- |
|  | 1e-03 | 1e-04 | 1e-05 |
| Reference | 18.744 | 10.588 | 6.979 |
| Tree | 21.531 | 11.821 | 7.552 |
| Tree Middle | 22.362 | 12.360 | 7.813 |
| Tree Variable | 22.041 | 12.323 | 7.826 |
| Tree Shadow | 19.935 | 11.275 | 7.353 |

created for each run. The resulting tree was then used to predict every present variable data vector within the file. Hence, the tree creation process was only performed once. As a consequence, the time measurements were performed separately for the tree creation and the prediction. The numbers listed are averages obtained for various runs and for the different variables. Results for the prediction are given for a single vector. For the optimized tree creation an additional weight creation process also adds to the overall time of the compression scheme. The time required for that purpose was not measured in detail, but in most cases times similar to the prediction itself were obtained. At least, this applied to the gradient-based approach when only a single variable was used for optimization. As can be concluded from the results listed below, the impact of the weight creation is then relatively small compared to that of the tree creation process itself.

Run times measured for the unweighted version are listed in Table 5.14. Especially the numbers obtained for the tree creation process are suboptimal. In the unweighted version, the same 'optimization' was performed, only that an equally weighted graph was used as input. Alternative greedy algorithms can be implemented instead, to significantly reduce the time required for the tree creation, if no optimization is considered.

The results listed in 5.15 are obtained by applying an optimized version to the test cases. This further emphasizes that the results obtained for the unweighted version should not

**Table 5.14:** Run times obtained for the tree creation process and for the prediction of a single data vector when applying the unoptimized tree compressor to the different test cases

|                      | Time for tree creation (s) | Run time per vector (s) |
| -------------------- | -------------------------- | ----------------------- |
| Wind Tunnel I        | 90.469                     | 0.565                   |
| Wind Tunnel II       | 45.333                     | 0.265                   |
| Car Venting System   | 0.616                      | 0.004                   |
| Mixing Chamber I     | 1.841                      | 0.010                   |
| Mixing Chamber II    | 3.566                      | 0.022                   |
| Mixing Pipe          | 0.123                      | 0.001                   |

be used to judge the performance of such an approach. If optimization is used, one can conclude from the results that the tree creation process requires most time by far. Even if a greedy algorithm is used, the time needed for the tree creation will presumably exceed that of the tree prediction.

**Table 5.15:** Run times obtained for the tree creation process and for the prediction of a single data vector when applying the optimized tree compressor to the different test cases

|                      | Time for tree creation (s) | Run time per vector (s) |
| -------------------- | -------------------------- | ----------------------- |
| Wind Tunnel I        | 81.481                     | 0.616                   |
| Wind Tunnel II       | 40.848                     | 0.308                   |
| Car Venting System   | 0.847                      | 0.006                   |
| Mixing Chamber I     | 2.980                      | 0.015                   |
| Mixing Chamber II    | 5.565                      | 0.033                   |
| Mixing Pipe          | 0.163                      | 0.001                   |

According to the implementation of the compression all operations after the quantization are performed on 32-bit integer values. The times listed in the table above correspond to the average throughputs shown in Table 5.16. With the exception of the 'Mixing Pipe' example the throughput remains roughly the same at around 250 MB/s. The 504,8 MB/s throughput that resulted from measuring the tree prediction for the 'Mixing Pipe' are probably a consequence of caching effects. Due to the small size of the example, it can be loaded into the cache of the CPU, which enables significantly faster access times than the otherwise used main memory.

**Table 5.16:** Throughput obtained by using the optimized tree prediction to compress the test cases

|                      | Data volume (Bytes) | Throughput (MB/s) |
| -------------------- | ------------------- | ----------------- |
| Wind Tunnel I        | 151053520           | 244.59            |
| Wind Tunnel II       | 75821048            | 246.30            |
| Car Venting System   | 1620472             | 286.89            |
| Mixing Chamber I     | 3725904             | 244.21            |
| Mixing Chamber II    | 7164116             | 217.71            |
| Mixing Pipe          | 329356              | 504.80            |

The memory consumption of the tree method during prediction is solely dependent on the size of the data vector itself and the number of predictions carried out. If one assumes that only one spanning tree is used for the prediction of the dataset and $N$ denotes the number of values in the dataset, then $N + (N - 1) \cdot 2 = 3N - 2$ integer values have to be held in memory. This includes the values themselves plus the $N - 1$ pairs representing the edge list of the tree that have to be held in memory during prediction. The memory consumption during the tree creation is not estimated that easily.

## 5.3 Wavelet Compression

The multitude of facets to be considered for the evaluation of the wavelet-based scheme is far less than that of the tree-based approach. Basically, there are two parameters that can be varied and should be considered during this evaluation. These parameters are the choice of the operator and the threshold that defines a strong coupling. Two feasible operators that may be used in this context were described in Chapter 4. Compression factors obtained for the wavelet method by using the graph Laplace operator are listed in Table 5.17. The table contains results for various thresholds as well as the three precision levels used for this evaluation.

Good compression factors were obtained for all test cases, while the results from the two wind tunnel simulations were compressed the strongest. For the majority of the test cases the variation of the threshold remains without a notable effect on the compression factor. Again, the behavior is different for the wind tunnel cases in which a relatively large impact on the compression strength was observed. For example, at the highest precision level the compression factor for 'Wind Tunnel I' by utilizing a threshold of 0.625 was 7.8% higher than that for a threshold of 0.125. The results for both wind tunnel experiments suggest to choose a threshold of either 0.5 or 0.625 to achieve the highest compression factors. The standard parameter often used in the context of AMG is 0.25.

Employing the distance-based operator described in Section 4.3.2 yielded the results listed in Table 5.18. They are almost identical to those obtained when using the graph Laplace operator. This suggests that the distances between neighboring cell centers are very similar for each cell. In fact, differences can only be observed in the case of the 'Car Venting System' and the 'Mixing Pipe'. Both of these test cases were simulated with the simulation software StarCD from CD-adapco [8], while the others were simulated with StarCCM+ [9]. Different meshing strategies seem to be the reason for this behavior.

In Table 5.19 the entropy results obtained by using the wavelet method with a coarsening threshold of 0.5 and the Laplace-Operator are listed. The wavelet transform obviously led to a significant reduction of the entropy, especially when applied to the wind tunnel experiments. While this is somewhat comprehensible from the results on the compression factor, it once again shows the effect of preprocessing.

**Table 5.17:** Compression factors obtained by applying the wavelet method by using the graph Laplace operator to the test cases. Results are listed for different thresholds for strong couplings as well as for different quantization levels.

| e-03 | Coupling threshold | | | | | |
|---|---|---|---|---|---|---|
| | 0.125 | 0.25 | 0.375 | 0.5 | 0.625 | 0.75 |
| Wind Tunnel I | 22.932 | 22.945 | 22.847 | 23.077 | 22.944 | 22.678 |
| Wind Tunnel II | 22.397 | 22.387 | 22.257 | 22.645 | 22.631 | 22.402 |
| Car Venting System | 9.864 | 9.895 | 9.923 | 9.904 | 9.874 | 9.826 |
| Mixing Chamber I | 19.731 | 19.713 | 19.655 | 19.590 | 19.511 | 19.429 |
| Mixing Chamber II | 15.556 | 15.507 | 15.477 | 15.435 | 15.387 | 15.335 |
| Mixing Pipe | 12.510 | 12.452 | 12.340 | 12.285 | 12.194 | 12.113 |

| e-04 | | | | | | |
|---|---|---|---|---|---|---|
| Wind Tunnel I | 14.900 | 15.068 | 14.962 | 15.540 | 15.540 | 15.299 |
| Wind Tunnel II | 14.231 | 14.259 | 14.117 | 14.597 | 14.777 | 14.633 |
| Car Venting System | 6.100 | 6.111 | 6.125 | 6.122 | 6.118 | 6.100 |
| Mixing Chamber I | 11.174 | 11.167 | 11.139 | 11.108 | 11.073 | 11.036 |
| Mixing Chamber II | 9.549 | 9.521 | 9.509 | 9.491 | 9.470 | 9.446 |
| Mixing Pipe | 8.146 | 8.120 | 8.071 | 8.043 | 8.005 | 7.969 |

| e-05 | | | | | | |
|---|---|---|---|---|---|---|
| Wind Tunnel I | 9.679 | 9.841 | 9.792 | 10.443 | 10.501 | 10.337 |
| Wind Tunnel II | 9.248 | 9.278 | 9.184 | 9.545 | 9.702 | 9.629 |
| Car Venting System | 4.283 | 4.289 | 4.296 | 4.296 | 4.295 | 4.289 |
| Mixing Chamber I | 7.211 | 7.208 | 7.195 | 7.181 | 7.165 | 7.149 |
| Mixing Chamber II | 6.545 | 6.529 | 6.523 | 6.514 | 6.504 | 6.492 |
| Mixing Pipe | 5.939 | 5.926 | 5.899 | 5.883 | 5.862 | 5.842 |

**Table 5.18:** Compression factors obtained by applying the wavelet method by using the distance-based operator to the test cases. Results are listed for different thresholds for strong couplings as well as for different quantization levels.

| e-03 | Coupling threshold | | | | | |
| --- | --- | --- | --- | --- | --- | --- |
| | 0.125 | 0.25 | 0.375 | 0.5 | 0.625 | 0.75 |
| Wind Tunnel I | 22.932 | 22.945 | 22.847 | 23.077 | 22.944 | 22.678 |
| Wind Tunnel II | 22.397 | 22.387 | 22.257 | 22.645 | 22.631 | 22.402 |
| Car Venting System | 9.547 | 9.517 | 9.375 | 9.274 | 9.167 | 8.971 |
| Mixing Chamber I | 19.731 | 19.713 | 19.655 | 19.590 | 19.511 | 19.429 |
| Mixing Chamber II | 15.556 | 15.507 | 15.477 | 15.435 | 15.387 | 15.335 |
| Mixing Pipe | 12.408 | 12.353 | 12.256 | 12.188 | 12.089 | 12.249 |
| e-04 | | | | | | |
| Wind Tunnel I | 14.900 | 15.068 | 14.962 | 15.540 | 15.540 | 15.299 |
| Wind Tunnel II | 14.231 | 14.259 | 14.117 | 14.597 | 14.777 | 14.633 |
| Car Venting System | 6.064 | 6.037 | 5.955 | 5.897 | 5.837 | 5.741 |
| Mixing Chamber I | 11.174 | 11.167 | 11.139 | 11.108 | 11.073 | 11.036 |
| Mixing Chamber II | 9.549 | 9.521 | 9.509 | 9.491 | 9.470 | 9.446 |
| Mixing Pipe | 8.092 | 8.066 | 8.024 | 7.990 | 7.945 | 8.014 |
| e-05 | | | | | | |
| Wind Tunnel I | 9.679 | 9.841 | 9.792 | 10.443 | 10.501 | 10.337 |
| Wind Tunnel II | 9.248 | 9.278 | 9.184 | 9.545 | 9.702 | 9.629 |
| Car Venting System | 4.293 | 4.272 | 4.227 | 4.194 | 4.159 | 4.106 |
| Mixing Chamber I | 7.211 | 7.208 | 7.195 | 7.181 | 7.165 | 7.149 |
| Mixing Chamber II | 6.545 | 6.529 | 6.523 | 6.514 | 6.504 | 6.492 |
| Mixing Pipe | 5.912 | 5.897 | 5.874 | 5.856 | 5.830 | 5.869 |

**Table 5.19:** Entropy results before and after preprocessing by using the wavelet method. The results for different precision levels are listed in separate columns.

| | Before | | | After | | |
| --- | --- | --- | --- | --- | --- | --- |
| | 1e-03 | 1e-04 | 1e-05 | 1e-03 | 1e-04 | 1e-05 |
| Wind Tunnel I | 7.702 | 10.839 | 14.060 | 2.229 | 4.014 | 6.210 |
| Wind Tunnel II | 7.506 | 10.712 | 13.985 | 2.342 | 4.402 | 7.088 |
| Car Venting System | 6.843 | 9.873 | 12.895 | 3.942 | 6.552 | 9.361 |
| Mixing Chamber I | 6.389 | 9.647 | 12.882 | 3.023 | 5.859 | 9.091 |
| Mixing Chamber II | 6.702 | 9.996 | 13.270 | 3.492 | 6.133 | 9.261 |
| Mixing Pipe | 7.104 | 9.985 | 12.625 | 5.085 | 7.899 | 10.680 |

### 5.3.1   Performance and Memory Requirements

The wavelet transform also comprises a two-part process similar to that of the tree prediction scheme. At first, the operators for the interpolation and update have to be created.
This is performed during a setup phase. The resulting hierarchy of transfer operators can
then be applied to every data vector to conduct the transformations. Hence, the setup
phase has to be carried out only once. Run times for the setup and for the transformation
of one data vector are listed in Table 5.20. A different workstation had to be used for performance measurements for 'Wind Tunnel I', because memory consumption peaked well
over 24 GB of memory. As described at the beginning of this chapter, the workstation used
for most testing only had 24 GB of memory installed. Instead, the tests were performed
on a system with 4 dual-core AMD Opteron 8218 Processors clocked at 2600 MHz. It had
64 GB of installed memory available.

**Table 5.20:** Run times obtained for test cases by using the wavelet compression scheme with a
coarsening threshold of 0.5 and the graph Laplace operator

|                     | Time for hierarchy setup (s) | Run time per vector (s) |
|---------------------|-----------------------------:|------------------------:|
| Wind Tunnel I       | 614.405                      | 19.293                  |
| Wind Tunnel II      | 356.223                      | 5.497                   |
| Car Venting System  | 2.606                        | 0.114                   |
| Mixing Chamber I    | 4.530                        | 0.185                   |
| Mixing Chamber II   | 10.615                       | 0.375                   |
| Mixing Pipe         | 0.541                        | 0.022                   |

It was stated above that the implementation is single-threaded. The LAMA library used
for matrix calculations is based on a highly parallel software architecture [22]. All vector
multiplications were in fact performed in parallel. According to the developers of the
library, the setup is only partially performed in parallel and also not optimal in that sense.
Consequently, the run time of the setup phase could potentially be reduced. Still, it is
likely that for the steady state files used for this evaluation, the setup time will exceed
the overall time to transform all solution vectors. The impact of the parallel execution
can be noticed by comparing the above results with those in Table 5.21. On both octa-
core machines used for testing, the parallel execution led to speed-ups around 1,5 to 3 for
both the setup and the transformation itself. The reason that the performance scaling
of the transformation is only around two lies in non-parallel tasks executed during the
transformation. For example, rounding and scaling operations for the entire vector are
also conducted during the transformation.

The times listed in both tables above correspond to the average throughput shown in Table
5.22. The throughput was between 3.5 and 12.7 MB/s for the single-core run, whereas 7.8
to 20.1 MB/s were achieved in the multi-core run.

As mentioned before, the test for 'Wind Tunnel I' had to be performed on a different workstation due to the memory consumption of the wavelet method. In Table 5.23 the memory
consumption for the matrix hierarchy is listed for two different coarsening thresholds. Obviously the matrices have quite a large number of entries. Most entries are found in the

**Table 5.21:** Run times obtained for test cases by using the wavelet compression scheme and restricting the processing to one core

|  | Time for hierarchy setup (s) | Run time per vector (s) |
|---|---|---|
| Wind Tunnel I | 1153.540 | 42.385 |
| Wind Tunnel II | 488.778 | 10.029 |
| Car Venting System | 5.778 | 0.200 |
| Mixing Chamber I | 10.455 | 0.293 |
| Mixing Chamber II | 32.064 | 0.618 |
| Mixing Pipe | 1.031 | 0.037 |

**Table 5.22:** Throughput obtained for test cases by using the wavelet compression scheme

|  | Data volume (bytes) | Single-core (MB/s) | Multi-core (MB/s) |
|---|---|---|---|
| Wind Tunnel I | 151053520 | 3.564 | 7.830 |
| Wind Tunnel II | 75821048 | 7.560 | 13.794 |
| Car Venting System | 1620472 | 8.117 | 14.192 |
| Mixing Chamber I | 3725904 | 12.717 | 20.114 |
| Mixing Chamber II | 7164116 | 11.586 | 19.113 |
| Mixing Pipe | 329356 | 8.796 | 14.674 |

hierarchy of Galerkin matrices which are only required during the setup phase. After the initial setup, they can be discarded, so that only the interpolation and restriction matrices remain in memory.

**Table 5.23:** Number of hierarchy levels and matrix entries as well as the memory consumption

| Threshold: 0.125 | Levels | Interpolation | Galerkin | Peak memory (MB) |
|---|---|---|---|---|
| Wind Tunnel I | 8 | 188411632 | 413386263 | 10020.506 |
| Wind Tunnel II | 8 | 101692923 | 220451455 | 5363.699 |
| Car Venting System | 6 | 2202604 | 4599546 | 114.077 |
| Mixing Chamber I | 6 | 2651928 | 4873091 | 131.526 |
| Mixing Chamber II | 6 | 6083765 | 12590421 | 315.651 |
| Mixing Pipe | 5 | 355339 | 776087 | 18.962 |
| Threshold: 0.75 |  |  |  |  |
| Wind Tunnel I | 14 | 201325369 | 679804771 | 13578.429 |
| Wind Tunnel II | 13 | 110483564 | 380799048 | 7524.141 |
| Car Venting System | 9 | 2410865 | 7966216 | 160.032 |
| Mixing Chamber I | 10 | 2601434 | 6366467 | 148.827 |
| Mixing Chamber II | 10 | 5899585 | 17038550 | 365.765 |
| Mixing Pipe | 8 | 348883 | 947014 | 20.945 |

# 6 Discussion

The strategy employed for compression was to reduce the entropy by exploiting correlations to achieve a more efficient encoding. This general approach was described and theoretically corroborated in Chapter 2. As the research was targeted at solution data from CFD simulations, which is generally stored as data sets of floating point values, a lossy compression was intended. For this purpose a uniform quantization was applied prior to the decorellation methods brought forward in this thesis. Thereafter, two entirely different strategies to exploit local correlations comprised in the data were applied. The tree predictor and the wavelet transformation introduced here were laid out to be suitable for the irregular volumetric grids often used for CFD simulations. The evaluation presented in the last chapter revealed that the treated preprocessing methods contributed to a reduction of the entropy and led to reasonable compression factors.

Both techniques introduced here make use of grid connectivity information to determine local correlations. To measure the impact of this approach an alternative and very simple predictor method was introduced and evaluated. In contrast to the tree predictor and the wavelet transform it does not require any connectivity information to perform the prediction. Instead, a prediction and differencing between neighboring storage locations is carried out and thus, the method relies on a meaningful order in which the values are stored to achieve decent compression factors. It is standing to reason that the order in which the values are stored by the simulation software are based on the structure of the grid. That this presumption is reasonable is shown by the compression factors obtained during the evaluation (see Section 5.1). To further support these results the same test cases were also compressed discarding the preprocessing and simply applying gzip as encoder. The compression scheme was not altered in that the quantization was applied. Consequently, it was still accountable for a notable reduction of the entropy. The compiled results in Table 6.1 clearly show the impact of the preprocessing and the effectiveness of this simple method.

More relevant than the comparison between the simple predictor and gzip is the analysis of the results achieved for the tree predictor and the wavelet transform. Results for the

**Table 6.1:** Compiled compression factors that were obtained by applying the gzip, the simple predictor, the unoptimized tree predictor and the wavelet transform to the test cases. For the wavelet transform the graph Laplace operator and a coarsening threshold of 0.5 were used. Results are listed for the three quantization levels.

| | gzip | | | Simple prediction | | |
|---|---|---|---|---|---|---|
| | 1e-03 | 1e-04 | 1e-05 | 1e-03 | 1e-04 | 1e-05 |
| Wind Tunnel I | 16.097 | 7.576 | 4.719 | 21.062 | 11.126 | 7.304 |
| Wind Tunnel II | 13.626 | 6.602 | 4.403 | 19.947 | 10.912 | 7.159 |
| Car Venting System | 5.160 | 3.417 | 2.518 | 7.693 | 4.997 | 3.633 |
| Mixing Chamber I | 9.515 | 5.380 | 3.870 | 15.874 | 9.079 | 6.198 |
| Mixing Chamber II | 7.471 | 4.765 | 3.564 | 12.333 | 7.758 | 5.559 |
| Mixing Pipe | 7.912 | 5.212 | 3.939 | 11.723 | 7.682 | 5.656 |

| | Tree prediction | | | Wavelet transform | | |
|---|---|---|---|---|---|---|
| | 1e-03 | 1e-04 | 1e-05 | 1e-03 | 1e-04 | 1e-05 |
| Wind Tunnel I | 25.277 | 12.512 | 7.842 | 23.077 | 15.540 | 10.443 |
| Wind Tunnel II | 22.383 | 11.794 | 7.557 | 22.645 | 14.597 | 9.545 |
| Car Venting System | 9.136 | 5.661 | 4.007 | 9.904 | 6.122 | 4.296 |
| Mixing Chamber I | 18.396 | 10.042 | 6.647 | 19.590 | 11.108 | 7.181 |
| Mixing Chamber II | 14.084 | 8.521 | 5.955 | 15.435 | 9.491 | 6.514 |
| Mixing Pipe | 13.062 | 8.288 | 5.986 | 12.285 | 8.043 | 5.883 |

unoptimized tree predictor as well as for the wavelet transform when using the graph Laplace operator and a coarsening threshold of 0.5 are also incorporated in the result summery shown in Table 6.1. Apparently, both of the introduced methods achieve higher compression factors than the simple method which indicates that the use of neighboring data points is beneficial for the decorellation. At least, this can be concluded from the comparison between the simple predictor and the tree predictor, as both use essentially the same mathematical predictor. The comparison of the results acquired for all three methods show a similar behavior for the different files. The application of the tree compression resulted in higher compression factors as compared to the application of the simple method. The wavelet method yielded even higher compression factors than the tree predictor.

The comparison between the simple compression and the tree compression reveals that compression factors obtained by applying the tree compression are between 10% and 17% higher for the two lower precisions, and between 5% and 7% higher for the relative precision 1e-05. Compared to these numbers the results obtained for the wavelet method indicate almost twice as good improvements upon those of the simple method. This is true at least for the two higher precision levels and with the exception of the 'Mixing Pipe' test case. In this case the compression factors obtained by applying the wavelet method were lower than those for the tree predictor. Interestingly, for the relative precision of 1e-03 the compression factors achieved with the wavelet method were less for 'Wind Tunnel I' than those of the tree compression, but significantly higher for the precision levels 1e-04 and 1e-05. The reason for the relatively low compression factors obtained for the 1e-03 precision level is probably related to the run-length encoding of the used encoder. Run-length encoding is used to highly efficiently encode streams of consecutive occurring '0' values.

Any deviations from '0' in-between such a stream prevents or causes an interruption of the run-length encoding. Due to the strong compression achieved for the relative precision of 1e-03 it is reasonable to assume that many '0' values and other small values result from the decorellation. Depending on their distribution the run-length encoding can be more or less effective which can impact the overall efficiency of the encoding. This coherence is reinforced by the entropy results shown in Tables 5.6 and 5.19. As listed there, the entropy was reduced from 7.702 to 2.422 by the tree predictor, whereas a reduction to 2.229 was achieved by the wavelet transform.

Across all compression methods the obtained results show that the two wind tunnel simulations were compressed the strongest. It is obvious from the entropy results listed in the previous chapter that the good compression achieved for these two test cases is not related to an initially lower entropy. Instead, each method was accountable for a substantial reduction of the entropy and therefore for the high compression factors. As pointed out before, the use of the wavelet transformation yielded the highest compression factors in all test cases with the exception of the 'Mixing Pipe'. Noticeably, the compression factors obtained for the wind tunnel simulations are significantly higher for medium and high precision levels than those obtained for the other methods. This difference is not as pronounced in the other cases. This behavior is probably related to the structure of the grid and the mathematical attributes of the wavelet method. As illustrated in Figure 6.1, most parts of the grids exhibit regular hexahedral structures. The compression behavior of the tree predictor can be expected to be independent thereof, because the regularity of the grid is not exploited. This is different for the wavelet approach. For regular 3D meshes the approximation order for the interpolation at the first level is of 2nd order under certain conditions. Roughly 50% of the values are decorrelated at the first level. Consequently, the higher order prediction can be expected to be noticeable in the results, especially, since the tree predictor is only of first order.

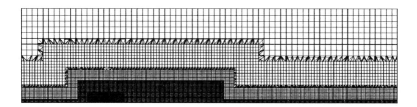

**Figure 6.1:** A 2D clip-plane along the x-axis of the 3D model of 'Wind Tunnel II' is shown. The regular structure of large parts of the grid can be observed.

Evidently, the wavelet transformation achieved higher compression factors than the unweighted tree predictor. The largest differences in terms of compression factor were obtained for the wind tunnel test cases, because their underlying grid has large regular parts. However, this comparison uses the unweighted version of the tree predictor and the wavelet transform based on the graph Laplace operator. The compression factor obtained for the two operators were not significantly different, as revealed by the evaluation of the wavelet approach. This finding is presumably related to the regularly spaced cell centers. In those cases where a difference was noticeable, the compression factors for the distance-based operator were slightly lower. A higher impact was ascertained by the variation of the coarsening threshold. The best results were achieved for thresholds 0.5 and 0.625, which means that a stricter selection of strong couplings led to an improved compression. While the associated results are listed in Table 6.1 and discussed above, the impact of the tree optimization has not yet been taken into account.

**Table 6.2:** Compression factors obtained by optimization based on the most suitable variable within each file as well as by optimizing for the full weighting

| | Single variable | | | All variables | | |
|---|---|---|---|---|---|---|
| | 1e-03 | 1e-04 | 1e-05 | 1e-03 | 1e-04 | 1e-05 |
| Wind Tunnel I | 27.237 | 14.197 | 9.078 | 29.134 | 14.834 | 9.461 |
| Wind Tunnel II | 24.331 | 13.547 | 8.584 | 26.639 | 14.261 | 8.843 |
| Car Venting System | 9.780 | 6.029 | 4.215 | 9.059 | 5.706 | 4.069 |
| Mixing Chamber I | 19.586 | 11.123 | 7.211 | 20.452 | 10.973 | 7.072 |
| Mixing Chamber II | 12.456 | 8.008 | 5.711 | 15.103 | 9.158 | 6.297 |
| Mixing Pipe | 16.915 | 10.067 | 6.917 | 16.733 | 9.881 | 6.821 |

The evaluation of the optimization has shown that it can be beneficial even if additional data has to be stored to ensure reversibility. The full weighting was the most promising of the evaluated weightings. While certain gradients of single variables could also be used to enhance the compression, this does not generally apply to all variables. In addition, the gain in compression factor was not as high in most other cases. This is summarized in Table 6.2. The results for the optimization variable yielding the highest compression factor for each particular file are listed in the columns under 'Single variable', while the respective results obtained for the full weighting are listed to the right. All displayed results comprise the overhead of storing the optimized tree by using the bit mask format. It is obvious from the side-by-side comparison, that the full weighting led to higher compression factors for 'Wind Tunnel I', 'Wind Tunnel II' and 'Mixing Chamber II'. For the others, the use of a single variable mostly led to higher compression factors, although the difference was usually not very large. As mentioned before, the full weighting has the advantage that it is universally applicable and does not need a weight selection process. Considering this comparison and the fact that no weight selection has to be carried out, the full weighting clearly seems to be the choice for optimizing the tree predictor. The results for other weightings were not as promising. Especially the geometry-based approach yielded only marginally improved results. The equally spaced cell centers seemed to be the reason for such poor improvement. This connection was further supported by the results obtained for the distance operator-based wavelet transform. Compared to the geometry-based weighting the dynamics-based weighting yielded much better results. However, compression factors were still significantly lower compared to those of the full weighting.

The comparison between the optimized tree predictor and the wavelet scheme shows a picture different from the previous comparison. Similarly high compression factors were found for the full weighting, and for the precision 1e-03 they even exceeded those of the wavelet transform, except for 'Mixing Chamber II'. In most other cases the compression factor was less than 5% lower than that obtained for the wavelet method. The differences were the highest for the wind tunnel test cases, presumably for the same reason as mentioned above. Nevertheless, the compression factors were only less than 10% lower for the highest precision. For the unweighted prediction the difference in both cases was more than 20% for the highest precision. As indicated by the results for the 'Mixing Pipe', a higher compression was reached when using the optimized tree predictor. Altogether, a strong improvement was achieved by utilizing optimization based on full weighting. While the wavelet method prooved to be still more effective for most cases, optimization reduced the previous gain in advantage significantly. Moreover, the weighting on which this comparison is based upon is very suitable for practical use, as it can be employed to implement a universally applicable compression scheme. No weight selection has to be carried out compared to other weightings. Previously, it was assumed that the prediction tree has to be stored with the compressed data. While this is true in general, it is possible in some settings to hide the tree within the topology description of the grid. Apparently, this can only be done for a single tree and if the grid is stored in a suitable format. For example, this is possible if the data to be compressed is stored as cell values and the face-based format is used to store the grid description. Then, the connectivities held by the tree could be complemented by the remaining connectivities of the graph. Although this would require some sort of reordering or separation of the connectivities to identify those of the tree, no information would be lost. The great advantage of such an approach is that one receives the full benefit of optimization, which would make it the most advantageous method in terms of the compression factor for any of the covered test cases. The fact that only a single tree can be used with this method is no problem, since multiple trees were not used anyway.

In addition to the optimization for steady state results, some of the weightings emerging in the transient case were also evaluated. In contrast to the steady state case, the use of all variable data of every time step for a weighting is impractical. The amount of data is simply too large. Also, correlations might vary too strongly over time to form an effective procedure. Several approaches to optimize for transient solution data were evaluated in Section 5.2.2. It was evident from the results that optimizing was most profitable if the full weighting was created from all variables of the middle time step. Due to the low number of time steps in this transient case, the middle time step of the entire file was chosen. For practical purposes the separation into blocks of time steps might be required when transient files with larger numbers of time steps are compressed. Nevertheless, for the transient case this optimization was feasible for practical use and beneficial for the compression.

Two significant findings were addressed in the discussion above: First, the wavelet scheme yielded the highest compression factors and secondly, an optimization for the tree predictor exists and achieves similarly good compression factors. However, these conclusions only concern the compression strength. Performance and memory consumption of the two methods exhibit a larger difference. Most computing time was spent during the setup phases of both methods. Noticeably, the creation of the wavelet hierarchy required significantly more time than the determination of an optimized prediction tree. Although this could be observed in all test cases, the results in Table 6.3 indicate that tendentially less nodes per second were processed for larger files. Consequently, it became most obvious for the large grids of 'Wind Tunnel I' and 'Wind Tunnel II'. Running on a single core, the creation of the wavelet hierarchy required almost 20 minutes for the 37 million cell 'Wind Tunnel I' example and a little more than 8 minutes for the 18 million cell 'Wind Tunnel II' case. In comparison hereto the creation of the minimal spanning tree required only 81.5 seconds when compressing 'Wind Tunnel I' and 40.9 seconds when applied to 'Wind Tunnel II'. Since only one tree was used for the prediction of all variables, it was only necessary in both cases to perform a setup phase once. As mention before, the LAMA library which was used for these operations is based on a highly parallel software design. Using all eight cores of the test machine reduced the hierarchy setup times by a factor of two to three. Still, the hierarchy setup required a significantly longer time. For the smaller test cases the differences between the measured run times were not as large. On a single core the hierarchy setup required between three to six times longer than the tree creation process. If parallel execution was used, this could be reduced by a factor of two. Nevertheless, parallel implementations of the tree predictor could also be used to further improve data throughput. Such implementations were not prepared for the evaluation of the method, however.

**Table 6.3:** Ratio between setup phase run-time and number of nodes (nodes/s)

|                     | Number of nodes | Tree creation | Hierarchy setup |
| ------------------- | --------------- | ------------- | --------------- |
| Wind Tunnel I       | 37763380        | 463462        | 32737           |
| Wind Tunnel II      | 18955262        | 464044        | 38781           |
| Car Venting System  | 405118          | 478298        | 70114           |
| Mixing Chamber I    | 931476          | 312576        | 89094           |
| Mixing Chamber II   | 1791029         | 321838        | 55858           |
| Mixing Pipe         | 82339           | 505147        | 79863           |

A similar behavior could be observed for the execution of the wavelet transform and the differencing performed to calculate prediction errors. The wavelet transform required significantly more time as it did not exceed 13 MB/s data throughput across the test files on a single core. On all eight cores the highest average throughput of 20.1 MB/s was achieved during compression of 'Mixing Chamber I'. In contrast, the tree predictor achieved an average throughput between 217 MB/s and 286 MB/s for all files except for the 'Mixing Pipe'. For the latter 504.8 MB/s were reached. For reference, the simple predictor achieved throughputs close to 1 GB/s. A relation between the number of nodes and the data throughput did not seem to exist. Still, the big difference in data throughput is particularly remarkable when large data sets are compressed. For industry applications it is questionable if such a throughput of 20 MB/s is sufficient, especially when considering that even larger examples are in use today.

**Table 6.4:** Memory in MB consumed by transfer operators required during transformation

| Threshold | 0.125 | 0.75 |
|---|---|---|
| Wind Tunnel I | 4981.243 | 5325.153 |
| Wind Tunnel II | 2676.279 | 2904.118 |
| Car Venting System | 57.956 | 63.325 |
| Mixing Chamber I | 72.398 | 71.582 |
| Mixing Chamber II | 163.157 | 159.508 |
| Mixing Pipe | 9.495 | 9.398 |

In addition to the suboptimal performance results, the memory consumption of the wavelet method was also identified as obstructive. Essentially, it was the reason for switching benchmark machines, since the large memory consumption well exceeded the 24 GB of installed memory. The corresponding results were listed in Table 5.23. Although these numbers only contain the memory required for the matrix hierarchy and do not include any additional memory required for setting up the matrices, the consumption is impressive. The numbers listed in the table are marked as peak values, because only the interpolation and restriction operators are necessary for calculating the transform after the hierarchy is set up. Nevertheless, even then the numbers are considerably higher compared to those of the tree predictor, as summarized in Table 6.4.

# 7 Summary and Conclusions

Two methods are presented for the compression of numerical data on irregular volumetric grids. They have the feature to be applicable to grids with non-unique cell types that are often used for CFD simulations. The two methods are based on the same general lossy compression scheme that includes quantization and rice encoding. The methods are characterized by two different decorrelation techniques that are proposed in this thesis. Solution data obtained from CFD simulations has been used for their evaluation, for which the compression factor as well as performance and memory consumption have been important measures.

Both methods show satisfactory results in terms of the compression factor. The wavelet compression yielded larger compression factors when compared to the unoptimized tree compression. For a wind tunnel simulation compression factors of 12.512 and 15.540 were obtained for a typical precision with the tree compression and the wavelet method, respectively. While the 20% stronger compression achieved with the wavelet transform represents a significant difference, a unique feature of the presented tree predictor is not considered in these numbers. A way to optimize the prediction tree is presented, for which several weightings have been evaluated. The full weighting appears to be the most practical and also one of the most beneficial approaches. With optimization the compression factor improved to 14.834 for the same wind tunnel simulation. Overall, the optimization cannot completely close the gap between the two methods, however, the differences become significantly smaller. Hence, the optimization proves to be very useful.

When utilizing the optimization both methods show fairly similar compression factors. In terms of performance and memory footprint the two methods exploit considerable differences. The required setup phase is the most time-consuming part in both cases. Here, the largest differences in run time and memory consumption have been identified. The setup for the wavelet hierarchy consumes by far more time and memory than the analogous tree creation process. While the tree creation process only requires 81.481 s, the hierarchy setup needs 1153.540 s until completion. In addition to the long run times memory consumption is another drawback of this method. The memory consumption of the sparse martrix format-based data structure utilized to hold the hierarchy of operators peaked at more than 10 GB during setup. A compressed sparse row (CSR) matrix format was used.

Although the compression factors achieved by the wavelet-based method are very promising, slow run times and large memory consumption make this method almost inapplicable in processes in industry. This is particularly the case when large amounts of data as in the field of CFD must be processed. The tree prediction combined with optimization seems to be the best choice for such purposes, as similarly high compression factors are obtained while requiring substantially less time and memory. Nevertheless, future efforts might bring forth possibilities to reduce time and memory requirements of the wavelet method, making it more attractive to application in industry.

As higher resolution grids will be used in the future, performance and memory consumption remain important measures for compression algorithms. In addition, presumably more transient problems will be simulated with high temporal resolution as the computational power and storage capacities rise. Consequently, the amount of produced simulation data will increase further, making compression techniques even more important. Higher resolution grids and the exploitation of temporal correlations will contribute to increased compression factors in the future.

# Bibliography

[1] ALEXA, M., AND MÜLLER, W. Representing Animations by Principal Components. *Computer Graphics Forum* (2000), 411–418.

[2] ALLIEZ, P., AND GOTSMAN, C. Recent Advances in Compression of 3D Meshes. In *Advances in Multiresolution for Geometric Modelling*, N. A. Dodgson, M. S. Floater, and M. A. Sabin, Eds. Springer-Verlag, Berlin etc., 2005, pp. 3–26.

[3] ANDERSON, J. D. *Computational Fluid Dynamics. The Basics with Applications.* McGraw-Hill, Inc., New York etc., 1995.

[4] BALSTER, E. J., FORTENER, B. T., AND TURRI, W. F. Integer Computation of JPEG 2000 Wavelet Transform and Quantization for Lossy Compression. *IEEE Transactions on Image Processing 20*, 8 (2011), 2386–2391.

[5] BRICEÑO, H. M., SANDER, P. V., MCMILLAN, L., GORTLER, S., AND HOPPE, H. Geometry videos: A new representation for 3d animations. *ACM Symposium on Computer Animation* (2003), 136–146.

[6] BURT, P. J., AND ADELSON, E. H. The Laplacian Pyramid as a Compact Image Code. *IEEE Transactions on Communications 31*, 4 (1983), 532–540.

[7] CALDERBANK, A. R., DAUBECHIES, I., SWELDENS, W., AND YEO, B.-L. Lossless image compression using integer to integer wavelet transforms. In *Proceedings of the International Conference on Image Processing* (1997), vol. I, pp. 596–599.

[8] CD-ADAPCO, 2012. http://www.cd-adapco.com/products/star_cd/index.html.

[9] CD-ADAPCO, 2012. http://www.cd-adapco.com/products/star_ccm_plus/index.html.

[10] CHEN, D., CHIANG, Y.-J., MEMON, N., AND WU, X. Geometry compression of tetrahedral meshes using optimized prediction. In *Proceedings of the European Conference on Signal Processing (EUSIPCO 05)* (2005).

[11] CHEN, D., CHIANG, Y.-J., MEMON, N., AND WU, X. Lossless Geometry Compression for Steady-State and Time-Varying Irregular Grids. In *Eurographics/IEEE-VGTC Symposium on Visualization*, T. Ertl, K. Joy, and B. Santos, Eds. The Eurographics Association, 2006.

[12] COHEN-OR, D., LEVIN, D., AND REMEZ, O. Progressive Compression of Arbitrary Triangular Meshes. In *Proceedings of the IEEE Visualization Conference* (1999), IEEE Computer Society and ACM, pp. 67–72.

[13] COVER, T. M., AND THOMAS, J. A. *Elements of Information Theory, 2nd ed.* John Wiley & Sons, Inc., New York, 2006.

[14] DAHMEN, W. Some Remarks on Multiscale Transformations, Stability and Biorthogonality. In *Curves and Surfaces II.* AKPeters, Boston, 1994, pp. 157–188.

[15] DAHMEN, W. Stability of Multiscale Transformations. *Fourier Anal. Appl. 2,* 4 (1996), 341–361.

[16] DAUBECHIES, I. *Ten Lectures on Wavelets.* CBMS-NSF Regional Conference Series in Applied Math. SIAM, Philadelphia, 1992.

[17] DAUBECHIES, I., AND SWELDENS, W. Factoring Wavelet Transforms into Lifting Steps. *J. Fourier Anal. Appl. 4,* 3 (1998), 247–269.

[18] DIESTEL, R. *Graphentheorie, 4. Aufl.* Springer-Verlag, Heidelberg, 2010.

[19] ENGELSON, V., FRITZSON, D., AND FRITZSON, P. Lossless Compression of High-Volume Numerical Data from Simulations. In *Data Compression Conference (DCC)* (2000), pp. 574–586.

[20] FENWICK, P. Universal Codes. In *Lossless Compression Handbook.* Academic Press, London, 2003, ch. 3, pp. 55–78.

[21] FLAIG, A. Airbus A380: Solutions to the Aerodynamic Challenges of Designing the World's Largest Passenger Aircraft, 2008.

[22] FÖRSTER, M., AND KRAUS, J. Scalable parallel AMG on ccNUMA machines with OpenMP. Personal communication.

[23] GAREY, M. R., AND JOHNSON, D. S. *Computers and Intractability; A Guide to the Theory of NP-Completeness.* W. H. Freeman & Co., New York, 1979.

[24] GUMHOLD, S., GUTHE, S., AND STRASSER, W. Tetrahedral Mesh Compression with the Cut-Border Machine. In *Proceedings of the Visualization Conference* (1999), IEEE Computer Society and ACM, pp. 51–58.

[25] HIRSCH, C. *Numerical Computation of Internal and External Flows. The Fundamentals of Computational Fluid Dynamics,* 2 ed. Butterworth-Heinemann, 2007.

[26] IBARRIA, L., LINDSTROM, P., ROSSIGNAC, J., AND SZYMCZAK, A. Out-of-core compression and decompression of large n-dimensional scalar fields. *Computer Graphics Forum 22,* 3 (2003), 343–348.

[27] IBARRIA, L., AND ROSSIGNAC, J. Dynapack: Space-time compression of the 3d animations of triangle meshes with fixed connectivity. In *Proceedings of the ACM SIGGRAPH/Eurographics Symposium on Computer Animation (SCA)* (2003), pp. 126–135.

[28] ISENBURG, M., AND ALLIEZ, P. Compressing Hexahedral Volume Meshes. *Graphical Models 65* (2003), 239–257.

[29] ISENBURG, M., AND SNOEYINK, J. Face Fixer: Compressing Polygon Meshes with Properties. In *Proceedings of the SIGGRAPH 2000 Conference* (2000), ACM Press/Addison-Wesley Publishing Co., pp. 263–270.

[30] JAWERTH, B., AND SWELDENS, W. An overview of wavelet based multiresolution analyses. *SIAM Rev. 36*, 3 (1994), 377–412.

[31] KALBERER, F., POLTHIER, K., AND VON TYCOWICZ, C. Lossless Compression of Adaptive Multiresolution Meshes. In *2009 XXII Brazilian Symposium on Computer Graphics and Image Processing (SIBGRAPI)* (2009), pp. 80–87.

[32] KARNI, Z., AND GOTSMAN, C. Spectral Compression of Mesh Geometry. In *Proceedings of the SIGGRAPH 2000 Conference* (2000), ACM Press/Addison-Wesley Publishing Co., pp. 279–286.

[33] KARNI, Z., AND GOTSMAN, C. 3D mesh compression using fixed spectral bases. *Proceedings of Graphics Interface* (2001), 1–8.

[34] KARNI, Z., AND GOTSMAN, C. Compression of soft-body animation sequences. *Computer & Graphics 28*, 1 (2004), 25–34.

[35] KHODAKOVSKY, A., SCHRÖDER, P., AND SWELDENS, W. Progressive Geometry Compression. In *Proceedings of the SIGGRAPH 2000 Conference* (2000), ACM Press/Addison-Wesley Publishing Co., pp. 271–278.

[36] KOMPATSIARIS, I., AND STRINTZIS, M. G. Hierarchical representation and coding of surfaces using 3D polygon meshes. In *Proceedings of the International Conference on Image Processing* (2000), vol. 1, pp. 21–24.

[37] KRONROD, B., AND GOTSMAN, C. Optimized Triangle Mesh Compression Using Prediction Trees. In *Proceedings of the First International Symposium on 3D Data Processing Visualization and Transmission* (2002).

[38] KÜRZ, C. MPEG für Simulationsergebnisse. Diplomarbeit, 2011.

[39] LEE, H., ALLIEZ, P., AND DESBRUN, M. Angle-Analyzer: A Triangle-Quad Mesh Codec. In *Eurographics Conference Proceedings* (2002), pp. 383–392.

[40] LENGYEL, J. E. Compression of Time-Dependent Geometry. In *Proceedings of the 1999 Symposium on Interactive 3D Graphics* (1999), ACM, pp. 89–95.

[41] LINDSTROM, P., AND ISENBURG, M. Lossless Compression of Hexahedral Meshes. *Proceedings of the IEEE Data Compression Conference* (2008), 192–201.

[42] MÜLLER, K., SMOLIC, A., KAUTZNER, M., EISERT, P., AND WIEGAND, T. Predictive Compression of Dynamic 3D Meshes. In *Proceedings of the IEEE International Conference on Image Processing* (2005), pp. 621–624.

[43] PAYAN, F., AND ANTONINI, M. Temporal wavelet-based compression for 3D animated models. *Computers & Graphics 31*, 1 (2007), 77–88.

[44] PIGEON, S. Huffman Coding. In *Lossless Compression Handbook*, K. Sayood, Ed. Academic Press, 2003, ch. 4, pp. 79–100.

[45] RETTENMEIER, M. Zwei Strategien zur verlustfreien Kompression von Simulationsergebnissen. Diplomarbeit, 2007.

[46] ROSSIGNAC, J. Edgebreaker: Connectivity compression for triangle meshes. *IEEE Transactions on Visualization and Computer Graphics 5*, 1 (1999), 47–61.

[47] SAID, A. Arithmetic Coding. In *Lossless Compression Handbook*. 2003, ch. 5, pp. 101–152.

[48] SALOMON, D., AND MOTTA, G. *Handbook of Data Compression*, 5 ed. Springer-Verlag, London, 2010.

[49] SATTLER, M., SARLETTE, R., AND KLEIN, R. Simple and efficient compression of animation sequences. In *Proceedings of the 2005 ACM SIGGRAPH/Eurographics symposium on Computer Animation* (2005), K. Anjyo and P. Faloutsos, Eds., ACM Press, pp. 209–217.

[50] SAYOOD, K. *Introduction to Data Compression*, 3 ed. Morgan Kaufmann, 2006.

[51] SCHMALZL, J. Using standard image compression algorithms to store data from computational fluid dynamics. *Computers & Geosciences 29*, 8 (2003), 1021–1031.

[52] SCHMIDT, A. Auswirkungen verlustbehafteter Kompression auf das Frequenzspektrum und die Gradienten von CFD-Simulationsergebnissen. Diplomarbeit, 2011.

[53] SCHRIJVER, A. *Combinatorial Optimization. Polyhedra and Efficiency.* Springer, Heidelberg, 2003.

[54] SECKER, A., AND TAUBMAN, D. S. Highly scalable video compression with scalable motion coding. *IEEE Transactions on Image Processing 13*, 8 (2004), 1029–1041.

[55] SHANNON, C. E. A Mathematical theory of Cummunication. *Bell System Technical Journal*, 27 (1948), 379–423 and 623–656.

[56] SHEPARD, D. A two-dimensional interpolation function for irregularly-spaced data. In *Proceedings of the 1968 ACM National Conference* (1968), ACM, pp. 517–524.

[57] SORKINE, O., COHEN-OR, D., AND TOLEDO, S. High-pass quantization for mesh encoding. In *Proceedings of the Eurographics/ACM SIGGRAPH Symposium on Geometry Processing* (2003), Eurographics Association, pp. 42–51.

[58] STÜBEN, K. Algebraic multigrid (AMG): experiences and comparisons. *Appl. Math. Comput.* (1983), 419–452.

[59] STÜBEN, K. Course on Algebraic Multigrid and SAMG. 2009.

[60] SWELDENS, W. The lifting scheme: a construction of second generation wavelets. *SIAM J. Math. Anal. 29*, 2 (1998), 511–546.

[61] SWELDENS, W., AND SCHRÖDER, P. Building Your Own Wavelets at Home. In *Wavelets in Computer Graphics*. ACM SIGGRAPH Course notes, 1996, pp. 15–87.

[62] SZYMCZAK, A., AND ROSSIGNAC, J. Grow & Fold: Compressing the Connectivity of Tetrahedral Meshes. *Computer-Aided Design 32*, 8/9 (2000), 527–538.

[63] TAUBIN, G., AND ROSSIGNAC, J. Geometric Compression Through Topological Surgery. *ACM Transactions on Graphics 17*, 2 (1998), 84–115.

[64] TOPCRUNCH.ORG, 2011. http://topcrunch.org.

[65] TROTTENBERG, U., OOSTERLEE, C. W., AND SCHÜLLER, A. *Multigrid Methods*. Academic Press, Inc., 2001.

[66] WASCHBÜSCH, M., GROSS, M., EBERHARD, F., LAMBORAY, E., AND WÜRMLIN, S. Progressive Compression of Point-Sampled Models. In *Proceedings of the Eurographics Symposium on Point-Based Graphics (SPBG)* (2004), pp. 95–102.

[67] WILLEMS, F. M. J., AND TJALKENS, T. J. Information Theory behind Source Coding. In *Lossless Compression Handbook*, K. Sayood, Ed. 2003, ch. 1, pp. 3–34.

[68] YANG, J.-H., KIM, C.-S., AND LEE, S.-U. Compression of 3-D Triangle Mesh Sequences Based on Vertex-Wise Motion Vector Prediction. *IEEE Transactions on Circuits and Systems for Video Technology 12*, 12 (2002), 1178–1184.

# A  Appendix

The appendix is separated into two parts. The six steady state test cases as well as the one transient test case are outlined in Section A.1. The outline includes a brief description of the underlying simulation, the file content and some statistics about data stored in the example files. The compression results obtained for the different methods and test cases are listed in detail in Sections A.2 - A.4. For each method the results are consolidated in separate sections. Compression factors are given for every variable contained in the test files.

Variable names are abbreviated according to the following table. The same abbriviations were already used in Chapter 5 and are here only listed again.

**Table A.1:** Variable names and their abbreviations

| Name | Abbreviation |
|------|--------------|
| Density | $\rho$ |
| Dissipation Rate | $\epsilon$ |
| Enthalpy | $H$ |
| Static Enthalpy | $H_s$ |
| Pressure | $P$ |
| Static Pressure | $P_s$ |
| Thermodynamic Pressure | $Pt$ |
| Turbulent Kinetic Energy | TKE |
| Turbulent Viscosity | TVis |
| Temperature | $T$ |
| Velocity Component U | $V_0$ |
| Velocity Component V | $V_1$ |
| Velocity Component W | $V_2$ |
| Mass Fraction Isocyanate | $w_{iso}$ |
| Mass Fraction Polyol | $w_{pol}$ |
| Molar Concentration Isocyanate | $c_{iso}$ |
| Molar Concentration Polyol | $c_{pol}$ |

## A.1 Test Cases

**Wind Tunnel I**

The test case is a result from virtual wind tunnel experiments as commonly performed by car manufacturers to determine the aerodynamic properties of car designs. The wind tunnel is modeled as a large box surrounding a car that is positioned in its middle. The grid fills the space between the car and the box and mostly consists of hexahedral cells. Consequently, large areas of the grid show regular structures. The resolution of the grid is adapted to the simulation in that cells far away from the car have a larger volume as those closer to the car.

The size of the grid can be described by the following numbers.

Number of vertices: 42339839

Number of cells: 37763380

Number of internal faces: 114784563

**Table A.2:** Minimal, maximal and average value of each variable data set contained in the file 'Wind Tunnel I'. In addition to the commonly stored variables such as density, pressure and velocity, this example contains additional velocity sets. They are marked by suffixes.

| Variable | Statistics | | | |
|---|---|---|---|---|
| | Minimum | Maximum | Average | Type |
| $\rho$ | 0.3418 | 1.2921 | 1.1739 | double |
| $P$ | -6415.4361 | 2756.8411 | -74.3894 | double |
| $T$ | 273.1500 | 1032.4235 | 301.7834 | double |
| $V_0$ | -58.7030 | 94.4985 | 36.2162 | double |
| $V_1$ | -96.1287 | 97.4899 | -0.3276 | double |
| $V_2$ | -73.4863 | 66.9747 | 0.4423 | double |
| $V_0$ L | -64.3112 | 122.8790 | 34.9256 | double |
| $V_1$ L | -251.1836 | 3708.2417 | 215.5535 | double |
| $V_2$ L | -1981.9025 | 1897.0444 | -36.6472 | double |
| $V_0$ vl | -874.5364 | 100.7006 | -18.3410 | double |
| $V_1$ vl | -96.0965 | 97.5164 | 4.2307 | double |
| $V_2$ vl | -928.5576 | 2049.2983 | 340.1405 | double |
| $V_0$ vr | -881.6960 | 98.4182 | -19.1495 | double |
| $V_1$ vr | -95.8266 | 97.8025 | -9.8870 | double |
| $V_2$ vr | -928.0895 | 2047.4812 | 339.5278 | double |
| $V_0$ hl | -870.0078 | 100.2096 | -18.3105 | double |
| $V_1$ hl | -97.2852 | 96.3314 | 0.2804 | double |
| $V_2$ hl | -1145.9651 | 1827.5582 | 120.5488 | double |
| $V_0$ hr | -877.4401 | 97.9897 | -19.1302 | double |
| $V_1$ hr | -92.1308 | 101.4952 | -2.0260 | double |
| $V_2$ hr | -1149.8298 | 1832.4667 | 121.1279 | double |

## Wind Tunnel II

This example file also contains the results of a wind tunnel experiment. Besides the different car model used for the simulations, the grid has less cells and only four variables are stored within the solution files. Nevertheless, the grid is very similar to the one of 'Wind Tunnel I' in that it mostly consists of hexahedral cells. Thus, there are also regular structures present for large parts of the grid.

The size of the grid can be described by the following numbers.

Number of vertices: 19419169
Number of cells: 18955262
Number of internal faces: 56832532

**Table A.3:** Minimal, maximal and average value of each variable data set contained in the file 'Wind Tunnel II'

| Variable | Statistics | | | |
|---|---|---|---|---|
| | Minimum | Maximum | Average | Type |
| $P$ | -2747.5674 | 1009.4172 | -83.5059 | double |
| $V_0$ | -23.7536 | 60.7614 | 27.1907 | double |
| $V_1$ | -51.7899 | 44.5620 | 0.0104 | double |
| $V_2$ | -31.4986 | 38.5671 | -0.3538 | double |

**Car Venting System**

The flow of air through the outlet of a car ventilation was simulated in this test case. The part of the duct that leads to the outlet as well as the space surrounding the outlet are modeled.

The size of the grid can be described by the following numbers.

Number of vertices: 443211

Number of cells: 405118

Number of internal faces: 1187304

**Table A.4:** Minimal, maximal and average value of each variable data set contained in the file 'Car Venting System'

| Variable | Statistics | | | |
|---|---|---|---|---|
| | Minimum | Maximum | Average | Type |
| $\epsilon$ | 1.2570 e-05 | 80305.6640 | 633.6796 | float |
| $P$ | -135.1884 | 112.0517 | 19.5738 | double |
| $Pt$ | 99862.2233 | 100111.6052 | 100018.4053 | double |
| TKE | 1.5383 e-05 | 17.3466 | 1.4546 | float |
| TVis | 1.2597 e-06 | 1.6504 e-02 | 1.1926 e-03 | float |
| $V_0$ | -8.5547 | 17.4352 | 4.3254 | float |
| $V_1$ | -8.8279 | 8.6796 | -1.2092 | float |
| $V_2$ | -10.1603 | 7.8290 | 0.3044 | float |

**Mixing Chamber I**

This example file is obtained from a simulation of a mixing process found in the production of polyurethane. The simulations were carried out with the intention to identify designs of a mixing chamber specially suitable for such a mixing process. The simulated chamber consists of two inlets from which polyol and isocyanate is injected. In the body of the chamber the two substances react to form PU foam and are then pushed out of the chamber through a larger outlet. The grid used to model the inside of the mixing chamber consists of irregular polyhedral cells. Opposed to the grids used for the wind tunnel simulations no regular structure is obvious.

The size of the grid can be described by the following numbers.

Number of vertices: 5247522
Number of cells: 931476
Number of internal faces: 6242762

**Table A.5:** Minimal, maximal and average value of each variable data set contained in the file 'Mixing Chamber I'

| Variable | Statistics | | | |
| --- | --- | --- | --- | --- |
| | Minimum | Maximum | Average | Type |
| $\rho$ | 1030 | 1200 | 1083.8125 | double |
| $w_{pol}$ | 0 | 1 | 0.6501 | double |
| $w_{iso}$ | 0 | 1 | 0.3499 | double |
| $c_{pol}$ | 0 | 57.1735 | 39.0756 | double |
| $c_{iso}$ | 0 | 66.6099 | 21.0850 | double |
| $P$ | -4501153.5703 | 13482499.3204 | 167992.9428 | double |
| $P_s$ | -4501148.7490 | 13482498.8539 | 167991.8530 | double |
| TVis | 2.4716 | 1.1228 | 1.0470e-02 | double |
| $V_0$ | -105.9902 | 72.8563 | -1.5098 | double |
| $V_1$ | -95.1498 | 99.6865 | -0.7776 | double |
| $V_2$ | -162.7767 | 156.1346 | -0.3988 | double |

**Mixing Chamber II**

'Mixing Chamber II' is very similar to 'Mixing Chamber I'. The results were obtained from the same simulation series, however, the design of the chamber was modified in that the inlets were arranged differently. In addition, the resolution of the grid was increased in comparison to that of 'Mixing Chamber I'. This difference in size becomes obvious from the following numbers.

Number of vertices: 10382292
Number of cells: 1791029
Number of internal faces: 12251664

**Table A.6:** Minimal, maximal and average value of each variable data set contained in the file 'Mixing Chamber II'

| Variable | Statistics | | | |
|---|---|---|---|---|
| | Minimum | Maximum | Average | Type |
| $\rho$ | 1.1841 | 1200.000 | 1008.6573 | double |
| $P$ | -1390844.5046 | 20408859.8053 | 170666.1749 | double |
| $V_0$ | -50.0853 | 81.9297 | 0.5115 | double |
| $V_1$ | -61.8625 | 70.8304 | 0.0107 | double |
| $V_2$ | -128.3220 | 119.3977 | -1.6612 | double |

**Mixing Pipe**

In this example, the mixing process of two air streams with different temperatures occurring in a mixing pipe was simulated. The main air stream flows through the pipe, while the other stream is added through a small inlet from the side of the mixing pipe. The grid of this example is very small, as one can observe from the following numbers.

Number of vertices: 90244

Number of cells: 82339

Number of internal faces: 240105

**Table A.7:** Minimal, maximal and average value of each variable data set contained in the file 'Mixing Pipe I'

| Variable | Statistics | | | |
|---|---|---|---|---|
| | Minimum | Maximum | Average | Type |
| $H_s$ | 297774.9008 | 375275.9862 | 337743.4555 | double |
| $\rho$ | 0.9337 | 1.1767 | 1.0420 | double |
| $H$ | 297774.9008 | 375275.9862 | 337743.4555 | double |
| $\epsilon$ | 3.8344e-02 | 418.1729 | 15.2625 | double |
| $P$ | -28.6685 | 27.2768 | -2.8908 | double |
| $T$ | 295.9989 | 373.0378 | 335.7291 | double |
| $Pt$ | 99971.3199 | 100026.8808 | 99997.0174 | double |
| TKE | 6.7469e-03 | 1.6406 | 0.1397 | double |
| TVis | 3.7439 | 8.3890e-04 | 2.0107e-04 | double |
| $V_0$ | -4.4495 | 6.3404 | 1.8169 | double |
| $V_1$ | -6.9608 | 11.7767 | 0.5135 | double |
| $V_2$ | -8.7513 | 5.5532 | -0.1637 | double |

**Fire Simulation**

This example file is obtained from a fire simulation of two connected rooms, where one of the rooms contains a fire source. The induced air flow is simulated over time, thus a transient simulation was performed. The file contains 5 variables and 20 time steps and the grid used for this simulation mostly consists of hexahedral cells.

The size of the grid can be described by the following numbers.

Number of vertices: 6138112
Number of cells: 1028120
Number of internal faces: 7201761

**Table A.8:** Minimal, maximal and average value of density data sets contained in the file 'Fire Simulation'

| Time Step | Statistics $\rho$ | | |
| --- | --- | --- | --- |
| | Minimum | Maximum | Average |
| 1 | 0.4718 | 1.1508 | 0.7760 |
| 2 | 0.0743 | 1.0655 | 0.3510 |
| 3 | 0.0588 | 0.9587 | 0.3467 |
| 4 | 0.0794 | 0.9953 | 0.3915 |
| 5 | 0.0950 | 1.0481 | 0.4256 |
| 6 | 0.0917 | 1.0751 | 0.4745 |
| 7 | 0.1175 | 1.1109 | 0.5110 |
| 8 | 0.1395 | 1.1130 | 0.5265 |
| 9 | 0.1532 | 1.0707 | 0.5261 |
| 10 | 0.1488 | 1.0760 | 0.5190 |
| 11 | 0.1417 | 1.0725 | 0.5080 |
| 12 | 0.1329 | 1.0699 | 0.5037 |
| 13 | 0.1290 | 1.0692 | 0.5007 |
| 14 | 0.1203 | 1.1017 | 0.4995 |
| 15 | 0.1156 | 1.1125 | 0.4906 |
| 16 | 0.1057 | 1.0882 | 0.4798 |
| 17 | 0.0935 | 1.0590 | 0.4807 |
| 18 | 0.1096 | 1.0460 | 0.4873 |
| 19 | 0.1210 | 1.0431 | 0.4917 |
| 20 | 0.1279 | 1.0520 | 0.4995 |

**Table A.9:** Minimal, maximal and average value of pressure data sets contained in the file 'Fire Simulation'

| Time step | Statistics $P$ | | |
| | Minimum | Maximum | Average |
| --- | --- | --- | --- |
| 1 | 27.6968 | 28.0518 | 27.9030 |
| 2 | -41.2038 | -40.3291 | -40.7596 |
| 3 | -42.3567 | -41.8856 | -42.0585 |
| 4 | -43.1015 | -41.9118 | -42.4777 |
| 5 | -42.9120 | -41.5763 | -42.2361 |
| 6 | -43.2716 | -41.4718 | -42.3599 |
| 7 | -43.5779 | -41.4985 | -42.4860 |
| 8 | -44.0333 | -41.5815 | -42.6889 |
| 9 | -44.2670 | -41.7076 | -42.8241 |
| 10 | -44.1686 | -41.8189 | -42.8771 |
| 11 | -44.0524 | -41.8871 | -42.8953 |
| 12 | -43.9052 | -41.8877 | -42.8612 |
| 13 | -43.8179 | -41.8392 | -42.7958 |
| 14 | -43.7667 | -41.8204 | -42.7686 |
| 15 | -43.8176 | -41.8546 | -42.8008 |
| 16 | -43.6603 | -41.8111 | -42.7176 |
| 17 | -43.6339 | -41.8605 | -42.7549 |
| 18 | -43.7810 | -41.9189 | -42.8500 |
| 19 | -43.9230 | -41.9717 | -42.9316 |
| 20 | -44.1143 | -42.0747 | -43.0695 |

**Table A.10:** Minimal, maximal and average value of velocity component U data sets contained in the file 'Fire Simulation'

| Time step | Statistics $V_0$ | | |
| | Minimum | Maximum | Average |
| --- | --- | --- | --- |
| 1 | -0.4387 | 0.4551 | 0.0014 |
| 2 | -1.3864 | 0.6563 | -0.7255 |
| 3 | -1.0255 | 0.8847 | -0.2435 |
| 4 | -1.9360 | 0.4678 | -1.1937 |
| 5 | -2.3686 | 0.0349 | -1.4463 |
| 6 | -2.6316 | 0.0348 | -1.7375 |
| 7 | -2.9865 | -0.5161 | -1.8187 |
| 8 | -3.2996 | -0.5337 | -1.8577 |
| 9 | -3.4746 | -0.5626 | -1.8728 |
| 10 | -3.1852 | -0.5614 | -1.8948 |
| 11 | -3.0032 | -0.5721 | -1.9008 |
| 12 | -2.8570 | -0.5698 | -1.8878 |
| 13 | -2.8260 | -0.5621 | -1.8671 |
| 14 | -2.8301 | -0.5454 | -1.8547 |
| 15 | -2.8482 | -0.5199 | -1.8458 |
| 16 | -2.7253 | -0.5239 | -1.7862 |
| 17 | -2.6219 | -0.5420 | -1.7656 |
| 18 | -2.6919 | -0.5504 | -1.7965 |
| 19 | -2.7977 | -0.5555 | -1.8101 |
| 20 | -2.8752 | -0.5590 | -1.8282 |

**Table A.11:** Minimal, maximal and average value of velocity component V data sets contained in the file 'Fire Simulation'

| Time step | Statistics $V_1$ | | |
| | Minimum | Maximum | Average |
|---|---|---|---|
| 1 | -0.4605 | 0.5106 | 0.0484 |
| 2 | -1.1719 | 1.1221 | -0.0809 |
| 3 | -0.7912 | 0.9334 | 0.1301 |
| 4 | -0.9088 | 1.2507 | 0.1237 |
| 5 | -1.0597 | 0.6241 | -0.4872 |
| 6 | -1.0479 | 0.4380 | -0.0804 |
| 7 | -0.3845 | 0.4122 | 0.0129 |
| 8 | -0.4431 | 0.4378 | -0.0067 |
| 9 | -0.4548 | 0.4277 | 0.0105 |
| 10 | -0.4200 | 0.4313 | 0.0105 |
| 11 | -0.4075 | 0.4133 | 0.0081 |
| 12 | -0.4107 | 0.3997 | -0.0102 |
| 13 | -0.3939 | 0.4005 | 0.0106 |
| 14 | -0.3887 | 0.3927 | 0.0138 |
| 15 | -0.3927 | 0.4198 | 0.0039 |
| 16 | -0.3353 | 0.4345 | 0.0479 |
| 17 | -0.3406 | 0.4011 | 0.0533 |
| 18 | -0.3711 | 0.3729 | 0.0223 |
| 19 | -0.4020 | 0.3403 | -0.0288 |
| 20 | -0.4538 | 0.3254 | -0.1083 |

**Table A.12:** Minimal, maximal and average value of velocity component W data sets contained in the file 'Fire Simulation'

| Time step | Statistics $V_2$ | | |
| | min | max | avg |
|---|---|---|---|
| 1 | -0.0828 | 1.5516 | 0.5457 |
| 2 | -0.1163 | 5.1348 | 1.1082 |
| 3 | -0.0251 | 6.0941 | 1.4429 |
| 4 | -0.1299 | 3.8496 | 0.7586 |
| 5 | -0.0738 | 2.8038 | 0.5586 |
| 6 | -0.0893 | 1.9733 | 0.3800 |
| 7 | -0.0981 | 0.9740 | 0.1809 |
| 8 | -0.1112 | 0.6466 | 0.1006 |
| 9 | -0.0978 | 0.5117 | 0.1031 |
| 10 | -0.0990 | 0.6886 | 0.1906 |
| 11 | -0.0944 | 1.0430 | 0.2669 |
| 12 | -0.0933 | 1.3370 | 0.3148 |
| 13 | -0.0921 | 1.4034 | 0.3245 |
| 14 | -0.0910 | 1.4454 | 0.3264 |
| 15 | -0.0956 | 1.4932 | 0.3099 |
| 16 | -0.0933 | 1.5309 | 0.3151 |
| 17 | -0.0867 | 1.6153 | 0.3441 |
| 18 | -0.0889 | 1.4564 | 0.3035 |
| 19 | -0.0899 | 1.2457 | 0.2535 |
| 20 | -0.0906 | 1.1112 | 0.2298 |

## A.2   Compression Factors Simple Compressor

**Table A.13:** Compression factors obtained for the data sets of 'Wind Tunnel I' by applying the simple compressor. Sizes of the un-/compressed data sets are also listed.

| | Compression factor | | | Orig. size | Compressed size | | |
|---|---|---|---|---|---|---|---|
| | 1e-03 | 1e-04 | 1e-05 | | 1e-03 | 1e-04 | 1e-05 |
| $\rho$ | 9933.484 | 386.537 | 95.930 | 302107040 | 30413 | 781574 | 3149234 |
| $P$ | 38.771 | 17.519 | 9.896 | 302107040 | 7792085 | 17244965 | 30528421 |
| $T$ | 64.775 | 28.098 | 15.092 | 302107040 | 4663980 | 10752037 | 20017361 |
| $V_0$ | 15.921 | 9.541 | 6.536 | 302107040 | 18974832 | 31664862 | 46222700 |
| $V_1$ | 18.542 | 10.276 | 6.782 | 302107040 | 16292874 | 29398452 | 44545285 |
| $V_2$ | 17.120 | 9.735 | 6.512 | 302107040 | 17646068 | 31033437 | 46395699 |
| $V_0$ L | 13.860 | 8.364 | 5.912 | 302107040 | 21796904 | 36119083 | 51103437 |
| $V_1$ L | 22.896 | 11.192 | 7.163 | 302107040 | 13194846 | 26992565 | 42173570 |
| $V_2$ L | 18.991 | 10.150 | 6.901 | 302107040 | 15907911 | 29764488 | 43775659 |
| $V_0$ vl | 19.542 | 10.268 | 6.795 | 302107040 | 15459218 | 29422944 | 44458973 |
| $V_1$ vl | 16.897 | 9.391 | 6.316 | 302107040 | 17878927 | 32170843 | 47833345 |
| $V_2$ vl | 24.147 | 11.108 | 7.095 | 302107040 | 12511222 | 27196204 | 42579605 |
| $V_0$ vr | 19.355 | 10.189 | 6.716 | 302107040 | 15608878 | 29649352 | 44984441 |
| $V_1$ vr | 16.053 | 9.012 | 6.157 | 302107040 | 18818923 | 33523373 | 49067021 |
| $V_2$ vr | 24.135 | 11.105 | 7.095 | 302107040 | 12517422 | 27204201 | 42580453 |
| $V_0$ hl | 19.675 | 10.398 | 6.900 | 302107040 | 15355053 | 29054088 | 43785684 |
| $V_1$ hl | 17.817 | 9.935 | 6.565 | 302107040 | 16956484 | 30408711 | 46015313 |
| $V_2$ hl | 23.095 | 10.828 | 6.987 | 302107040 | 13081163 | 27901383 | 43239396 |
| $V_0$ hr | 19.478 | 10.254 | 6.776 | 302107040 | 15509782 | 29461515 | 44582844 |
| $V_1$ hr | 16.651 | 9.271 | 6.260 | 302107040 | 18143993 | 32585708 | 48257437 |
| $V_2$ hr | 23.098 | 10.826 | 6.986 | 302107040 | 13079339 | 27906452 | 43246197 |
| Total | 21.062 | 11.126 | 7.304 | 6344247840 | 301220317 | 570236237 | 868542075 |

**Table A.14:** Compression factors obtained for the data sets of 'Wind Tunnel II' by applying the simple compressor. Sizes of the un-/compressed data sets are also listed.

| | Compression factor | | | Orig. size | Compressed size | | |
|---|---|---|---|---|---|---|---|
| | 1e-03 | 1e-04 | 1e-05 | | 1e-03 | 1e-04 | 1e-05 |
| $P$ | 27.635 | 13.456 | 8.203 | 151642096 | 5487284 | 11269584 | 18487196 |
| $V_0$ | 14.771 | 8.828 | 6.103 | 151642096 | 10266520 | 17177209 | 24845726 |
| $V_1$ | 20.718 | 11.186 | 7.336 | 151642096 | 7319437 | 13556162 | 20671440 |
| $V_2$ | 20.669 | 11.165 | 7.318 | 151642096 | 7336522 | 13581956 | 20721404 |
| Total | 19.947 | 10.912 | 7.159 | 606568384 | 30409763 | 55584931 | 84725766 |

**Table A.15:** Compression factors obtained for the data sets of 'Car Venting System' by applying the simple compressor. Sizes of the un-/compressed data sets are also listed.

| | Compression factor | | | Orig. size | Compressed size | | |
|---|---|---|---|---|---|---|---|
| | 1e-03 | 1e-04 | 1e-05 | | 1e-03 | 1e-04 | 1e-05 |
| $\epsilon$ | 10.185 | 5.821 | 3.905 | 1620472 | 159105 | 278400 | 414929 |
| $P$ | 12.221 | 7.869 | 5.731 | 3240944 | 265191 | 411849 | 565503 |
| Pt | 208.233 | 45.704 | 19.544 | 3240944 | 15564 | 70911 | 165829 |
| TKE | 5.665 | 3.695 | 2.708 | 1620472 | 286061 | 438517 | 598472 |
| TVis | 4.822 | 3.214 | 2.410 | 1620472 | 336053 | 504240 | 672340 |
| $V_0$ | 4.611 | 3.154 | 2.377 | 1620472 | 351408 | 513856 | 681612 |
| $V_1$ | 4.648 | 3.147 | 2.372 | 1620472 | 348620 | 514964 | 683208 |
| $V_2$ | 4.706 | 3.178 | 2.390 | 1620472 | 344316 | 509884 | 678028 |
| Total | 7.693 | 4.997 | 3.633 | 16204720 | 2106318 | 3242621 | 4459921 |

**Table A.16:** Compression factors obtained for the data sets of 'Mixing Chamber I' by applying the simple compressor. Sizes of the un-/compressed data sets are also listed.

| | Compression factor | | | Orig. size | Compressed size | | |
| | 1e-03 | 1e-04 | 1e-05 | | 1e-03 | 1e-04 | 1e-05 |
|---|---|---|---|---|---|---|---|
| $\rho$ | 29.999 | 13.724 | 8.112 | 7451808 | 248398 | 542960 | 918635 |
| $w_{iso}$ | 14.962 | 8.576 | 5.939 | 7451808 | 498061 | 868948 | 1254804 |
| $w_{pol}$ | 14.955 | 8.575 | 5.939 | 7451808 | 498289 | 869044 | 1254824 |
| $c_{iso}$ | 15.192 | 8.660 | 5.979 | 7451808 | 490518 | 860468 | 1246254 |
| $c_{pol}$ | 15.185 | 8.659 | 5.979 | 7451808 | 490738 | 860556 | 1246278 |
| $P$ | 23.805 | 11.929 | 7.447 | 7451808 | 313035 | 624669 | 1000682 |
| $P_s$ | 23.807 | 11.929 | 7.447 | 7451808 | 313006 | 624664 | 1000666 |
| TVis | 18.197 | 10.109 | 6.745 | 7451808 | 409508 | 737177 | 1104785 |
| $V_0$ | 11.611 | 7.297 | 5.295 | 7451808 | 641803 | 1021209 | 1407377 |
| $V_1$ | 11.581 | 7.274 | 5.281 | 7451808 | 643435 | 1024510 | 1411082 |
| $V_2$ | 12.078 | 7.497 | 5.400 | 7451808 | 616969 | 993998 | 1379888 |
| Total | 15.874 | 9.079 | 6.198 | 81969888 | 5163760 | 9028203 | 13225275 |

**Table A.17:** Compression factors obtained for the data sets of 'Mixing Chamber II' by applying the simple compressor. Sizes of the un-/compressed data sets are also listed.

| | Compression factor | | | Orig. size | Compressed size | | |
| | 1e-03 | 1e-04 | 1e-05 | | 1e-03 | 1e-04 | 1e-05 |
|---|---|---|---|---|---|---|---|
| $\rho$ | 8.361 | 5.860 | 4.506 | 14328232 | 1713783 | 2445172 | 3179541 |
| $P$ | 37.250 | 16.167 | 9.092 | 14328232 | 384651 | 886274 | 1575916 |
| $V_0$ | 11.301 | 7.162 | 5.222 | 14328232 | 1267850 | 2000461 | 2743633 |
| $V_1$ | 11.695 | 7.311 | 5.300 | 14328232 | 1225151 | 1959937 | 2703385 |
| $V_2$ | 11.769 | 7.374 | 5.335 | 14328232 | 1217434 | 1942945 | 2685497 |
| Total | 12.333 | 7.758 | 5.559 | 71641160 | 5808869 | 9234789 | 12887972 |

**Table A.18:** Compression factors obtained for the data sets of 'Mixing Pipe' by applying the simple compressor. Sizes of the un-/compressed data sets are also listed.

| | Compression factor | | | Orig. size | Compressed size | | |
| | 1e-03 | 1e-04 | 1e-05 | | 1e-03 | 1e-04 | 1e-05 |
|---|---|---|---|---|---|---|---|
| $H_s$ | 14.195 | 8.756 | 6.345 | 658712 | 46403 | 75229 | 103821 |
| $\rho$ | 14.327 | 8.890 | 6.349 | 658712 | 45977 | 74095 | 103750 |
| $\epsilon$ | 12.535 | 7.909 | 5.635 | 658712 | 52551 | 83283 | 116887 |
| $H$ | 14.195 | 8.756 | 6.345 | 658712 | 46403 | 75229 | 103821 |
| $P$ | 10.028 | 6.620 | 4.927 | 658712 | 65687 | 99507 | 133683 |
| $T$ | 14.195 | 8.756 | 6.345 | 658712 | 46403 | 75229 | 103821 |
| Pt | 552.148 | 83.977 | 29.499 | 658712 | 1193 | 7844 | 22330 |
| TKE | 10.110 | 6.682 | 4.963 | 658712 | 65156 | 98575 | 132727 |
| TVis | 8.362 | 5.832 | 4.477 | 658712 | 78779 | 112955 | 147127 |
| $V_0$ | 8.644 | 5.966 | 4.556 | 658712 | 76203 | 110411 | 144567 |
| $V_1$ | 8.967 | 6.162 | 4.671 | 658712 | 73457 | 106899 | 141019 |
| $V_2$ | 8.657 | 6.001 | 4.574 | 658712 | 76087 | 109759 | 144007 |
| Total | 11.723 | 7.682 | 5.656 | 7904544 | 674299 | 1029015 | 1397560 |

# A.3 Compression Factors Tree Predictor

## A.3.1 Unweighted Approach

**Table A.19:** Compression factors obtained for the data sets of 'Wind Tunnel I' by applying the unweighted tree predictor. Sizes of the un-/compressed data sets are also listed.

| | Compression factor | | | Orig. size | Compressed size | | |
| | 1e-03 | 1e-04 | 1e-05 | | 1e-03 | 1e-04 | 1e-05 |
|---|---|---|---|---|---|---|---|
| $\rho$ | 10794.549 | 588.538 | 133.551 | 302107040 | 27987 | 513318 | 2262113 |
| $P$ | 48.922 | 20.764 | 11.109 | 302107040 | 6175253 | 14549620 | 27194776 |
| $T$ | 85.174 | 34.933 | 17.523 | 302107040 | 3546960 | 8648120 | 17241057 |
| $V_0$ | 18.437 | 10.558 | 7.017 | 302107040 | 16385858 | 28614394 | 43050967 |
| $V_1$ | 22.028 | 11.537 | 7.315 | 302107040 | 13714801 | 26185341 | 41297910 |
| $V_2$ | 20.222 | 10.981 | 7.078 | 302107040 | 14939504 | 27511731 | 42684209 |
| $V_0$ L | 15.450 | 8.709 | 6.011 | 302107040 | 19553800 | 34689321 | 50262301 |
| $V_1$ L | 26.893 | 12.294 | 7.595 | 302107040 | 11233564 | 24573853 | 39779533 |
| $V_2$ L | 21.336 | 10.414 | 6.800 | 302107040 | 14159275 | 29010364 | 44426081 |
| $V_0$ vl | 22.089 | 10.721 | 6.856 | 302107040 | 13676608 | 28178149 | 44062597 |
| $V_1$ vl | 20.363 | 10.736 | 6.921 | 302107040 | 14835838 | 28140021 | 43648985 |
| $V_2$ vl | 32.857 | 14.024 | 8.195 | 302107040 | 9194674 | 21542628 | 36863397 |
| $V_0$ vr | 22.129 | 10.753 | 6.861 | 302107040 | 13652078 | 28096357 | 44033861 |
| $V_1$ vr | 19.962 | 10.387 | 6.749 | 302107040 | 15134199 | 29083921 | 44764181 |
| $V_2$ vr | 32.847 | 14.022 | 8.195 | 302107040 | 9197291 | 21545865 | 36865561 |
| $V_0$ hl | 22.063 | 10.706 | 6.854 | 302107040 | 13692656 | 28219169 | 44079917 |
| $V_1$ hl | 21.212 | 11.227 | 7.150 | 302107040 | 14242144 | 26908188 | 42251593 |
| $V_2$ hl | 31.545 | 13.583 | 7.947 | 302107040 | 9577010 | 22242260 | 38013817 |
| $V_0$ hr | 22.108 | 10.734 | 6.858 | 302107040 | 13664992 | 28144557 | 44048841 |
| $V_1$ hr | 20.393 | 10.629 | 6.833 | 302107040 | 14814386 | 28424177 | 44213245 |
| $V_2$ hr | 31.553 | 13.592 | 7.953 | 302107040 | 9574685 | 22227017 | 37984249 |
| Total | 25.277 | 12.512 | 7.842 | 6344247840 | 250993563 | 507048371 | 809029191 |

**Table A.20:** Compression factors obtained for the data sets of 'Wind Tunnel II' by applying the unweighted tree predictor. Sizes of the un-/compressed data sets are also listed.

| | Compression factor | | | Orig. size | Compressed size | | |
| | 1e-03 | 1e-04 | 1e-05 | | 1e-03 | 1e-04 | 1e-05 |
|---|---|---|---|---|---|---|---|
| $P$ | 34.152 | 15.604 | 9.106 | 151642096 | 4440209 | 9718330 | 16652275 |
| $V_0$ | 15.374 | 9.021 | 6.199 | 151642096 | 9863328 | 16809621 | 24460755 |
| $V_1$ | 24.363 | 12.443 | 7.889 | 151642096 | 6224161 | 12186490 | 19222050 |
| $V_2$ | 23.076 | 11.925 | 7.610 | 151642096 | 6571285 | 12715813 | 19925994 |
| Total | 22.383 | 11.794 | 7.557 | 606568384 | 27098983 | 51430254 | 80261074 |

**Table A.21:** Compression factors obtained for the data sets of 'Car Venting System' by applying the unweighted tree predictor. Sizes of the un-/compressed data sets are also listed.

| | Compression factor | | | Orig. size | Compressed size | | |
| | 1e-03 | 1e-04 | 1e-05 | | 1e-03 | 1e-04 | 1e-05 |
|---|---|---|---|---|---|---|---|
| $\epsilon$ | 12.626 | 6.849 | 4.392 | 1620472 | 128349 | 236591 | 368959 |
| $P$ | 14.643 | 8.942 | 6.326 | 3240944 | 221326 | 362447 | 512326 |
| Pt | 276.319 | 58.509 | 24.989 | 3240944 | 11729 | 55392 | 129697 |
| TKE | 6.594 | 4.116 | 2.956 | 1620472 | 245768 | 393677 | 548112 |
| TVis | 5.788 | 3.625 | 2.635 | 1620472 | 279974 | 446980 | 615088 |
| $V_0$ | 5.516 | 3.605 | 2.629 | 1620472 | 293762 | 449548 | 616284 |
| $V_1$ | 5.443 | 3.517 | 2.577 | 1620472 | 297731 | 460796 | 628788 |
| $V_2$ | 5.490 | 3.547 | 2.594 | 1620472 | 295162 | 456884 | 624680 |
| Total | 9.136 | 5.661 | 4.007 | 16204720 | 1773801 | 2862315 | 4043934 |

**Table A.22:** Compression factors obtained for the data sets of 'Mixing Chamber I' by applying the unweighted tree predictor. Sizes of the un-/compressed data sets are also listed.

|  | Compression factor | | | Orig. size | Compressed size | | |
|---|---|---|---|---|---|---|---|
|  | 1e-03 | 1e-04 | 1e-05 |  | 1e-03 | 1e-04 | 1e-05 |
| $\rho$ | 35.840 | 16.151 | 9.017 | 7451808 | 207916 | 461371 | 826455 |
| $w_{iso}$ | 17.735 | 9.589 | 6.413 | 7451808 | 420170 | 777080 | 1161973 |
| $w_{pol}$ | 17.937 | 9.604 | 6.414 | 7451808 | 415434 | 775932 | 1161857 |
| $c_{iso}$ | 18.037 | 9.695 | 6.461 | 7451808 | 413148 | 768639 | 1153424 |
| $c_{pol}$ | 18.253 | 9.710 | 6.461 | 7451808 | 408252 | 767447 | 1153332 |
| $P$ | 28.272 | 13.703 | 8.197 | 7451808 | 263575 | 543818 | 909102 |
| $P_s$ | 28.281 | 13.703 | 8.197 | 7451808 | 263495 | 543794 | 909070 |
| TVis | 18.912 | 10.323 | 6.809 | 7451808 | 394032 | 721871 | 1094359 |
| $V_0$ | 13.241 | 7.917 | 5.613 | 7451808 | 562785 | 941202 | 1327482 |
| $V_1$ | 13.119 | 7.876 | 5.593 | 7451808 | 568005 | 946190 | 1332398 |
| $V_2$ | 13.825 | 8.138 | 5.722 | 7451808 | 538995 | 915734 | 1302333 |
| Total | 18.396 | 10.042 | 6.647 | 81969888 | 4455807 | 8163078 | 12331785 |

**Table A.23:** Compression factors obtained for the data sets of 'Mixing Chamber II' by applying the unweighted tree predictor. Sizes of the un-/compressed data sets are also listed.

|  | Compression factor | | | Orig. size | Compressed size | | |
|---|---|---|---|---|---|---|---|
|  | 1e-03 | 1e-04 | 1e-05 |  | 1e-03 | 1e-04 | 1e-05 |
| $\rho$ | 8.940 | 6.140 | 4.670 | 14328232 | 1602795 | 2333655 | 3067874 |
| $P$ | 45.547 | 19.416 | 10.244 | 14328232 | 314584 | 737973 | 1398757 |
| $V_0$ | 13.136 | 7.904 | 5.608 | 14328232 | 1090786 | 1812737 | 2554849 |
| $V_1$ | 13.697 | 8.068 | 5.688 | 14328232 | 1046067 | 1775873 | 2519233 |
| $V_2$ | 13.877 | 8.198 | 5.753 | 14328232 | 1032504 | 1747829 | 2490541 |
| Total | 14.084 | 8.521 | 5.955 | 71641160 | 5086736 | 8408067 | 12031254 |

**Table A.24:** Compression factors obtained for the data sets of 'Mixing Pipe' by applying the unweighted tree predictor. Sizes of the un-/compressed data sets are also listed.

|  | Compression factor | | | Orig. size | Compressed size | | |
|---|---|---|---|---|---|---|---|
|  | 1e-03 | 1e-04 | 1e-05 |  | 1e-03 | 1e-04 | 1e-05 |
| $H_s$ | 15.612 | 9.387 | 6.684 | 658712 | 42192 | 70173 | 98553 |
| $\rho$ | 16.306 | 9.554 | 6.704 | 658712 | 40397 | 68944 | 98250 |
| $\epsilon$ | 14.098 | 8.641 | 6.017 | 658712 | 46724 | 76231 | 109483 |
| $H$ | 15.612 | 9.387 | 6.684 | 658712 | 42192 | 70173 | 98553 |
| $P$ | 10.527 | 6.880 | 5.071 | 658712 | 62573 | 95747 | 129907 |
| $T$ | 15.612 | 9.387 | 6.684 | 658712 | 42192 | 70173 | 98553 |
| Pt | 511.820 | 89.608 | 30.781 | 658712 | 1287 | 7351 | 21400 |
| TKE | 11.218 | 7.206 | 5.248 | 658712 | 58718 | 91407 | 125527 |
| TVis | 9.002 | 6.133 | 4.652 | 658712 | 73171 | 107407 | 141587 |
| $V_0$ | 9.558 | 6.395 | 4.800 | 658712 | 68915 | 103003 | 137235 |
| $V_1$ | 10.626 | 6.930 | 5.100 | 658712 | 61991 | 95055 | 129167 |
| $V_2$ | 10.167 | 6.714 | 4.981 | 658712 | 64790 | 98115 | 132239 |
| Total | 13.062 | 8.288 | 5.986 | 7904544 | 605142 | 953779 | 1320454 |

## A.3.2 Distance-based Optimization

**Table A.25:** Compression factors obtained for the data sets of 'Wind Tunnel I' by applying the weighted tree predictor. Distance-based weights were used for the optimization. Sizes of the un-/compressed data sets are also listed.

| | Compression factor | | | Orig. size | Compressed size | | |
| | 1e-03 | 1e-04 | 1e-05 | | 1e-03 | 1e-04 | 1e-05 |
|---|---|---|---|---|---|---|---|
| $\rho$ | 9705.627 | 567.689 | 128.926 | 302107040 | 31127 | 532170 | 2343255 |
| $P$ | 50.001 | 21.388 | 11.425 | 302107040 | 6041986 | 14124862 | 26442693 |
| $T$ | 84.336 | 34.898 | 17.593 | 302107040 | 3582172 | 8656764 | 17171639 |
| $V_0$ | 18.157 | 10.419 | 6.974 | 302107040 | 16638654 | 28995522 | 43316452 |
| $V_1$ | 22.046 | 11.630 | 7.366 | 302107040 | 13703371 | 25976408 | 41011168 |
| $V_2$ | 20.227 | 11.043 | 7.103 | 302107040 | 14935935 | 27356737 | 42529384 |
| $V_0$ L | 15.647 | 8.855 | 6.111 | 302107040 | 19307271 | 34116780 | 49435390 |
| $V_1$ L | 28.477 | 13.215 | 7.982 | 302107040 | 10608974 | 22860273 | 37850081 |
| $V_2$ L | 23.333 | 11.311 | 7.298 | 302107040 | 12947470 | 26709439 | 41394610 |
| $V_0$ vl | 22.921 | 11.193 | 7.095 | 302107040 | 13180510 | 26990690 | 42577848 |
| $V_1$ vl | 20.288 | 10.721 | 6.916 | 302107040 | 14890822 | 28177853 | 43682433 |
| $V_2$ vl | 32.110 | 14.003 | 8.298 | 302107040 | 9408440 | 21575099 | 36408922 |
| $V_0$ vr | 22.859 | 11.160 | 7.068 | 302107040 | 13215973 | 27069749 | 42742769 |
| $V_1$ vr | 19.865 | 10.334 | 6.721 | 302107040 | 15207667 | 29235339 | 44950185 |
| $V_2$ vr | 32.101 | 14.002 | 8.298 | 302107040 | 9411192 | 21575912 | 36405243 |
| $V_0$ hl | 22.937 | 11.206 | 7.133 | 302107040 | 13171069 | 26960479 | 42356245 |
| $V_1$ hl | 21.166 | 11.242 | 7.164 | 302107040 | 14273507 | 26873773 | 42170761 |
| $V_2$ hl | 30.420 | 13.651 | 8.014 | 302107040 | 9931208 | 22130651 | 37696234 |
| $V_0$ hr | 22.901 | 11.186 | 7.083 | 302107040 | 13191905 | 27007581 | 42653869 |
| $V_1$ hr | 20.270 | 10.599 | 6.823 | 302107040 | 14904430 | 28502029 | 44278401 |
| $V_2$ hr | 30.431 | 13.652 | 8.013 | 302107040 | 9927574 | 22128997 | 37703816 |
| Total | 25.529 | 12.751 | 7.979 | 6344247840 | 248511257 | 497557197 | 795121398 |

**Table A.26:** Compression factors obtained for the data sets of 'Wind Tunnel II' by applying the weighted tree predictor. Distance-based weights were used for the optimization. Sizes of the un-/compressed data sets are also listed.

| | Compression factor | | | Orig. size | Compressed size | | |
| | 1e-03 | 1e-04 | 1e-05 | | 1e-03 | 1e-04 | 1e-05 |
|---|---|---|---|---|---|---|---|
| $P$ | 44.317 | 19.839 | 11.090 | 151642096 | 3421726 | 7643507 | 13674217 |
| $V_0$ | 14.258 | 8.644 | 6.025 | 151642096 | 10635569 | 17542471 | 25167350 |
| $V_1$ | 24.843 | 12.648 | 7.999 | 151642096 | 6103978 | 11989218 | 18957115 |
| $V_2$ | 23.034 | 11.806 | 7.513 | 151642096 | 6583314 | 12844765 | 20183297 |
| Total | 22.680 | 12.127 | 7.778 | 606568384 | 26744587 | 50019961 | 77981979 |

**Table A.27:** Compression factors obtained for the data sets of 'Car Venting System' by applying the weighted tree predictor. Distance-based weights were used for the optimization. Sizes of the un-/compressed data sets are also listed.

| | Compression factor | | | Orig. size | Compressed size | | |
| | 1e-03 | 1e-04 | 1e-05 | | 1e-03 | 1e-04 | 1e-05 |
|---|---|---|---|---|---|---|---|
| $\epsilon$ | 12.417 | 6.807 | 4.387 | 1620472 | 130500 | 238056 | 369393 |
| $P$ | 17.176 | 10.029 | 6.909 | 3240944 | 188687 | 323152 | 469122 |
| Pt | 390.193 | 70.056 | 29.691 | 3240944 | 8306 | 46262 | 109156 |
| TKE | 6.669 | 4.153 | 2.986 | 1620472 | 242987 | 390221 | 542731 |
| TVis | 6.047 | 3.753 | 2.703 | 1620472 | 267978 | 431764 | 599548 |
| $V_0$ | 5.710 | 3.706 | 2.693 | 1620472 | 283815 | 437229 | 601804 |
| $V_1$ | 5.836 | 3.711 | 2.684 | 1620472 | 277650 | 436652 | 603728 |
| $V_2$ | 5.811 | 3.714 | 2.686 | 1620472 | 278862 | 436324 | 603332 |
| Total | 9.653 | 5.915 | 4.156 | 16204720 | 1678785 | 2739660 | 3898814 |

**Table A.28:** Compression factors obtained for the data sets of 'Mixing Chamber I' by applying the weighted tree predictor. Distance-based weights were used for the optimization. Sizes of the un-/compressed data sets are also listed.

| | Compression factor | | | Orig. size | Compressed size | | |
| | 1e-03 | 1e-04 | 1e-05 | | 1e-03 | 1e-04 | 1e-05 |
|---|---|---|---|---|---|---|---|
| $\rho$ | 37.658 | 16.915 | 9.308 | 7451808 | 197881 | 440555 | 800599 |
| $w_{iso}$ | 18.596 | 9.918 | 6.561 | 7451808 | 400719 | 751362 | 1135817 |
| $w_{pol}$ | 18.869 | 9.931 | 6.561 | 7451808 | 394915 | 750322 | 1135725 |
| $c_{iso}$ | 18.910 | 10.030 | 6.610 | 7451808 | 394061 | 742926 | 1127290 |
| $c_{pol}$ | 19.198 | 10.044 | 6.611 | 7451808 | 388157 | 741906 | 1127218 |
| $P$ | 29.779 | 14.242 | 8.422 | 7451808 | 250235 | 523211 | 884774 |
| $P_s$ | 29.780 | 14.244 | 8.422 | 7451808 | 250225 | 523146 | 884810 |
| TVis | 19.393 | 10.578 | 6.944 | 7451808 | 384257 | 704454 | 1073055 |
| $V_0$ | 13.589 | 8.053 | 5.682 | 7451808 | 548365 | 925386 | 1311490 |
| $V_1$ | 13.471 | 8.008 | 5.658 | 7451808 | 553182 | 930546 | 1316926 |
| $V_2$ | 14.163 | 8.281 | 5.795 | 7451808 | 526134 | 899864 | 1285929 |
| Total | 19.116 | 10.332 | 6.784 | 81969888 | 4288131 | 7933678 | 12083633 |

**Table A.29:** Compression factors obtained for the data sets of 'Mixing Chamber II' by applying the weighted tree predictor. Distance-based weights were used for the optimization. Sizes of the un-/compressed data sets are also listed.

| | Compression factor | | | Orig. size | Compressed size | | |
| | 1e-03 | 1e-04 | 1e-05 | | 1e-03 | 1e-04 | 1e-05 |
|---|---|---|---|---|---|---|---|
| $\rho$ | 8.882 | 6.114 | 4.656 | 14328232 | 1613166 | 2343603 | 3077656 |
| $P$ | 46.438 | 19.803 | 10.407 | 14328232 | 308546 | 723536 | 1376740 |
| $V_0$ | 13.197 | 7.916 | 5.613 | 14328232 | 1085755 | 1810037 | 2552541 |
| $V_1$ | 13.757 | 8.086 | 5.696 | 14328232 | 1041540 | 1771929 | 2515349 |
| $V_2$ | 13.882 | 8.215 | 5.762 | 14328232 | 1032159 | 1744081 | 2486613 |
| Total | 14.099 | 8.536 | 5.966 | 71641160 | 5081166 | 8393186 | 12008899 |

**Table A.30:** Compression factors obtained for the data sets of 'Mixing Pipe' by applying the weighted tree predictor. Distance-based weights were used for the optimization. Sizes of the un-/compressed data sets are also listed.

| | Compression factor | | | Orig. size | Compressed size | | |
| | 1e-03 | 1e-04 | 1e-05 | | 1e-03 | 1e-04 | 1e-05 |
|---|---|---|---|---|---|---|---|
| $H_s$ | 14.466 | 8.828 | 6.394 | 658712 | 45536 | 74618 | 103023 |
| $\rho$ | 14.457 | 8.980 | 6.412 | 658712 | 45563 | 73350 | 102725 |
| $\epsilon$ | 11.986 | 7.625 | 5.469 | 658712 | 54956 | 86387 | 120439 |
| $H$ | 14.466 | 8.828 | 6.394 | 658712 | 45536 | 74618 | 103023 |
| $P$ | 10.424 | 6.845 | 5.052 | 658712 | 63192 | 96231 | 130379 |
| $T$ | 14.466 | 8.828 | 6.394 | 658712 | 45536 | 74618 | 103023 |
| Pt | 629.744 | 89.196 | 32.725 | 658712 | 1046 | 7385 | 20129 |
| TKE | 9.789 | 6.513 | 4.866 | 658712 | 67291 | 101135 | 135375 |
| TVis | 8.274 | 5.792 | 4.453 | 658712 | 79615 | 113719 | 147935 |
| $V_0$ | 9.019 | 6.141 | 4.657 | 658712 | 73035 | 107267 | 141447 |
| $V_1$ | 10.409 | 6.854 | 5.058 | 658712 | 63282 | 96103 | 130227 |
| $V_2$ | 10.075 | 6.680 | 4.963 | 658712 | 65378 | 98607 | 132735 |
| Total | 12.161 | 7.873 | 5.768 | 7904544 | 649966 | 1004038 | 1370460 |

## A.3.3 Gradient Optimization

### *Wind Tunnel I*

**Table A.31:** Compression factors obtained for the data sets of 'Wind Tunnel I' by applying the weighted tree predictor. Gradient-based optimization was utilized in combination with the variable 'Pressure'. Sizes of the un-/compressed data sets are also listed.

| | Compression factor | | | Orig. size | Compressed size | | |
| | 1e-03 | 1e-04 | 1e-05 | | 1e-03 | 1e-04 | 1e-05 |
|---|---|---|---|---|---|---|---|
| $\rho$ | 10725.186 | 586.971 | 135.769 | 302107040 | 28168 | 514688 | 2225161 |
| $P$ | 173.834 | 39.370 | 15.611 | 302107040 | 1737905 | 7673588 | 19351961 |
| $T$ | 86.835 | 36.208 | 18.583 | 302107040 | 3479092 | 8343683 | 16257435 |
| $V_0$ | 18.753 | 11.094 | 7.486 | 302107040 | 16109625 | 27232776 | 40355570 |
| $V_1$ | 22.008 | 11.556 | 7.374 | 302107040 | 13727392 | 26143726 | 40969370 |
| $V_2$ | 20.488 | 11.096 | 7.215 | 302107040 | 14745527 | 27225748 | 41872546 |
| $V_0$ L | 15.839 | 9.087 | 6.507 | 302107040 | 19073396 | 33246462 | 46427019 |
| $V_1$ L | 27.374 | 12.880 | 8.358 | 302107040 | 11036188 | 23456373 | 36144516 |
| $V_2$ L | 22.240 | 11.300 | 8.132 | 302107040 | 13583692 | 26736277 | 37152036 |
| $V_0$ vl | 22.549 | 11.137 | 7.630 | 302107040 | 13397732 | 27125408 | 39593699 |
| $V_1$ vl | 20.558 | 10.832 | 6.974 | 302107040 | 14695336 | 27891518 | 43317733 |
| $V_2$ vl | 36.164 | 15.112 | 9.054 | 302107040 | 8353803 | 19990630 | 33366323 |
| $V_0$ vr | 22.551 | 11.135 | 7.567 | 302107040 | 13396774 | 27132109 | 39921940 |
| $V_1$ vr | 20.132 | 10.466 | 6.810 | 302107040 | 15006487 | 28864648 | 44361117 |
| $V_2$ vr | 36.157 | 15.115 | 9.061 | 302107040 | 8355334 | 19986600 | 33341621 |
| $V_0$ hl | 22.533 | 11.145 | 7.702 | 302107040 | 13407277 | 27106177 | 39226317 |
| $V_1$ hl | 21.328 | 11.317 | 7.229 | 302107040 | 14164801 | 26696042 | 41788188 |
| $V_2$ hl | 34.769 | 14.662 | 8.846 | 302107040 | 8688899 | 20604063 | 34151037 |
| $V_0$ hr | 22.559 | 11.139 | 7.604 | 302107040 | 13391772 | 27122616 | 39729253 |
| $V_1$ hr | 20.390 | 10.673 | 6.876 | 302107040 | 14816237 | 28305081 | 43937293 |
| $V_2$ hr | 34.719 | 14.636 | 8.803 | 302107040 | 8701609 | 20641003 | 34319186 |
| Total | 26.446 | 13.161 | 8.484 | 6344247840 | 239897046 | 482039783 | 747809321 |

**Table A.32:** Compression factors obtained for the data sets of 'Wind Tunnel I' by applying the weighted tree predictor. Gradient-based optimization was utilized in combination with the variable 'Density'. Sizes of the un-/compressed data sets are also listed.

| | Compression factor | | | Orig. size | Compressed size | | |
| | 1e-03 | 1e-04 | 1e-05 | | 1e-03 | 1e-04 | 1e-05 |
|---|---|---|---|---|---|---|---|
| $\rho$ | 17236.666 | 8378.596 | 876.417 | 302107040 | 17527 | 36057 | 344707 |
| $P$ | 48.916 | 20.738 | 10.992 | 302107040 | 6176096 | 14567481 | 27484256 |
| $T$ | 84.698 | 34.856 | 18.190 | 302107040 | 3566880 | 8667309 | 16608525 |
| $V_0$ | 18.158 | 10.460 | 7.060 | 302107040 | 16637326 | 28882497 | 42789826 |
| $V_1$ | 21.931 | 11.414 | 7.301 | 302107040 | 13775181 | 26468559 | 41379044 |
| $V_2$ | 20.103 | 10.982 | 7.120 | 302107040 | 15028162 | 27508430 | 42430621 |
| $V_0$ L | 15.630 | 8.866 | 6.199 | 302107040 | 19328215 | 34074503 | 48732248 |
| $V_1$ L | 27.651 | 13.113 | 8.178 | 302107040 | 10925584 | 23038358 | 36941017 |
| $V_2$ L | 23.260 | 11.257 | 7.308 | 302107040 | 12988235 | 26836741 | 41340994 |
| $V_0$ vl | 22.308 | 11.285 | 7.247 | 302107040 | 13542440 | 26769814 | 41689504 |
| $V_1$ vl | 20.558 | 10.916 | 7.050 | 302107040 | 14695406 | 27676527 | 42851691 |
| $V_2$ vl | 41.466 | 17.778 | 9.737 | 302107040 | 7285677 | 16993446 | 31025749 |
| $V_0$ vr | 22.270 | 11.178 | 7.179 | 302107040 | 13565384 | 27027771 | 42081156 |
| $V_1$ vr | 20.500 | 10.776 | 6.966 | 302107040 | 14736822 | 28036318 | 43371135 |
| $V_2$ vr | 41.511 | 17.811 | 9.760 | 302107040 | 7277754 | 16961366 | 30954064 |
| $V_0$ hl | 22.298 | 11.347 | 7.334 | 302107040 | 13548715 | 26623766 | 41190474 |
| $V_1$ hl | 21.273 | 11.266 | 7.214 | 302107040 | 14201708 | 26815513 | 41877617 |
| $V_2$ hl | 40.008 | 17.310 | 9.523 | 302107040 | 7551089 | 17453034 | 31723686 |
| $V_0$ hr | 22.314 | 11.277 | 7.228 | 302107040 | 13539018 | 26789844 | 41797567 |
| $V_1$ hr | 20.608 | 10.859 | 6.988 | 302107040 | 14660048 | 27820657 | 43231773 |
| $V_2$ hr | 39.848 | 17.074 | 9.393 | 302107040 | 7581505 | 17694424 | 32162309 |
| Total | 26.365 | 13.307 | 8.326 | 6344247840 | 240628772 | 476742415 | 762007963 |

**Table A.33:** Compression factors obtained for the data sets of 'Wind Tunnel I' by applying the weighted tree predictor. Gradient-based optimization was utilized in combination with the variable 'Temperature'. Sizes of the un-/compressed data sets are also listed.

| | Compression factor | | | Orig. size | Compressed size | | |
| | 1e-03 | 1e-04 | 1e-05 | | 1e-03 | 1e-04 | 1e-05 |
|---|---|---|---|---|---|---|---|
| $\rho$ | 14107.263 | 1147.784 | 261.440 | 302107040 | 21415 | 263209 | 1155550 |
| $P$ | 49.414 | 20.794 | 11.419 | 302107040 | 6113821 | 14528337 | 26455906 |
| $T$ | 305.054 | 74.903 | 30.295 | 302107040 | 990341 | 4033321 | 9972158 |
| $V_0$ | 18.813 | 11.486 | 7.794 | 302107040 | 16058644 | 26302889 | 38763929 |
| $V_1$ | 22.411 | 11.941 | 7.697 | 302107040 | 13480499 | 25299570 | 39251843 |
| $V_2$ | 20.753 | 11.481 | 7.525 | 302107040 | 14557413 | 26314226 | 40148168 |
| $V_0$ L | 16.360 | 9.666 | 6.570 | 302107040 | 18466062 | 31253082 | 45980466 |
| $V_1$ L | 28.422 | 13.688 | 8.440 | 302107040 | 10629242 | 22070745 | 35795924 |
| $V_2$ L | 24.014 | 11.803 | 7.551 | 302107040 | 12580358 | 25595664 | 40007879 |
| $V_0$ vl | 22.519 | 11.900 | 7.660 | 302107040 | 13415385 | 25386543 | 39438303 |
| $V_1$ vl | 20.901 | 11.275 | 7.212 | 302107040 | 14454219 | 26793549 | 41887609 |
| $V_2$ vl | 39.767 | 16.251 | 8.571 | 302107040 | 7596846 | 18590069 | 35246983 |
| $V_0$ vr | 22.508 | 11.803 | 7.624 | 302107040 | 13422341 | 25595966 | 39626776 |
| $V_1$ vr | 20.791 | 11.011 | 7.021 | 302107040 | 14530764 | 27436309 | 43027692 |
| $V_2$ vr | 39.793 | 16.266 | 8.580 | 302107040 | 7592027 | 18572967 | 35211529 |
| $V_0$ hl | 22.503 | 11.936 | 7.704 | 302107040 | 13424916 | 25311334 | 39212286 |
| $V_1$ hl | 21.709 | 11.750 | 7.492 | 302107040 | 13915963 | 25711832 | 40323361 |
| $V_2$ hl | 38.289 | 15.778 | 8.374 | 302107040 | 7890112 | 19147243 | 36076834 |
| $V_0$ hr | 22.534 | 11.872 | 7.648 | 302107040 | 13406691 | 25446089 | 39500419 |
| $V_1$ hr | 20.965 | 11.181 | 7.089 | 302107040 | 14409980 | 27018814 | 42614657 |
| $V_2$ hr | 38.156 | 15.637 | 8.332 | 302107040 | 7917688 | 19319925 | 36256726 |
| Total | 27.011 | 13.792 | 8.505 | 6344247840 | 234874727 | 459991683 | 745954998 |

**Table A.34:** Compression factors obtained for the data sets of 'Wind Tunnel I' by applying the weighted tree predictor. Gradient-based optimization was utilized in combination with the variable 'Velocity Component U'. Sizes of the un-/compressed data sets are also listed.

| | Compression factor | | | Orig. size | Compressed size | | |
| | 1e-03 | 1e-04 | 1e-05 | | 1e-03 | 1e-04 | 1e-05 |
|---|---|---|---|---|---|---|---|
| $\rho$ | 11775.298 | 738.753 | 188.546 | 302107040 | 25656 | 408942 | 1602297 |
| $P$ | 53.794 | 23.744 | 12.484 | 302107040 | 5597238 | 12723478 | 24200466 |
| $T$ | 114.428 | 46.122 | 22.759 | 302107040 | 2640148 | 6550170 | 13273963 |
| $V_0$ | 35.999 | 16.083 | 9.209 | 302107040 | 8391987 | 18784327 | 32807373 |
| $V_1$ | 24.348 | 12.609 | 7.829 | 302107040 | 12408117 | 23960323 | 38587041 |
| $V_2$ | 22.759 | 12.162 | 7.679 | 302107040 | 13274072 | 24839847 | 39342511 |
| $V_0$ L | 21.068 | 11.159 | 7.507 | 302107040 | 14339473 | 27073816 | 40240763 |
| $V_1$ L | 31.549 | 14.732 | 9.298 | 302107040 | 9575810 | 20506286 | 32490755 |
| $V_2$ L | 24.004 | 12.779 | 8.826 | 302107040 | 12585564 | 23640780 | 34229537 |
| $V_0$ vl | 27.600 | 13.862 | 9.192 | 302107040 | 10945801 | 21794120 | 32868000 |
| $V_1$ vl | 22.050 | 11.355 | 7.208 | 302107040 | 13700895 | 26605224 | 41915601 |
| $V_2$ vl | 33.687 | 14.581 | 8.954 | 302107040 | 8968008 | 20718978 | 33741162 |
| $V_0$ vr | 27.542 | 13.815 | 9.032 | 302107040 | 10968965 | 21868711 | 33449705 |
| $V_1$ vr | 21.338 | 10.813 | 6.992 | 302107040 | 14158375 | 27939546 | 43204653 |
| $V_2$ vr | 33.684 | 14.585 | 8.962 | 302107040 | 8968983 | 20714054 | 33708189 |
| $V_0$ hl | 27.616 | 13.906 | 9.396 | 302107040 | 10939528 | 21725267 | 32151248 |
| $V_1$ hl | 23.215 | 12.102 | 7.529 | 302107040 | 13013242 | 24963409 | 40126132 |
| $V_2$ hl | 32.317 | 14.161 | 8.795 | 302107040 | 9348296 | 21333777 | 34351055 |
| $V_0$ hr | 27.588 | 13.844 | 9.127 | 302107040 | 10950575 | 21822576 | 33099031 |
| $V_1$ hr | 21.937 | 11.172 | 7.082 | 302107040 | 13771828 | 27041903 | 42656569 |
| $V_2$ hr | 32.294 | 14.132 | 8.737 | 302107040 | 9354833 | 21377650 | 34576195 |
| Total | 29.656 | 14.538 | 9.160 | 6344247840 | 213927394 | 436393189 | 692622246 |

**Table A.35:** Compression factors obtained for the data sets of 'Wind Tunnel I' by applying the weighted tree predictor. Gradient-based optimization was utilized in combination with the variable 'Velocity Component V'. Sizes of the un-/compressed data sets are also listed.

| | Compression factor | | | Orig. size | Compressed size | | |
| | 1e-03 | 1e-04 | 1e-05 | | 1e-03 | 1e-04 | 1e-05 |
|---|---|---|---|---|---|---|---|
| $\rho$ | 11631.133 | 696.210 | 169.813 | 302107040 | 25974 | 433931 | 1779056 |
| $P$ | 49.694 | 21.242 | 11.285 | 302107040 | 6079360 | 14222226 | 26771530 |
| $T$ | 98.697 | 41.047 | 20.397 | 302107040 | 3060967 | 7359950 | 14811313 |
| $V_0$ | 20.326 | 11.665 | 7.638 | 302107040 | 14863284 | 25899126 | 39550588 |
| $V_1$ | 45.966 | 17.799 | 9.766 | 302107040 | 6572420 | 16973351 | 30935396 |
| $V_2$ | 21.392 | 12.004 | 7.812 | 302107040 | 14122525 | 25166329 | 38670691 |
| $V_0$ L | 16.962 | 10.139 | 7.250 | 302107040 | 17810445 | 29796149 | 41667573 |
| $V_1$ L | 30.495 | 15.726 | 9.597 | 302107040 | 9906720 | 19210181 | 31478192 |
| $V_2$ L | 23.331 | 13.704 | 10.004 | 302107040 | 12948718 | 22045526 | 30200120 |
| $V_0$ vl | 24.054 | 13.213 | 9.004 | 302107040 | 12559424 | 22864351 | 33553664 |
| $V_1$ vl | 26.592 | 13.161 | 7.916 | 302107040 | 11360814 | 22954593 | 38163497 |
| $V_2$ vl | 32.861 | 13.951 | 8.611 | 302107040 | 9193598 | 21654155 | 35083248 |
| $V_0$ vr | 24.062 | 13.170 | 8.914 | 302107040 | 12555226 | 22938768 | 33892037 |
| $V_1$ vr | 25.426 | 12.161 | 7.589 | 302107040 | 11881763 | 24841666 | 39810377 |
| $V_2$ vr | 32.848 | 13.952 | 8.617 | 302107040 | 9197132 | 21653272 | 35061328 |
| $V_0$ hl | 24.046 | 13.267 | 9.109 | 302107040 | 12563694 | 22770694 | 33165055 |
| $V_1$ hl | 28.394 | 14.783 | 8.555 | 302107040 | 10639842 | 20435505 | 35314636 |
| $V_2$ hl | 31.507 | 13.545 | 8.481 | 302107040 | 9588625 | 22303953 | 35622783 |
| $V_0$ hr | 24.067 | 13.206 | 8.964 | 302107040 | 12552925 | 22877261 | 33701264 |
| $V_1$ hr | 26.251 | 12.699 | 7.637 | 302107040 | 11508466 | 23790329 | 39557681 |
| $V_2$ hr | 31.506 | 13.527 | 8.451 | 302107040 | 9588931 | 22334349 | 35749769 |
| Total | 29.025 | 14.668 | 9.268 | 6344247840 | 218580853 | 432525665 | 684539798 |

**Table A.36:** Compression factors obtained for the data sets of 'Wind Tunnel I' by applying the weighted tree predictor. Gradient-based optimization was utilized in combination with the variable 'Velocity Component W'. Sizes of the un-/compressed data sets are also listed.

| | Compression factor | | | Orig. size | Compressed size | | |
| | 1e-03 | 1e-04 | 1e-05 | | 1e-03 | 1e-04 | 1e-05 |
|---|---|---|---|---|---|---|---|
| $\rho$ | 11746.910 | 687.108 | 172.976 | 302107040 | 25718 | 439679 | 1746525 |
| $P$ | 51.123 | 21.589 | 11.409 | 302107040 | 5909424 | 13993570 | 26480199 |
| $T$ | 99.257 | 41.754 | 20.725 | 302107040 | 3043697 | 7235410 | 14576685 |
| $V_0$ | 20.690 | 11.855 | 7.718 | 302107040 | 14601509 | 25483836 | 39145631 |
| $V_1$ | 23.342 | 12.620 | 8.082 | 302107040 | 12942878 | 23938900 | 37379611 |
| $V_2$ | 41.083 | 16.933 | 9.451 | 302107040 | 7353581 | 17841229 | 31966586 |
| $V_0$ L | 17.104 | 10.284 | 7.278 | 302107040 | 17663441 | 29375469 | 41512068 |
| $V_1$ L | 30.293 | 15.864 | 9.634 | 302107040 | 9972810 | 19043673 | 31357391 |
| $V_2$ L | 24.165 | 14.389 | 10.489 | 302107040 | 12502100 | 20995666 | 28802805 |
| $V_0$ vl | 24.217 | 13.770 | 9.271 | 302107040 | 12474840 | 21939333 | 32586161 |
| $V_1$ vl | 21.430 | 11.157 | 7.120 | 302107040 | 14097354 | 27077599 | 42430437 |
| $V_2$ vl | 35.664 | 14.848 | 9.054 | 302107040 | 8471009 | 20346142 | 33366748 |
| $V_0$ vr | 24.214 | 13.682 | 9.162 | 302107040 | 12476296 | 22080298 | 32972382 |
| $V_1$ vr | 20.777 | 10.510 | 6.864 | 302107040 | 14540207 | 28744006 | 44015033 |
| $V_2$ vr | 35.661 | 14.858 | 9.072 | 302107040 | 8471542 | 20332341 | 33300918 |
| $V_0$ hl | 24.205 | 13.816 | 9.399 | 302107040 | 12481065 | 21866132 | 32143234 |
| $V_1$ hl | 22.465 | 11.975 | 7.445 | 302107040 | 13447779 | 25228041 | 40577809 |
| $V_2$ hl | 34.223 | 14.446 | 8.962 | 302107040 | 8827576 | 20912845 | 33710240 |
| $V_0$ hr | 24.222 | 13.748 | 9.226 | 302107040 | 12472568 | 21974307 | 32745659 |
| $V_1$ hr | 21.342 | 10.928 | 6.961 | 302107040 | 14155416 | 27646010 | 43399557 |
| $V_2$ hr | 34.195 | 14.375 | 8.852 | 302107040 | 8834721 | 21015740 | 34128438 |
| Total | 28.226 | 14.501 | 9.217 | 6344247840 | 224765531 | 437511276 | 688344117 |

## Wind Tunnel II

**Table A.37:** Compression factors obtained for the data sets of 'Wind Tunnel II' by applying the weighted tree predictor. Gradient-based optimization was utilized in combination with the variable 'Pressure'. Sizes of the un-/compressed data sets are also listed.

| | Compression factor | | | Orig. size | Compressed size | | |
| | 1e-03 | 1e-04 | 1e-05 | | 1e-03 | 1e-04 | 1e-05 |
|---|---|---|---|---|---|---|---|
| $P$ | 193.657 | 32.088 | 14.984 | 151642096 | 783044 | 4725758 | 10120025 |
| $V_0$ | 15.574 | 9.498 | 6.512 | 151642096 | 9736769 | 15965229 | 23287760 |
| $V_1$ | 24.561 | 12.545 | 7.937 | 151642096 | 6174098 | 12088197 | 19104662 |
| $V_2$ | 23.633 | 12.500 | 7.892 | 151642096 | 6416589 | 12131832 | 19215408 |
| Total | 26.246 | 13.506 | 8.457 | 606568384 | 23110500 | 44911016 | 71727855 |

**Table A.38:** Compression factors obtained for the data sets of 'Wind Tunnel II' by applying the weighted tree predictor. Gradient-based optimization was utilized in combination with the variable 'Velocity Component U'. Sizes of the un-/compressed data sets are also listed.

| | Compression factor | | | Orig. size | Compressed size | | |
| | 1e-03 | 1e-04 | 1e-05 | | 1e-03 | 1e-04 | 1e-05 |
|---|---|---|---|---|---|---|---|
| $P$ | 38.656 | 18.749 | 10.640 | 151642096 | 3922858 | 8088007 | 14251824 |
| $V_0$ | 46.267 | 17.724 | 9.925 | 151642096 | 3277537 | 8555638 | 15278597 |
| $V_1$ | 28.143 | 13.811 | 8.486 | 151642096 | 5388344 | 10979659 | 17870469 |
| $V_2$ | 28.953 | 15.094 | 9.386 | 151642096 | 5237528 | 10046649 | 16156104 |
| Total | 34.027 | 16.102 | 9.544 | 606568384 | 17826267 | 37669953 | 63556994 |

**Table A.39:** Compression factors obtained for the data sets of 'Wind Tunnel II' by applying the weighted tree predictor. Gradient-based optimization was utilized in combination with the variable 'Velocity Component V'. Sizes of the un-/compressed data sets are also listed.

| | Compression factor | | | Orig. size | Compressed size | | |
| | 1e-03 | 1e-04 | 1e-05 | | 1e-03 | 1e-04 | 1e-05 |
|---|---|---|---|---|---|---|---|
| $P$ | 35.182 | 16.094 | 9.305 | 151642096 | 4310177 | 9421991 | 16296330 |
| $V_0$ | 17.226 | 10.102 | 6.860 | 151642096 | 8803083 | 15011223 | 22104243 |
| $V_1$ | 64.777 | 20.509 | 11.133 | 151642096 | 2340970 | 7393814 | 13620364 |
| $V_2$ | 26.288 | 13.747 | 8.575 | 151642096 | 5768434 | 11030826 | 17685064 |
| Total | 28.581 | 14.153 | 8.702 | 606568384 | 21222664 | 42857854 | 69706001 |

**Table A.40:** Compression factors obtained for the data sets of 'Wind Tunnel II' by applying the weighted tree predictor. Gradient-based optimization was utilized in combination with the variable 'Velocity Component W'. Sizes of the un-/compressed data sets are also listed.

| | Compression factor | | | Orig. size | Compressed size | | |
| | 1e-03 | 1e-04 | 1e-05 | | 1e-03 | 1e-04 | 1e-05 |
|---|---|---|---|---|---|---|---|
| $P$ | 36.825 | 17.063 | 9.796 | 151642096 | 4117958 | 8886976 | 15480532 |
| $V_0$ | 18.469 | 11.200 | 7.715 | 151642096 | 8210618 | 13539479 | 19654472 |
| $V_1$ | 27.661 | 14.264 | 8.805 | 151642096 | 5482176 | 10631111 | 17221628 |
| $V_2$ | 58.343 | 20.626 | 11.342 | 151642096 | 2599137 | 7352097 | 13370054 |
| Total | 29.719 | 15.010 | 9.229 | 606568384 | 20409889 | 40409663 | 65726686 |

## Car Venting System

**Table A.41:** Compression factors obtained for the data sets of 'Car Venting System' by applying the weighted tree predictor. Gradient-based optimization was utilized in combination with the variable 'Dissipation Rate'. Sizes of the un-/compressed data sets are also listed.

| | Compression factor | | | Orig. size | Compressed size | | |
|---|---|---|---|---|---|---|---|
| | 1e-03 | 1e-04 | 1e-05 | | 1e-03 | 1e-04 | 1e-05 |
| $\epsilon$ | 25.418 | 10.422 | 5.805 | 1620472 | 63753 | 155489 | 279166 |
| $P$ | 15.261 | 9.274 | 6.516 | 3240944 | 212366 | 349458 | 497401 |
| Pt | 339.259 | 65.107 | 28.000 | 3240944 | 9553 | 49779 | 115748 |
| TKE | 7.663 | 4.698 | 3.283 | 1620472 | 211455 | 344933 | 493659 |
| TVis | 6.400 | 3.960 | 2.820 | 1620472 | 253215 | 409252 | 574560 |
| $V_0$ | 5.921 | 3.834 | 2.761 | 1620472 | 273689 | 422664 | 586864 |
| $V_1$ | 5.638 | 3.634 | 2.645 | 1620472 | 287396 | 445860 | 612600 |
| $V_2$ | 5.732 | 3.703 | 2.684 | 1620472 | 282721 | 437664 | 603644 |
| Total | 10.165 | 6.197 | 4.306 | 16204720 | 1594148 | 2615099 | 3763642 |

**Table A.42:** Compression factors obtained for the data sets of 'Car Venting System' by applying the weighted tree predictor. Gradient-based optimization was utilized in combination with the variable 'Pressure'. Sizes of the un-/compressed data sets are also listed.

| | Compression factor | | | Orig. size | Compressed size | | |
|---|---|---|---|---|---|---|---|
| | 1e-03 | 1e-04 | 1e-05 | | 1e-03 | 1e-04 | 1e-05 |
| $\epsilon$ | 13.310 | 7.118 | 4.516 | 1620472 | 121747 | 227669 | 358829 |
| $P$ | 22.449 | 11.873 | 7.822 | 3240944 | 144369 | 272977 | 414316 |
| Pt | 724.719 | 94.720 | 38.548 | 3240944 | 4472 | 34216 | 84075 |
| TKE | 6.775 | 4.189 | 3.000 | 1620472 | 239180 | 386820 | 540166 |
| TVis | 5.872 | 3.676 | 2.660 | 1620472 | 275989 | 440808 | 609236 |
| $V_0$ | 5.749 | 3.714 | 2.693 | 1620472 | 281872 | 436360 | 601712 |
| $V_1$ | 5.611 | 3.608 | 2.635 | 1620472 | 288795 | 449084 | 614968 |
| $V_2$ | 5.705 | 3.651 | 2.654 | 1620472 | 284027 | 443788 | 610612 |
| Total | 9.878 | 6.020 | 4.227 | 16204720 | 1640451 | 2691722 | 3833914 |

**Table A.43:** Compression factors obtained for the data sets of 'Car Venting System' by applying the weighted tree predictor. Gradient-based optimization was utilized in combination with the variable 'Thermodynamic Pressure'. Sizes of the un-/compressed data sets are also listed.

| | Compression factor | | | Orig. size | Compressed size | | |
|---|---|---|---|---|---|---|---|
| | 1e-03 | 1e-04 | 1e-05 | | 1e-03 | 1e-04 | 1e-05 |
| $\epsilon$ | 12.911 | 7.029 | 4.555 | 1620472 | 125508 | 230527 | 355728 |
| $P$ | 14.670 | 9.360 | 7.051 | 3240944 | 220927 | 346260 | 459668 |
| Pt | 7753.455 | 683.311 | 52.050 | 3240944 | 418 | 4743 | 62266 |
| TKE | 6.715 | 4.173 | 3.026 | 1620472 | 241314 | 388339 | 535469 |
| TVis | 5.901 | 3.670 | 2.677 | 1620472 | 274602 | 441572 | 605244 |
| $V_0$ | 5.555 | 3.654 | 2.685 | 1620472 | 291717 | 443522 | 603528 |
| $V_1$ | 5.481 | 3.540 | 2.606 | 1620472 | 295659 | 457760 | 621864 |
| $V_2$ | 5.503 | 3.585 | 2.640 | 1620472 | 294449 | 451988 | 613912 |
| Total | 9.289 | 5.861 | 4.201 | 16204720 | 1744594 | 2764711 | 3857679 |

**Table A.44:** Compression factors obtained for the data sets of 'Car Venting System' by applying the weighted tree predictor. Gradient-based optimization was utilized in combination with the variable 'Turbulence Kinetic Energy'. Sizes of the un-/compressed data sets are also listed.

| | Compression factor | | | Orig. size | Compressed size | | |
| | 1e-03 | 1e-04 | 1e-05 | | 1e-03 | 1e-04 | 1e-05 |
|---|---|---|---|---|---|---|---|
| $\epsilon$ | 17.658 | 8.732 | 5.235 | 1620472 | 91771 | 185582 | 309527 |
| $P$ | 15.246 | 9.201 | 6.481 | 3240944 | 212572 | 352242 | 500061 |
| Pt | 323.900 | 63.504 | 27.219 | 3240944 | 10006 | 51035 | 119070 |
| TKE | 9.903 | 5.447 | 3.639 | 1620472 | 163635 | 297484 | 445325 |
| TVis | 7.014 | 4.130 | 2.956 | 1620472 | 231047 | 392352 | 548144 |
| $V_0$ | 6.047 | 3.851 | 2.787 | 1620472 | 267994 | 420780 | 581440 |
| $V_1$ | 5.742 | 3.662 | 2.677 | 1620472 | 282229 | 442560 | 605304 |
| $V_2$ | 5.852 | 3.718 | 2.707 | 1620472 | 276904 | 435864 | 598640 |
| Total | 10.549 | 6.286 | 4.371 | 16204720 | 1536158 | 2577899 | 3707511 |

**Table A.45:** Compression factors obtained for the data sets of 'Car Venting System' by applying the weighted tree predictor. Gradient-based optimization was utilized in combination with the variable 'Turbulent Viscosity'. Sizes of the un-/compressed data sets are also listed.

| | Compression factor | | | Orig. size | Compressed size | | |
| | 1e-03 | 1e-04 | 1e-05 | | 1e-03 | 1e-04 | 1e-05 |
|---|---|---|---|---|---|---|---|
| $\epsilon$ | 16.511 | 8.397 | 5.088 | 1620472 | 98147 | 192974 | 318512 |
| $P$ | 15.137 | 9.174 | 6.459 | 3240944 | 214106 | 353287 | 501788 |
| Pt | 318.520 | 63.359 | 27.030 | 3240944 | 10175 | 51152 | 119902 |
| TKE | 8.166 | 4.820 | 3.335 | 1620472 | 198436 | 336232 | 485871 |
| TVis | 9.740 | 5.028 | 3.310 | 1620472 | 166373 | 322287 | 489496 |
| $V_0$ | 6.053 | 3.891 | 2.791 | 1620472 | 267718 | 416433 | 580604 |
| $V_1$ | 5.787 | 3.702 | 2.682 | 1620472 | 280024 | 437724 | 604260 |
| $V_2$ | 5.925 | 3.774 | 2.721 | 1620472 | 273478 | 429324 | 595632 |
| Total | 10.743 | 6.381 | 4.384 | 16204720 | 1508457 | 2539413 | 3696065 |

**Table A.46:** Compression factors obtained for the data sets of 'Car Venting System' by applying the weighted tree predictor. Gradient-based optimization was utilized in combination with the variable 'Velocity Component U'. Sizes of the un-/compressed data sets are also listed.

| | Compression factor | | | Orig. size | Compressed size | | |
| | 1e-03 | 1e-04 | 1e-05 | | 1e-03 | 1e-04 | 1e-05 |
|---|---|---|---|---|---|---|---|
| $\epsilon$ | 15.719 | 8.030 | 4.924 | 1620472 | 103089 | 201791 | 329074 |
| $P$ | 16.075 | 9.524 | 6.637 | 3240944 | 201610 | 340283 | 488330 |
| Pt | 367.038 | 68.036 | 29.059 | 3240944 | 8830 | 47636 | 111530 |
| TKE | 7.565 | 4.550 | 3.195 | 1620472 | 214207 | 356160 | 507169 |
| TVis | 6.436 | 3.938 | 2.807 | 1620472 | 251790 | 411476 | 577252 |
| $V_0$ | 7.952 | 4.568 | 3.127 | 1620472 | 203772 | 354744 | 518208 |
| $V_1$ | 5.743 | 3.670 | 2.661 | 1620472 | 282189 | 441600 | 608920 |
| $V_2$ | 5.970 | 3.803 | 2.737 | 1620472 | 271444 | 426056 | 592084 |
| Total | 10.544 | 6.282 | 4.341 | 16204720 | 1536931 | 2579746 | 3732567 |

**Table A.47:** Compression factors obtained for the data sets of 'Car Venting System' by applying the weighted tree predictor. Gradient-based optimization was utilized in combination with the variable 'Velocity Component V'. Sizes of the un-/compressed data sets are also listed.

| | Compression factor | | | Orig. size | Compressed size | | |
| --- | --- | --- | --- | --- | --- | --- | --- |
| | 1e-03 | 1e-04 | 1e-05 | | 1e-03 | 1e-04 | 1e-05 |
| $\epsilon$ | 14.216 | 7.491 | 4.691 | 1620472 | 113988 | 216313 | 345464 |
| $P$ | 15.320 | 9.290 | 6.539 | 3240944 | 211549 | 348848 | 495666 |
| Pt | 341.080 | 63.473 | 26.747 | 3240944 | 9502 | 51060 | 121170 |
| TKE | 7.164 | 4.374 | 3.102 | 1620472 | 226190 | 370461 | 522329 |
| TVis | 6.411 | 3.920 | 2.792 | 1620472 | 252770 | 413360 | 580344 |
| $V_0$ | 5.840 | 3.764 | 2.719 | 1620472 | 277489 | 430534 | 596056 |
| $V_1$ | 7.736 | 4.393 | 3.026 | 1620472 | 209477 | 368898 | 535428 |
| $V_2$ | 5.780 | 3.691 | 2.670 | 1620472 | 280375 | 439076 | 606820 |
| Total | 10.247 | 6.142 | 4.261 | 16204720 | 1581340 | 2638550 | 3803277 |

**Table A.48:** Compression factors obtained for the data sets of 'Car Venting System' by applying the weighted tree predictor. Gradient-based optimization was utilized in combination with the variable 'Velocity Component W'. Sizes of the un-/compressed data sets are also listed.

| | Compression factor | | | Orig. size | Compressed size | | |
| --- | --- | --- | --- | --- | --- | --- | --- |
| | 1e-03 | 1e-04 | 1e-05 | | 1e-03 | 1e-04 | 1e-05 |
| $\epsilon$ | 14.774 | 7.695 | 4.790 | 1620472 | 109685 | 210578 | 338274 |
| $P$ | 15.651 | 9.382 | 6.579 | 3240944 | 207076 | 345456 | 492589 |
| Pt | 345.922 | 64.863 | 27.877 | 3240944 | 9369 | 49966 | 116258 |
| TKE | 7.351 | 4.467 | 3.155 | 1620472 | 220434 | 362765 | 513632 |
| TVis | 6.421 | 3.928 | 2.795 | 1620472 | 252357 | 412564 | 579812 |
| $V_0$ | 6.003 | 3.871 | 2.782 | 1620472 | 269940 | 418575 | 582412 |
| $V_1$ | 5.737 | 3.663 | 2.655 | 1620472 | 282454 | 442364 | 610332 |
| $V_2$ | 7.870 | 4.433 | 3.049 | 1620472 | 205904 | 365510 | 531516 |
| Total | 10.4062 | 6.2140 | 4.3042 | 16204720 | 1557219 | 2607778 | 3764825 |

## Mixing Chamber I

**Table A.49:** Compression factors obtained for the data sets of 'Mixing Chamber I' by applying the weighted tree predictor. Gradient-based optimization was utilized in combination with the variable 'Pressure'. Sizes of the un-/compressed data sets are also listed.

| | Compression factor | | | Orig. size | Compressed size | | |
|---|---|---|---|---|---|---|---|
| | 1e-03 | 1e-04 | 1e-05 | | 1e-03 | 1e-04 | 1e-05 |
| $\rho$ | 38.269 | 16.896 | 9.333 | 7451808 | 194720 | 441031 | 798401 |
| $w_{iso}$ | 18.787 | 9.872 | 6.572 | 7451808 | 396648 | 754828 | 1133840 |
| $w_{pol}$ | 18.777 | 9.879 | 6.572 | 7451808 | 396868 | 754288 | 1133896 |
| $c_{iso}$ | 19.113 | 9.983 | 6.622 | 7451808 | 389885 | 746424 | 1125287 |
| $c_{pol}$ | 19.099 | 9.991 | 6.622 | 7451808 | 390173 | 745828 | 1125335 |
| $P$ | 113.024 | 28.120 | 12.396 | 7451808 | 65931 | 265002 | 601160 |
| $P_s$ | 101.175 | 26.012 | 12.274 | 7451808 | 73653 | 286477 | 607146 |
| TVis | 19.576 | 10.594 | 6.948 | 7451808 | 380661 | 703429 | 1072515 |
| $V_0$ | 13.283 | 7.948 | 5.624 | 7451808 | 560989 | 937574 | 1324958 |
| $V_1$ | 13.249 | 7.914 | 5.604 | 7451808 | 562462 | 941542 | 1329634 |
| $V_2$ | 13.887 | 8.193 | 5.745 | 7451808 | 536603 | 909540 | 1297065 |
| Total | 20.759 | 10.950 | 7.097 | 81969888 | 3948593 | 7485963 | 11549237 |

**Table A.50:** Compression factors obtained for the data sets of 'Mixing Chamber I' by applying the weighted tree predictor. Gradient-based optimization was utilized in combination with the variable 'Density'. Sizes of the un-/compressed data sets are also listed.

| | Compression factor | | | Orig. size | Compressed size | | |
|---|---|---|---|---|---|---|---|
| | 1e-03 | 1e-04 | 1e-05 | | 1e-03 | 1e-04 | 1e-05 |
| $\rho$ | 291.610 | 38.165 | 14.267 | 7451808 | 25554 | 195253 | 522295 |
| $w_{iso}$ | 21.077 | 13.293 | 8.692 | 7451808 | 353559 | 560563 | 857344 |
| $w_{pol}$ | 21.098 | 13.338 | 8.694 | 7451808 | 353195 | 558683 | 857136 |
| $c_{iso}$ | 21.450 | 13.491 | 8.779 | 7451808 | 347403 | 552356 | 848801 |
| $c_{pol}$ | 21.478 | 13.537 | 8.782 | 7451808 | 346947 | 550468 | 848549 |
| $P$ | 29.036 | 14.218 | 8.412 | 7451808 | 256644 | 524124 | 885886 |
| $P_s$ | 29.042 | 14.220 | 8.411 | 7451808 | 256588 | 524050 | 885914 |
| TVis | 19.241 | 10.626 | 6.976 | 7451808 | 387298 | 701265 | 1068282 |
| $V_0$ | 13.584 | 8.246 | 5.789 | 7451808 | 548555 | 903645 | 1287250 |
| $V_1$ | 13.402 | 8.130 | 5.725 | 7451808 | 556005 | 916530 | 1301690 |
| $V_2$ | 14.443 | 8.562 | 5.938 | 7451808 | 515962 | 870298 | 1254985 |
| Total | 20.764 | 11.954 | 7.720 | 81969888 | 3947710 | 6857235 | 10618132 |

**Table A.51:** Compression factors obtained for the data sets of 'Mixing Chamber I' by applying the weighted tree predictor. Gradient-based optimization was utilized in combination with the variable 'Static Pressure'. Sizes of the un-/compressed data sets are also listed.

| | Compression factor | | | Orig. size | Compressed size | | |
|---|---|---|---|---|---|---|---|
| | 1e-03 | 1e-04 | 1e-05 | | 1e-03 | 1e-04 | 1e-05 |
| $\rho$ | 38.246 | 16.897 | 9.335 | 7451808 | 194841 | 441018 | 798277 |
| $w_{iso}$ | 18.790 | 9.875 | 6.573 | 7451808 | 396575 | 754648 | 1133712 |
| $w_{pol}$ | 18.775 | 9.885 | 6.572 | 7451808 | 396891 | 753824 | 1133792 |
| $c_{iso}$ | 19.119 | 9.986 | 6.623 | 7451808 | 389753 | 746212 | 1125179 |
| $c_{pol}$ | 19.099 | 9.996 | 6.622 | 7451808 | 390173 | 745444 | 1125227 |
| $P$ | 100.638 | 25.961 | 12.275 | 7451808 | 74046 | 287039 | 607070 |
| $P_s$ | 112.783 | 28.127 | 12.397 | 7451808 | 66072 | 264930 | 601089 |
| TVis | 19.574 | 10.596 | 6.948 | 7451808 | 380692 | 703275 | 1072546 |
| $V_0$ | 13.281 | 7.949 | 5.624 | 7451808 | 561070 | 937507 | 1325014 |
| $V_1$ | 13.249 | 7.915 | 5.605 | 7451808 | 562430 | 941518 | 1329538 |
| $V_2$ | 13.887 | 8.194 | 5.745 | 7451808 | 536604 | 909387 | 1297029 |
| Total | 20.7564 | 10.9515 | 7.0979 | 81969888 | 3949147 | 7484802 | 11548473 |

**Table A.52:** Compression factors obtained for the data sets of 'Mixing Chamber I' by applying the weighted tree predictor. Gradient-based optimization was utilized in combination with the variable 'Turbulent Viscosity'. Sizes of the un-/compressed data sets are also listed.

| | Compression factor | | | Orig. size | Compressed size | | |
| | 1e-03 | 1e-04 | 1e-05 | | 1e-03 | 1e-04 | 1e-05 |
|---|---|---|---|---|---|---|---|
| $\rho$ | 37.321 | 16.696 | 9.184 | 7451808 | 199669 | 446335 | 811355 |
| $w_{iso}$ | 18.360 | 9.785 | 6.495 | 7451808 | 405877 | 761574 | 1147264 |
| $w_{pol}$ | 18.352 | 9.781 | 6.495 | 7451808 | 406053 | 761854 | 1147328 |
| $c_{iso}$ | 18.688 | 9.894 | 6.544 | 7451808 | 398743 | 753138 | 1138700 |
| $c_{pol}$ | 18.668 | 9.891 | 6.544 | 7451808 | 399183 | 753386 | 1138784 |
| $P$ | 29.342 | 14.002 | 8.264 | 7451808 | 253963 | 532209 | 901746 |
| $P_s$ | 29.351 | 14.003 | 8.264 | 7451808 | 253884 | 532161 | 901738 |
| TVis | 40.245 | 17.105 | 9.702 | 7451808 | 185162 | 435652 | 768096 |
| $V_0$ | 13.586 | 8.140 | 5.753 | 7451808 | 548481 | 915483 | 1295202 |
| $V_1$ | 13.502 | 8.107 | 5.735 | 7451808 | 551884 | 919166 | 1299446 |
| $V_2$ | 14.220 | 8.403 | 5.885 | 7451808 | 524034 | 886751 | 1266201 |
| Total | 19.862 | 10.649 | 6.937 | 81969888 | 4126933 | 7697709 | 11815860 |

**Table A.53:** Compression factors obtained for the data sets of 'Mixing Chamber I' by applying the weighted tree predictor. Gradient-based optimization was utilized in combination with the variable 'Mass Fraction Polyol'. Sizes of the un-/compressed data sets are also listed.

| | Compression factor | | | Orig. size | Compressed size | | |
| | 1e-03 | 1e-04 | 1e-05 | | 1e-03 | 1e-04 | 1e-05 |
|---|---|---|---|---|---|---|---|
| $\rho$ | 60.186 | 29.847 | 14.208 | 7451808 | 123813 | 249667 | 524483 |
| $w_{iso}$ | 46.470 | 15.617 | 8.776 | 7451808 | 160359 | 477168 | 849090 |
| $w_{pol}$ | 47.866 | 15.685 | 8.777 | 7451808 | 155679 | 475084 | 849026 |
| $c_{iso}$ | 28.970 | 15.493 | 8.861 | 7451808 | 257222 | 480964 | 840993 |
| $c_{pol}$ | 29.500 | 15.552 | 8.862 | 7451808 | 252607 | 479160 | 840893 |
| $P$ | 29.643 | 14.305 | 8.422 | 7451808 | 251386 | 520922 | 884838 |
| $P_s$ | 29.643 | 14.306 | 8.422 | 7451808 | 251382 | 520878 | 884849 |
| TVis | 19.553 | 10.645 | 6.974 | 7451808 | 381112 | 700004 | 1068551 |
| $V_0$ | 14.040 | 8.269 | 5.787 | 7451808 | 530762 | 901147 | 1287602 |
| $V_1$ | 13.762 | 8.143 | 5.722 | 7451808 | 541483 | 915126 | 1302222 |
| $V_2$ | 14.935 | 8.576 | 5.937 | 7451808 | 498951 | 868870 | 1255217 |
| Total | 24.075 | 12.440 | 7.742 | 81969888 | 3404756 | 6588990 | 10587764 |

**Table A.54:** Compression factors obtained for the data sets of 'Mixing Chamber I' by applying the weighted tree predictor. Gradient-based optimization was utilized in combination with the variable 'Mass Fraction Isocyanate'. Sizes of the un-/compressed data sets are also listed.

| | Compression factor | | | Orig. size | Compressed size | | |
| | 1e-03 | 1e-04 | 1e-05 | | 1e-03 | 1e-04 | 1e-05 |
|---|---|---|---|---|---|---|---|
| $\rho$ | 60.161 | 29.847 | 14.208 | 7451808 | 123865 | 249666 | 524483 |
| $w_{iso}$ | 46.536 | 15.616 | 8.776 | 7451808 | 160129 | 477176 | 849090 |
| $w_{pol}$ | 47.960 | 15.685 | 8.777 | 7451808 | 155377 | 475088 | 849026 |
| $c_{iso}$ | 28.969 | 15.493 | 8.861 | 7451808 | 257232 | 480965 | 840993 |
| $c_{pol}$ | 29.528 | 15.552 | 8.862 | 7451808 | 252361 | 479169 | 840893 |
| $P$ | 29.672 | 14.305 | 8.422 | 7451808 | 251140 | 520926 | 884838 |
| $P_s$ | 29.679 | 14.306 | 8.422 | 7451808 | 251084 | 520886 | 884849 |
| TVis | 19.554 | 10.645 | 6.974 | 7451808 | 381091 | 700024 | 1068551 |
| $V_0$ | 14.049 | 8.269 | 5.787 | 7451808 | 530434 | 901151 | 1287602 |
| $V_1$ | 13.760 | 8.143 | 5.722 | 7451808 | 541560 | 915126 | 1302222 |
| $V_2$ | 14.938 | 8.577 | 5.937 | 7451808 | 498842 | 868862 | 1255217 |
| Total | 24.087 | 12.440 | 7.742 | 81969888 | 3403115 | 6589039 | 10587764 |

**Table A.55:** Compression factors obtained for the data sets of 'Mixing Chamber I' by applying the weighted tree predictor. Gradient-based optimization was utilized in combination with the variable 'Molar Concentration Polyol'. Sizes of the un-/compressed data sets are also listed.

| | Compression factor | | | Orig. size | Compressed size | | |
|---|---|---|---|---|---|---|---|
| | 1e-03 | 1e-04 | 1e-05 | | 1e-03 | 1e-04 | 1e-05 |
| $\rho$ | 57.912 | 29.775 | 14.207 | 7451808 | 128674 | 250274 | 524532 |
| $w_{iso}$ | 28.191 | 15.232 | 8.771 | 7451808 | 264329 | 489219 | 849570 |
| $w_{pol}$ | 28.685 | 15.284 | 8.772 | 7451808 | 259777 | 487563 | 849478 |
| $c_{iso}$ | 48.184 | 15.886 | 8.864 | 7451808 | 154654 | 469084 | 840640 |
| $c_{pol}$ | 49.733 | 15.943 | 8.866 | 7451808 | 149836 | 467408 | 840512 |
| $P$ | 29.598 | 14.307 | 8.422 | 7451808 | 251765 | 520833 | 884810 |
| $P_s$ | 29.603 | 14.308 | 8.422 | 7451808 | 251728 | 520807 | 884832 |
| TVis | 19.555 | 10.646 | 6.974 | 7451808 | 381073 | 699984 | 1068497 |
| $V_0$ | 14.042 | 8.269 | 5.787 | 7451808 | 530690 | 901222 | 1287602 |
| $V_1$ | 13.760 | 8.143 | 5.722 | 7451808 | 541565 | 915166 | 1302234 |
| $V_2$ | 14.928 | 8.577 | 5.937 | 7451808 | 499197 | 868812 | 1255193 |
| Total | 24.015 | 12.438 | 7.742 | 81969888 | 3413288 | 6590372 | 10587900 |

**Table A.56:** Compression factors obtained for the data sets of 'Mixing Chamber I' by applying the weighted tree predictor. Gradient-based optimization was utilized in combination with the variable 'Molar Concentration Isocyanate'. Sizes of the un-/compressed data sets are also listed.

| | Compression factor | | | Orig. size | Compressed size | | |
|---|---|---|---|---|---|---|---|
| | 1e-03 | 1e-04 | 1e-05 | | 1e-03 | 1e-04 | 1e-05 |
| $\rho$ | 57.823 | 29.762 | 14.207 | 7451808 | 128872 | 250381 | 524527 |
| $w_{iso}$ | 28.195 | 15.227 | 8.771 | 7451808 | 264295 | 489376 | 849557 |
| $w_{pol}$ | 28.683 | 15.288 | 8.773 | 7451808 | 259795 | 487416 | 849449 |
| $c_{iso}$ | 48.249 | 15.879 | 8.865 | 7451808 | 154444 | 469280 | 840610 |
| $c_{pol}$ | 49.660 | 15.945 | 8.866 | 7451808 | 150056 | 467348 | 840478 |
| $P$ | 29.615 | 14.306 | 8.421 | 7451808 | 251626 | 520898 | 884874 |
| $P_s$ | 29.617 | 14.306 | 8.421 | 7451808 | 251609 | 520902 | 884881 |
| TVis | 19.558 | 10.645 | 6.974 | 7451808 | 381019 | 700020 | 1068562 |
| $V_0$ | 14.054 | 8.269 | 5.787 | 7451808 | 530223 | 901142 | 1287586 |
| $V_1$ | 13.774 | 8.143 | 5.722 | 7451808 | 541004 | 915162 | 1302206 |
| $V_2$ | 14.941 | 8.577 | 5.936 | 7451808 | 498733 | 868800 | 1255285 |
| Total | 24.026 | 12.437 | 7.742 | 81969888 | 3411676 | 6590725 | 10588015 |

**Table A.57:** Compression factors obtained for the data sets of 'Mixing Chamber I' by applying the weighted tree predictor. Gradient-based optimization was utilized in combination with the variable 'Velocity Component U'. Sizes of the un-/compressed data sets are also listed.

| | Compression factor | | | Orig. size | Compressed size | | |
|---|---|---|---|---|---|---|---|
| | 1e-03 | 1e-04 | 1e-05 | | 1e-03 | 1e-04 | 1e-05 |
| $\rho$ | 39.601 | 17.625 | 9.514 | 7451808 | 188171 | 422809 | 783251 |
| $w_{iso}$ | 19.392 | 10.147 | 6.659 | 7451808 | 384279 | 734407 | 1119070 |
| $w_{pol}$ | 19.284 | 10.142 | 6.658 | 7451808 | 386431 | 734779 | 1119158 |
| $c_{iso}$ | 19.744 | 10.264 | 6.710 | 7451808 | 377423 | 726015 | 1110547 |
| $c_{pol}$ | 19.635 | 10.259 | 6.709 | 7451808 | 379507 | 726351 | 1110655 |
| $P$ | 29.296 | 14.061 | 8.277 | 7451808 | 254362 | 529962 | 900278 |
| $P_s$ | 29.299 | 14.062 | 8.277 | 7451808 | 254334 | 529940 | 900294 |
| TVis | 19.594 | 10.741 | 7.059 | 7451808 | 380305 | 693782 | 1055699 |
| $V_0$ | 27.077 | 12.168 | 7.505 | 7451808 | 275203 | 612389 | 992948 |
| $V_1$ | 14.334 | 8.424 | 5.872 | 7451808 | 519870 | 884638 | 1268998 |
| $V_2$ | 15.307 | 8.830 | 6.076 | 7451808 | 486832 | 843908 | 1226389 |
| Total | 21.090 | 11.019 | 7.074 | 81969888 | 3886717 | 7438980 | 11587287 |

**Table A.58:** Compression factors obtained for the data sets of 'Mixing Chamber I' by applying the weighted tree predictor. Gradient-based optimization was utilized in combination with the variable 'Velocity Component V'. Sizes of the un-/compressed data sets are also listed.

| | Compression factor | | | Orig. size | Compressed size | | |
| --- | --- | --- | --- | --- | --- | --- | --- |
| | 1e-03 | 1e-04 | 1e-05 | | 1e-03 | 1e-04 | 1e-05 |
| $\rho$ | 38.941 | 17.288 | 9.384 | 7451808 | 191363 | 431031 | 794093 |
| $w_{iso}$ | 19.028 | 10.004 | 6.594 | 7451808 | 391616 | 744861 | 1130055 |
| $w_{pol}$ | 18.943 | 9.997 | 6.594 | 7451808 | 393388 | 745417 | 1130135 |
| $c_{iso}$ | 19.369 | 10.118 | 6.644 | 7451808 | 384727 | 736512 | 1121505 |
| $c_{pol}$ | 19.278 | 10.110 | 6.644 | 7451808 | 386547 | 737044 | 1121581 |
| $P$ | 29.158 | 14.005 | 8.248 | 7451808 | 255568 | 532067 | 903494 |
| $P_s$ | 29.159 | 14.005 | 8.248 | 7451808 | 255560 | 532066 | 903478 |
| TVis | 19.640 | 10.761 | 7.070 | 7451808 | 379423 | 692463 | 1053988 |
| $V_0$ | 14.428 | 8.465 | 5.895 | 7451808 | 516475 | 880280 | 1264006 |
| $V_1$ | 26.996 | 12.105 | 7.471 | 7451808 | 276034 | 615621 | 997426 |
| $V_2$ | 15.273 | 8.837 | 6.080 | 7451808 | 487912 | 843232 | 1225565 |
| Total | 20.918 | 10.943 | 7.039 | 81969888 | 3918613 | 7490594 | 11645326 |

**Table A.59:** Compression factors obtained for the data sets of 'Mixing Chamber I' by applying the weighted tree predictor. Gradient-based optimization was utilized in combination with the variable 'Velocity Component W'. Sizes of the un-/compressed data sets are also listed.

| | Compression factor | | | Orig. size | Compressed size | | |
| --- | --- | --- | --- | --- | --- | --- | --- |
| | 1e-03 | 1e-04 | 1e-05 | | 1e-03 | 1e-04 | 1e-05 |
| $\rho$ | 40.675 | 17.869 | 9.564 | 7451808 | 183202 | 417028 | 779121 |
| $w_{iso}$ | 19.729 | 10.209 | 6.683 | 7451808 | 377710 | 729959 | 1115023 |
| $w_{pol}$ | 19.542 | 10.200 | 6.683 | 7451808 | 381314 | 730603 | 1115103 |
| $c_{iso}$ | 20.092 | 10.328 | 6.734 | 7451808 | 370885 | 721511 | 1106549 |
| $c_{pol}$ | 19.898 | 10.318 | 6.734 | 7451808 | 374497 | 722207 | 1106613 |
| $P$ | 29.170 | 14.002 | 8.256 | 7451808 | 255460 | 532178 | 902590 |
| $P_s$ | 29.167 | 14.002 | 8.256 | 7451808 | 255488 | 532204 | 902578 |
| TVis | 19.625 | 10.756 | 7.069 | 7451808 | 379709 | 692806 | 1054117 |
| $V_0$ | 14.627 | 8.563 | 5.946 | 7451808 | 509465 | 870210 | 1253178 |
| $V_1$ | 14.494 | 8.526 | 5.925 | 7451808 | 514138 | 874013 | 1257790 |
| $V_2$ | 29.007 | 12.685 | 7.723 | 7451808 | 256900 | 587471 | 964843 |
| Total | 21.243 | 11.062 | 7.092 | 81969888 | 3858768 | 7410190 | 11557505 |

## Mixing Chamber II

**Table A.60:** Compression factors obtained for the data sets of 'Mixing Chamber II' by applying the weighted tree predictor. Gradient-based optimization was utilized in combination with the variable 'Pressure'. Sizes of the un-/compressed data sets are also listed.

| | Compression factor | | | Orig. size | Compressed size | | |
| | 1e-03 | 1e-04 | 1e-05 | | 1e-03 | 1e-04 | 1e-05 |
|---|---|---|---|---|---|---|---|
| $\rho$ | 8.921 | 6.155 | 4.680 | 14328232 | 1606107 | 2327887 | 3061572 |
| $P$ | 340.548 | 55.641 | 17.180 | 14328232 | 42074 | 257511 | 834020 |
| $V_0$ | 13.142 | 7.948 | 5.641 | 14328232 | 1090296 | 1802665 | 2540037 |
| $V_1$ | 13.606 | 8.086 | 5.707 | 14328232 | 1053101 | 1771925 | 2510497 |
| $V_2$ | 13.869 | 8.237 | 5.784 | 14328232 | 1033138 | 1739469 | 2477185 |
| Total | 14.849 | 9.069 | 6.271 | 71641160 | 4824716 | 7899457 | 11423311 |

**Table A.61:** Compression factors obtained for the data sets of 'Mixing Chamber II' by applying the weighted tree predictor. Gradient-based optimization was utilized in combination with the variable 'Density'. Sizes of the un-/compressed data sets are also listed.

| | Compression factor | | | Orig. size | Compressed size | | |
| | 1e-03 | 1e-04 | 1e-05 | | 1e-03 | 1e-04 | 1e-05 |
|---|---|---|---|---|---|---|---|
| $\rho$ | 14.623 | 8.440 | 5.897 | 14328232 | 979848 | 1697655 | 2429762 |
| $P$ | 46.491 | 19.667 | 10.346 | 14328232 | 308194 | 728548 | 1384909 |
| $V_0$ | 14.103 | 8.272 | 5.792 | 14328232 | 1015960 | 1732181 | 2473837 |
| $V_1$ | 14.546 | 8.393 | 5.849 | 14328232 | 985043 | 1707081 | 2449629 |
| $V_2$ | 14.675 | 8.537 | 5.925 | 14328232 | 976400 | 1678406 | 2418397 |
| Total | 16.796 | 9.497 | 6.421 | 71641160 | 4265445 | 7543871 | 11156534 |

**Table A.62:** Compression factors obtained for the data sets of 'Mixing Chamber II' by applying the weighted tree predictor. Gradient-based optimization was utilized in combination with the variable 'Velocity Component U'. Sizes of the un-/compressed data sets are also listed.

| | Compression factor | | | Orig. size | Compressed size | | |
| | 1e-03 | 1e-04 | 1e-05 | | 1e-03 | 1e-04 | 1e-05 |
|---|---|---|---|---|---|---|---|
| $\rho$ | 9.431 | 6.400 | 4.823 | 14328232 | 1519252 | 2238666 | 2970942 |
| $P$ | 47.158 | 19.970 | 10.455 | 14328232 | 303837 | 717495 | 1370525 |
| $V_0$ | 26.738 | 11.916 | 7.396 | 14328232 | 535875 | 1202485 | 1937297 |
| $V_1$ | 14.918 | 8.601 | 5.953 | 14328232 | 960470 | 1665893 | 2406901 |
| $V_2$ | 15.906 | 9.013 | 6.155 | 14328232 | 900832 | 1589664 | 2327953 |
| Total | 16.976 | 9.663 | 6.505 | 71641160 | 4220266 | 7414203 | 11013618 |

**Table A.63:** Compression factors obtained for the data sets of 'Mixing Chamber II' by applying the weighted tree predictor. Gradient-based optimization was utilized in combination with the variable 'Velocity Component V'. Sizes of the un-/compressed data sets are also listed.

| | Compression factor | | | Orig. size | Compressed size | | |
| | 1e-03 | 1e-04 | 1e-05 | | 1e-03 | 1e-04 | 1e-05 |
|---|---|---|---|---|---|---|---|
| $\rho$ | 9.375 | 6.363 | 4.802 | 14328232 | 1528312 | 2251805 | 2984050 |
| $P$ | 46.920 | 19.794 | 10.380 | 14328232 | 305375 | 723884 | 1380349 |
| $V_0$ | 14.404 | 8.432 | 5.873 | 14328232 | 994718 | 1699253 | 2439857 |
| $V_1$ | 28.361 | 12.327 | 7.543 | 14328232 | 505210 | 1162354 | 1899445 |
| $V_2$ | 15.099 | 8.762 | 6.037 | 14328232 | 948962 | 1635283 | 2373509 |
| Total | 16.729 | 9.587 | 6.467 | 71641160 | 4282577 | 7472579 | 11077210 |

**Table A.64:** Compression factors obtained for the data sets of 'Mixing Chamber II' by applying the weighted tree predictor. Gradient-based optimization was utilized in combination with the variable 'Velocity Component W'. Sizes of the un-/compressed data sets are also listed.

| | Compression factor | | | Orig. size | Compressed size | | |
| | 1e-03 | 1e-04 | 1e-05 | | 1e-03 | 1e-04 | 1e-05 |
|---|---|---|---|---|---|---|---|
| $\rho$ | 9.347 | 6.369 | 4.806 | 14328232 | 1532996 | 2249604 | 2981083 |
| $P$ | 47.292 | 19.969 | 10.456 | 14328232 | 302972 | 717535 | 1370331 |
| $V_0$ | 15.019 | 8.663 | 5.985 | 14328232 | 954035 | 1653977 | 2394049 |
| $V_1$ | 14.885 | 8.615 | 5.961 | 14328232 | 962570 | 1663225 | 2403613 |
| $V_2$ | 28.554 | 12.459 | 7.631 | 14328232 | 501787 | 1150070 | 1877689 |
| Total | 16.839 | 9.636 | 6.497 | 71641160 | 4254360 | 7434411 | 11026765 |

## Mixing Pipe

**Table A.65:** Compression factors obtained for the data sets of 'Mixing Pipe' by applying the weighted tree predictor. Gradient-based optimization was utilized in combination with the variable 'Pressure'. Sizes of the un-/compressed data sets are also listed.

| | Compression factor | | | Orig. size | Compressed size | | |
| | 1e-03 | 1e-04 | 1e-05 | | 1e-03 | 1e-04 | 1e-05 |
|---|---|---|---|---|---|---|---|
| $H_s$ | 23.492 | 12.229 | 8.023 | 658712 | 28040 | 53866 | 82099 |
| $\rho$ | 24.502 | 12.500 | 8.055 | 658712 | 26884 | 52698 | 81781 |
| $\epsilon$ | 19.341 | 10.879 | 7.109 | 658712 | 34057 | 60548 | 92655 |
| $H$ | 23.492 | 12.229 | 8.023 | 658712 | 28040 | 53866 | 82099 |
| $P$ | 15.753 | 8.904 | 6.100 | 658712 | 41814 | 73979 | 107987 |
| $T$ | 23.492 | 12.229 | 8.023 | 658712 | 28040 | 53866 | 82099 |
| Pt | 2225.378 | 178.949 | 52.105 | 658712 | 296 | 3681 | 12642 |
| TKE | 14.641 | 8.646 | 5.989 | 658712 | 44991 | 76183 | 109987 |
| TVis | 10.871 | 6.992 | 5.135 | 658712 | 60591 | 94211 | 128283 |
| $V_0$ | 10.765 | 6.918 | 5.089 | 658712 | 61191 | 95223 | 129443 |
| $V_1$ | 12.138 | 7.573 | 5.442 | 658712 | 54267 | 86987 | 121051 |
| $V_2$ | 11.478 | 7.298 | 5.295 | 658712 | 57387 | 90263 | 124391 |
| Total | 16.977 | 9.938 | 6.847 | 7904544 | 465598 | 795371 | 1154517 |

**Table A.66:** Compression factors obtained for the data sets of 'Mixing Pipe' by applying the weighted tree predictor. Gradient-based optimization was utilized in combination with the variable 'Density'. Sizes of the un-/compressed data sets are also listed.

| | Compression factor | | | Orig. size | Compressed size | | |
| | 1e-03 | 1e-04 | 1e-05 | | 1e-03 | 1e-04 | 1e-05 |
|---|---|---|---|---|---|---|---|
| $H_s$ | 28.564 | 14.323 | 8.930 | 658712 | 23061 | 45990 | 73767 |
| $\rho$ | 32.890 | 14.773 | 9.038 | 658712 | 20028 | 44588 | 72885 |
| $\epsilon$ | 21.480 | 11.735 | 7.541 | 658712 | 30667 | 56131 | 87347 |
| $H$ | 28.564 | 14.323 | 8.930 | 658712 | 23061 | 45990 | 73767 |
| $P$ | 12.637 | 7.851 | 5.589 | 658712 | 52124 | 83907 | 117859 |
| $T$ | 28.564 | 14.323 | 8.930 | 658712 | 23061 | 45990 | 73767 |
| Pt | 1108.943 | 131.663 | 42.569 | 658712 | 594 | 5003 | 15474 |
| TKE | 16.080 | 9.219 | 6.305 | 658712 | 40965 | 71451 | 104475 |
| TVis | 11.640 | 7.356 | 5.354 | 658712 | 56591 | 89543 | 123031 |
| $V_0$ | 11.004 | 7.060 | 5.176 | 658712 | 59859 | 93303 | 127259 |
| $V_1$ | 12.025 | 7.604 | 5.481 | 658712 | 54777 | 86627 | 120183 |
| $V_2$ | 11.343 | 7.321 | 5.307 | 658712 | 58071 | 89979 | 124127 |
| Total | 17.849 | 10.421 | 7.096 | 7904544 | 442859 | 758502 | 1113941 |

**Table A.67:** Compression factors obtained for the data sets of 'Mixing Pipe' by applying the weighted tree predictor. Gradient-based optimization was utilized in combination with the variable 'Enthalpy'. Sizes of the un-/compressed data sets are also listed.

| | Compression factor | | | Orig. size | Compressed size | | |
| | 1e-03 | 1e-04 | 1e-05 | | 1e-03 | 1e-04 | 1e-05 |
|---|---|---|---|---|---|---|---|
| $H_s$ | 32.382 | 14.614 | 9.012 | 658712 | 20342 | 45075 | 73096 |
| $\rho$ | 29.081 | 14.674 | 8.942 | 658712 | 22651 | 44890 | 73666 |
| $\epsilon$ | 21.466 | 11.812 | 7.552 | 658712 | 30687 | 55768 | 87219 |
| $H$ | 32.382 | 14.614 | 9.012 | 658712 | 20342 | 45075 | 73096 |
| $P$ | 12.646 | 7.842 | 5.579 | 658712 | 52088 | 83995 | 118071 |
| $T$ | 32.382 | 14.614 | 9.012 | 658712 | 20342 | 45075 | 73096 |
| Pt | 1007.205 | 130.232 | 42.034 | 658712 | 654 | 5058 | 15671 |
| TKE | 16.088 | 9.256 | 6.312 | 658712 | 40944 | 71167 | 104359 |
| TVis | 11.641 | 7.379 | 5.355 | 658712 | 56587 | 89267 | 123003 |
| $V_0$ | 11.007 | 7.066 | 5.169 | 658712 | 59843 | 93223 | 127443 |
| $V_1$ | 12.039 | 7.619 | 5.494 | 658712 | 54717 | 86459 | 119899 |
| $V_2$ | 11.339 | 7.308 | 5.303 | 658712 | 58095 | 90139 | 124215 |
| Total | 18.076 | 10.467 | 7.103 | 7904544 | 437292 | 755191 | 1112834 |

**Table A.68:** Compression factors obtained for the data sets of 'Mixing Pipe' by applying the weighted tree predictor. Gradient-based optimization was utilized in combination with the variable 'Static Enthalpy'. Sizes of the un-/compressed data sets are also listed.

| | Compression factor | | | Orig. size | Compressed size | | |
| | 1e-03 | 1e-04 | 1e-05 | | 1e-03 | 1e-04 | 1e-05 |
|---|---|---|---|---|---|---|---|
| $H_s$ | 32.382 | 14.614 | 9.012 | 658712 | 20342 | 45075 | 73096 |
| $\rho$ | 29.081 | 14.674 | 8.942 | 658712 | 22651 | 44890 | 73666 |
| $\epsilon$ | 21.466 | 11.812 | 7.552 | 658712 | 30687 | 55768 | 87219 |
| $H$ | 32.382 | 14.614 | 9.012 | 658712 | 20342 | 45075 | 73096 |
| $P$ | 12.646 | 7.842 | 5.579 | 658712 | 52088 | 83995 | 118071 |
| $T$ | 32.382 | 14.614 | 9.012 | 658712 | 20342 | 45075 | 73096 |
| Pt | 1007.205 | 130.232 | 42.034 | 658712 | 654 | 5058 | 15671 |
| TKE | 16.088 | 9.256 | 6.312 | 658712 | 40944 | 71167 | 104359 |
| TVis | 11.641 | 7.379 | 5.355 | 658712 | 56587 | 89267 | 123003 |
| $V_0$ | 11.007 | 7.066 | 5.169 | 658712 | 59843 | 93223 | 127443 |
| $V_1$ | 12.039 | 7.619 | 5.494 | 658712 | 54717 | 86459 | 119899 |
| $V_2$ | 11.339 | 7.308 | 5.303 | 658712 | 58095 | 90139 | 124215 |
| Total | 18.076 | 10.467 | 7.103 | 7904544 | 437292 | 755191 | 1112834 |

**Table A.69:** Compression factors obtained for the data sets of 'Mixing Pipe' by applying the weighted tree predictor. Gradient-based optimization was utilized in combination with the variable 'Thermodynamic Pressure'. Sizes of the un-/compressed data sets are also listed.

| | Compression factor | | | Orig. size | Compressed size | | |
| | 1e-03 | 1e-04 | 1e-05 | | 1e-03 | 1e-04 | 1e-05 |
|---|---|---|---|---|---|---|---|
| $H_s$ | 14.962 | 9.351 | 7.189 | 658712 | 44026 | 70446 | 91631 |
| $\rho$ | 15.699 | 9.519 | 7.215 | 658712 | 41960 | 69197 | 91298 |
| $\epsilon$ | 13.594 | 8.522 | 6.240 | 658712 | 48457 | 77299 | 105559 |
| $H$ | 14.962 | 9.351 | 7.189 | 658712 | 44026 | 70446 | 91631 |
| $P$ | 10.312 | 6.885 | 5.442 | 658712 | 63876 | 95667 | 121051 |
| $T$ | 14.962 | 9.351 | 7.189 | 658712 | 44026 | 70446 | 91631 |
| Pt | 6653.657 | 1689.005 | 130.103 | 658712 | 99 | 390 | 5063 |
| TKE | 10.862 | 7.148 | 5.406 | 658712 | 60644 | 92151 | 121847 |
| TVis | 8.763 | 6.085 | 4.801 | 658712 | 75171 | 108255 | 137191 |
| $V_0$ | 9.403 | 6.329 | 4.922 | 658712 | 70051 | 104083 | 133839 |
| $V_1$ | 10.500 | 6.913 | 5.220 | 658712 | 62733 | 95287 | 126191 |
| $V_2$ | 10.061 | 6.707 | 5.089 | 658712 | 65471 | 98219 | 129431 |
| Total | 12.738 | 8.304 | 6.342 | 7904544 | 620540 | 951886 | 1246363 |

**Table A.70:** Compression factors obtained for the data sets of 'Mixing Pipe' by applying the weighted tree predictor. Gradient-based optimization was utilized in combination with the variable 'Temperature'. Sizes of the un-/compressed data sets are also listed.

| | Compression factor | | | Orig. size | Compressed size | | |
| | 1e-03 | 1e-04 | 1e-05 | | 1e-03 | 1e-04 | 1e-05 |
|---|---|---|---|---|---|---|---|
| $H_s$ | 32.382 | 14.614 | 9.012 | 658712 | 20342 | 45075 | 73096 |
| $\rho$ | 29.081 | 14.674 | 8.942 | 658712 | 22651 | 44890 | 73666 |
| $\epsilon$ | 21.466 | 11.812 | 7.552 | 658712 | 30687 | 55768 | 87219 |
| $H$ | 32.382 | 14.614 | 9.012 | 658712 | 20342 | 45075 | 73096 |
| $P$ | 12.646 | 7.842 | 5.579 | 658712 | 52088 | 83995 | 118071 |
| $T$ | 32.382 | 14.614 | 9.012 | 658712 | 20342 | 45075 | 73096 |
| Pt | 1007.205 | 130.232 | 42.034 | 658712 | 654 | 5058 | 15671 |
| TKE | 16.088 | 9.256 | 6.312 | 658712 | 40944 | 71167 | 104359 |
| TVis | 11.641 | 7.379 | 5.355 | 658712 | 56587 | 89267 | 123003 |
| $V_0$ | 11.007 | 7.066 | 5.169 | 658712 | 59843 | 93223 | 127443 |
| $V_1$ | 12.039 | 7.619 | 5.494 | 658712 | 54717 | 86459 | 119899 |
| $V_2$ | 11.339 | 7.308 | 5.303 | 658712 | 58095 | 90139 | 124215 |
| Total | 18.076 | 10.467 | 7.103 | 7904544 | 437292 | 755191 | 1112834 |

**Table A.71:** Compression factors obtained for the data sets of 'Mixing Pipe' by applying the weighted tree predictor. Gradient-based optimization was utilized in combination with the variable 'Turbulent Viscosity'. Sizes of the un-/compressed data sets are also listed.

| | Compression factor | | | Orig. size | Compressed size | | |
| | 1e-03 | 1e-04 | 1e-05 | | 1e-03 | 1e-04 | 1e-05 |
|---|---|---|---|---|---|---|---|
| $H_s$ | 24.230 | 12.446 | 8.109 | 658712 | 27186 | 52924 | 81228 |
| $\rho$ | 24.574 | 12.619 | 8.123 | 658712 | 26805 | 52199 | 81092 |
| $\epsilon$ | 25.524 | 13.054 | 7.995 | 658712 | 25808 | 50462 | 82391 |
| $H$ | 24.230 | 12.446 | 8.109 | 658712 | 27186 | 52924 | 81228 |
| $P$ | 12.084 | 7.519 | 5.413 | 658712 | 54513 | 87603 | 121699 |
| $T$ | 24.230 | 12.446 | 8.109 | 658712 | 27186 | 52924 | 81228 |
| Pt | 1591.092 | 119.397 | 38.805 | 658712 | 414 | 5517 | 16975 |
| TKE | 18.546 | 10.053 | 6.621 | 658712 | 35517 | 65527 | 99483 |
| TVis | 15.318 | 8.642 | 5.968 | 658712 | 43003 | 76219 | 110367 |
| $V_0$ | 11.454 | 7.233 | 5.259 | 658712 | 57507 | 91071 | 125255 |
| $V_1$ | 11.877 | 7.459 | 5.382 | 658712 | 55460 | 88311 | 122391 |
| $V_2$ | 10.992 | 7.080 | 5.180 | 658712 | 59925 | 93035 | 127171 |
| Total | 17.944 | 10.283 | 6.992 | 7904544 | 440510 | 768716 | 1130508 |

**Table A.72:** Compression factors obtained for the data sets of 'Mixing Pipe' by applying the weighted tree predictor. Gradient-based optimization was utilized in combination with the variable 'Turbulence Kinetic Energy'. Sizes of the un-/compressed data sets are also listed.

| | Compression factor | | | Orig. size | Compressed size | | |
| | 1e-03 | 1e-04 | 1e-05 | | 1e-03 | 1e-04 | 1e-05 |
|---|---|---|---|---|---|---|---|
| $H_s$ | 23.345 | 12.465 | 8.137 | 658712 | 28216 | 52847 | 80957 |
| $\rho$ | 24.328 | 12.674 | 8.150 | 658712 | 27076 | 51975 | 80821 |
| $\epsilon$ | 28.637 | 14.615 | 8.659 | 658712 | 23002 | 45070 | 76075 |
| $H$ | 23.345 | 12.465 | 8.137 | 658712 | 28216 | 52847 | 80957 |
| $P$ | 11.860 | 7.569 | 5.446 | 658712 | 55542 | 87031 | 120955 |
| $T$ | 23.345 | 12.465 | 8.137 | 658712 | 28216 | 52847 | 80957 |
| Pt | 577.818 | 125.326 | 39.107 | 658712 | 1140 | 5256 | 16844 |
| TKE | 23.885 | 11.509 | 7.266 | 658712 | 27578 | 57235 | 90651 |
| TVis | 12.248 | 7.714 | 5.523 | 658712 | 53779 | 85387 | 119259 |
| $V_0$ | 11.224 | 7.202 | 5.248 | 658712 | 58687 | 91459 | 125519 |
| $V_1$ | 11.820 | 7.508 | 5.409 | 658712 | 55729 | 87739 | 121787 |
| $V_2$ | 10.993 | 7.137 | 5.216 | 658712 | 59919 | 92291 | 126279 |
| Total | 17.680 | 10.374 | 7.051 | 7904544 | 447100 | 761984 | 1121061 |

**Table A.73:** Compression factors obtained for the data sets of 'Mixing Pipe' by applying the weighted tree predictor. Gradient-based optimization was utilized in combination with the variable 'Dissipation Rate'. Sizes of the un-/compressed data sets are also listed.

| | Compression factor | | | Orig. size | Compressed size | | |
| | 1e-03 | 1e-04 | 1e-05 | | 1e-03 | 1e-04 | 1e-05 |
|---|---|---|---|---|---|---|---|
| $H_s$ | 21.533 | 12.454 | 8.270 | 658712 | 30591 | 52892 | 79649 |
| $\rho$ | 22.721 | 12.680 | 8.283 | 658712 | 28991 | 51950 | 79525 |
| $\epsilon$ | 36.092 | 15.455 | 8.917 | 658712 | 18251 | 42622 | 73871 |
| $H$ | 21.533 | 12.454 | 8.270 | 658712 | 30591 | 52892 | 79649 |
| $P$ | 11.297 | 7.590 | 5.545 | 658712 | 58308 | 86783 | 118791 |
| $T$ | 21.533 | 12.454 | 8.270 | 658712 | 30591 | 52892 | 79649 |
| Pt | 626.152 | 123.841 | 40.921 | 658712 | 1052 | 5319 | 16097 |
| TKE | 19.169 | 10.909 | 7.081 | 658712 | 34364 | 60383 | 93019 |
| TVis | 11.712 | 7.633 | 5.555 | 658712 | 56243 | 86303 | 118571 |
| $V_0$ | 10.918 | 7.187 | 5.281 | 658712 | 60335 | 91659 | 124731 |
| $V_1$ | 11.446 | 7.497 | 5.456 | 658712 | 57550 | 87867 | 120735 |
| $V_2$ | 10.726 | 7.127 | 5.256 | 658712 | 61415 | 92423 | 125335 |
| Total | 16.880 | 10.346 | 7.124 | 7904544 | 468282 | 763985 | 1109622 |

**Table A.74:** Compression factors obtained for the data sets of 'Mixing Pipe' by applying the weighted tree predictor. Gradient-based optimization was utilized in combination with the variable 'Velocity Component U'. Sizes of the un-/compressed data sets are also listed.

| | Compression factor | | | Orig. size | Compressed size | | |
| | 1e-03 | 1e-04 | 1e-05 | | 1e-03 | 1e-04 | 1e-05 |
|---|---|---|---|---|---|---|---|
| $H_s$ | 21.945 | 11.671 | 7.763 | 658712 | 30016 | 56438 | 84850 |
| $\rho$ | 22.662 | 11.893 | 7.801 | 658712 | 29067 | 55386 | 84442 |
| $\epsilon$ | 19.946 | 11.199 | 7.222 | 658712 | 33025 | 58820 | 91203 |
| $H$ | 21.945 | 11.671 | 7.763 | 658712 | 30016 | 56438 | 84850 |
| $P$ | 11.909 | 7.452 | 5.374 | 658712 | 55310 | 88395 | 122563 |
| $T$ | 21.945 | 11.671 | 7.763 | 658712 | 30016 | 56438 | 84850 |
| Pt | 1081.629 | 112.909 | 38.523 | 658712 | 609 | 5834 | 17099 |
| TKE | 15.179 | 8.864 | 6.081 | 658712 | 43396 | 74315 | 108315 |
| TVis | 11.254 | 7.154 | 5.218 | 658712 | 58531 | 92071 | 126239 |
| $V_0$ | 14.032 | 8.183 | 5.744 | 658712 | 46942 | 80499 | 114671 |
| $V_1$ | 11.378 | 7.243 | 5.268 | 658712 | 57891 | 90943 | 125035 |
| $V_2$ | 11.021 | 7.089 | 5.185 | 658712 | 59767 | 92923 | 127043 |
| Total | 16.656 | 9.777 | 6.749 | 7904544 | 474586 | 808500 | 1171160 |

**Table A.75:** Compression factors obtained for the data sets of 'Mixing Pipe' by applying the weighted tree predictor. Gradient-based optimization was utilized in combination with the variable 'Velocity Component V'. Sizes of the un-/compressed data sets are also listed.

| | Compression factor | | | Orig. size | Compressed size | | |
| | 1e-03 | 1e-04 | 1e-05 | | 1e-03 | 1e-04 | 1e-05 |
|---|---|---|---|---|---|---|---|
| $H_s$ | 20.906 | 11.360 | 7.655 | 658712 | 31508 | 57983 | 86050 |
| $\rho$ | 21.557 | 11.553 | 7.651 | 658712 | 30557 | 57017 | 86094 |
| $\epsilon$ | 18.874 | 10.549 | 6.914 | 658712 | 34901 | 62446 | 95271 |
| $H$ | 20.906 | 11.360 | 7.655 | 658712 | 31508 | 57983 | 86050 |
| $P$ | 11.943 | 7.489 | 5.395 | 658712 | 55153 | 87959 | 122107 |
| $T$ | 20.906 | 11.360 | 7.655 | 658712 | 31508 | 57983 | 86050 |
| Pt | 899.880 | 107.826 | 38.333 | 658712 | 732 | 6109 | 17184 |
| TKE | 14.295 | 8.436 | 5.873 | 658712 | 46081 | 78079 | 112167 |
| TVis | 10.556 | 6.843 | 5.052 | 658712 | 62399 | 96267 | 130399 |
| $V_0$ | 10.325 | 6.734 | 4.990 | 658712 | 63799 | 97819 | 132003 |
| $V_1$ | 16.448 | 9.115 | 6.207 | 658712 | 40047 | 72267 | 106131 |
| $V_2$ | 10.995 | 7.094 | 5.188 | 658712 | 59910 | 92859 | 126963 |
| Total | 16.194 | 9.584 | 6.662 | 7904544 | 488103 | 824771 | 1186469 |

**Table A.76:** Compression factors obtained for the data sets of 'Mixing Pipe' by applying the weighted tree predictor. Gradient-based optimization was utilized in combination with the variable 'Velocity Component W'. Sizes of the un-/compressed data sets are also listed.

| | Compression factor | | | Orig. size | Compressed size | | |
| | 1e-03 | 1e-04 | 1e-05 | | 1e-03 | 1e-04 | 1e-05 |
|---|---|---|---|---|---|---|---|
| $H_s$ | 20.925 | 11.321 | 7.623 | 658712 | 31479 | 58183 | 86412 |
| $\rho$ | 21.696 | 11.567 | 7.647 | 658712 | 30361 | 56947 | 86137 |
| $\epsilon$ | 17.780 | 10.258 | 6.790 | 658712 | 37048 | 64217 | 97019 |
| $H$ | 20.925 | 11.321 | 7.623 | 658712 | 31479 | 58183 | 86412 |
| $P$ | 11.868 | 7.456 | 5.377 | 658712 | 55501 | 88343 | 122495 |
| $T$ | 20.925 | 11.321 | 7.623 | 658712 | 31479 | 58183 | 86412 |
| Pt | 970.121 | 113.064 | 37.772 | 658712 | 679 | 5826 | 17439 |
| TKE | 13.699 | 8.270 | 5.800 | 658712 | 48086 | 79651 | 113575 |
| TVis | 10.425 | 6.807 | 5.033 | 658712 | 63183 | 96767 | 130879 |
| $V_0$ | 10.461 | 6.810 | 5.032 | 658712 | 62967 | 96731 | 130907 |
| $V_1$ | 11.515 | 7.322 | 5.310 | 658712 | 57207 | 89963 | 124059 |
| $V_2$ | 15.072 | 8.647 | 5.981 | 658712 | 43704 | 76175 | 110127 |
| Total | 16.028 | 9.533 | 6.632 | 7904544 | 493173 | 829169 | 1191873 |

## A.3.4 Full Weighting

**Table A.77:** Compression factors and sizes of compressed data vectors obtained for 'Wind Tunnel I' by using full optimization

| | Compression factor | | | Orig. size | Compressed size | | |
|---|---|---|---|---|---|---|---|
| | 1e-03 | 1e-04 | 1e-05 | | 1e-03 | 1e-04 | 1e-05 |
| $\rho$ | 12411.957 | 786.977 | 195.682 | 302107040 | 24340 | 383883 | 1543865 |
| $P$ | 55.374 | 22.445 | 11.661 | 302107040 | 5455716 | 13459723 | 25907726 |
| $T$ | 118.435 | 46.538 | 22.420 | 302107040 | 2550835 | 6491556 | 13474653 |
| $V_0$ | 26.175 | 13.159 | 8.243 | 302107040 | 11541975 | 22957630 | 36648281 |
| $V_1$ | 30.851 | 14.977 | 8.983 | 302107040 | 9792355 | 20172041 | 33629850 |
| $V_2$ | 26.048 | 13.680 | 8.477 | 302107040 | 11598312 | 22083557 | 35639345 |
| $V_0$ L | 20.753 | 13.431 | 8.480 | 302107040 | 14557217 | 22494017 | 35625931 |
| $V_1$ L | 56.210 | 22.447 | 10.885 | 302107040 | 5374614 | 13458399 | 27753200 |
| $V_2$ L | 26.706 | 22.467 | 13.440 | 302107040 | 11312135 | 13446925 | 22478918 |
| $V_0$ vl | 56.851 | 23.261 | 12.415 | 302107040 | 5314024 | 12987815 | 24334184 |
| $V_1$ vl | 25.667 | 11.971 | 7.420 | 302107040 | 11770201 | 25236341 | 40716909 |
| $V_2$ vl | 29.348 | 12.313 | 7.669 | 302107040 | 10294026 | 24534798 | 39393801 |
| $V_0$ vr | 54.937 | 23.078 | 12.416 | 302107040 | 5499118 | 13090708 | 24331637 |
| $V_1$ vr | 23.422 | 10.829 | 7.009 | 302107040 | 12898458 | 27896734 | 43101513 |
| $V_2$ vr | 29.335 | 12.310 | 7.669 | 302107040 | 10298471 | 24542324 | 39393231 |
| $V_0$ hl | 57.587 | 23.193 | 12.434 | 302107040 | 5246101 | 13025558 | 24297091 |
| $V_1$ hl | 27.945 | 13.435 | 7.943 | 302107040 | 10810754 | 22487352 | 38034705 |
| $V_2$ hl | 27.822 | 11.969 | 7.601 | 302107040 | 10858731 | 25240773 | 39744670 |
| $V_0$ hr | 56.222 | 23.252 | 12.405 | 302107040 | 5373487 | 12992992 | 24352774 |
| $V_1$ hr | 25.164 | 11.653 | 7.210 | 302107040 | 12005594 | 25926133 | 41902877 |
| $V_2$ hr | 27.852 | 11.970 | 7.600 | 302107040 | 10846873 | 25237811 | 39751317 |
| Total | 34.588 | 16.345 | 9.730 | 6344247840 | 183423337 | 388147070 | 652056478 |

**Table A.78:** Compression factors and sizes of compressed data vectors obtained for 'Wind Tunnel II' by using full optimization

| | Compression factor | | | Orig. size | Compressed size | | |
|---|---|---|---|---|---|---|---|
| | 1e-03 | 1e-04 | 1e-05 | | 1e-03 | 1e-04 | 1e-05 |
| $P$ | 46.663 | 19.007 | 10.501 | 151642096 | 3249737 | 7978157 | 14440145 |
| $V_0$ | 34.401 | 15.733 | 9.233 | 151642096 | 4408069 | 9638273 | 16424355 |
| $V_1$ | 35.919 | 15.992 | 9.388 | 151642096 | 4221768 | 9482117 | 16152322 |
| $V_2$ | 40.047 | 18.205 | 10.477 | 151642096 | 3786564 | 8329696 | 14474309 |
| Total | 38.718 | 17.121 | 9.864 | 606568384 | 15666138 | 35428243 | 61491131 |

**Table A.79:** Compression factors and sizes of compressed data vectors obtained for 'Car Venting System' by using full optimization

| | Compression factor | | | Orig. size | Compressed size | | |
|---|---|---|---|---|---|---|---|
| | 1e-03 | 1e-04 | 1e-05 | | 1e-03 | 1e-04 | 1e-05 |
| $\epsilon$ | 16.346 | 8.276 | 5.045 | 1620472 | 121747 | 227669 | 358829 |
| $P$ | 15.655 | 9.366 | 6.559 | 3240944 | 144369 | 272977 | 414316 |
| Pt | 353.159 | 65.703 | 28.165 | 3240944 | 4472 | 34216 | 84075 |
| TKE | 7.980 | 4.734 | 3.294 | 1620472 | 239180 | 386820 | 540166 |
| TVis | 8.316 | 4.587 | 3.113 | 1620472 | 275989 | 440808 | 609236 |
| $V_0$ | 6.219 | 3.953 | 2.823 | 1620472 | 281872 | 436360 | 601712 |
| $V_1$ | 5.853 | 3.720 | 2.689 | 1620472 | 288795 | 449084 | 614968 |
| $V_2$ | 7.198 | 4.231 | 2.947 | 1620472 | 284027 | 443788 | 610612 |
| Total | 9.878 | 6.020 | 4.227 | 16204720 | 1640451 | 2691722 | 3833914 |

**Table A.80:** Compression factors and sizes of compressed data vectors obtained for 'Mixing Chamber I' by using full optimization

|  | Compression factor | | | Orig. size | Compressed size | | |
|  | 1e-03 | 1e-04 | 1e-05 |  | 1e-03 | 1e-04 | 1e-05 |
|---|---|---|---|---|---|---|---|
| $\rho$ | 57.001 | 23.398 | 11.402 | 7451808 | 130731 | 318482 | 653581 |
| $w_{iso}$ | 27.526 | 12.326 | 7.543 | 7451808 | 270720 | 604536 | 987881 |
| $w_{pol}$ | 27.396 | 12.307 | 7.542 | 7451808 | 272004 | 605496 | 988017 |
| $c_{iso}$ | 27.990 | 12.496 | 7.609 | 7451808 | 266231 | 596340 | 979318 |
| $c_{pol}$ | 27.872 | 12.475 | 7.608 | 7451808 | 267359 | 597316 | 979470 |
| $P$ | 34.779 | 14.965 | 8.578 | 7451808 | 214259 | 497951 | 868702 |
| $P_s$ | 34.774 | 14.965 | 8.578 | 7451808 | 214293 | 497945 | 868682 |
| TVis | 22.988 | 11.859 | 7.548 | 7451808 | 324155 | 628359 | 987233 |
| $V_0$ | 17.488 | 9.485 | 6.367 | 7451808 | 426112 | 785607 | 1170338 |
| $V_1$ | 17.192 | 9.376 | 6.315 | 7451808 | 433437 | 794802 | 1180078 |
| $V_2$ | 18.250 | 9.765 | 6.498 | 7451808 | 408316 | 763130 | 1146757 |
| Total | 25.396 | 12.253 | 7.583 | 81969888 | 3227617 | 6689964 | 10810057 |

**Table A.81:** Compression factors and sizes of compressed data vectors obtained for 'Mixing Chamber II' by using full optimization

|  | Compression factor | | | Orig. size | Compressed size | | |
|  | 1e-03 | 1e-04 | 1e-05 |  | 1e-03 | 1e-04 | 1e-05 |
|---|---|---|---|---|---|---|---|
| $\rho$ | 13.056 | 7.869 | 5.610 | 14328232 | 1097479 | 1820772 | 2554027 |
| $P$ | 52.722 | 20.587 | 10.618 | 14328232 | 271772 | 695969 | 1349382 |
| $V_0$ | 16.896 | 9.185 | 6.224 | 14328232 | 848001 | 1559905 | 2301965 |
| $V_1$ | 16.917 | 9.177 | 6.219 | 14328232 | 846971 | 1561357 | 2303901 |
| $V_2$ | 17.375 | 9.413 | 6.334 | 14328232 | 824665 | 1522126 | 2262193 |
| Total | 18.422 | 10.006 | 6.651 | 71641160 | 3888888 | 7160129 | 10771468 |

**Table A.82:** Compression factors and sizes of compressed data vectors obtained for 'Mixing Pipe' by using full optimization

|  | Compression factor | | | Orig. size | Compressed size | | |
|  | 1e-03 | 1e-04 | 1e-05 |  | 1e-03 | 1e-04 | 1e-05 |
|---|---|---|---|---|---|---|---|
| $H_s$ | 26.240 | 13.053 | 8.377 | 658712 | 25103 | 50465 | 78631 |
| $\rho$ | 27.955 | 13.385 | 8.414 | 658712 | 23563 | 49213 | 78285 |
| $\epsilon$ | 20.886 | 11.445 | 7.351 | 658712 | 31538 | 57557 | 89607 |
| $H$ | 26.240 | 13.053 | 8.377 | 658712 | 25103 | 50465 | 78631 |
| $P$ | 15.557 | 8.839 | 6.069 | 658712 | 42341 | 74527 | 108539 |
| $T$ | 26.240 | 13.053 | 8.377 | 658712 | 25103 | 50465 | 78631 |
| Pt | 2271.421 | 176.598 | 51.684 | 658712 | 290 | 3730 | 12745 |
| TKE | 15.697 | 9.033 | 6.173 | 658712 | 41963 | 72919 | 106711 |
| TVis | 11.440 | 7.225 | 5.258 | 658712 | 57579 | 91167 | 125283 |
| $V_0$ | 10.999 | 7.015 | 5.141 | 658712 | 59887 | 93899 | 128131 |
| $V_1$ | 12.360 | 7.655 | 5.484 | 658712 | 53296 | 86047 | 120111 |
| $V_2$ | 11.638 | 7.362 | 5.330 | 658712 | 56599 | 89479 | 1235955 |
| Total | 17.869 | 10.267 | 7.002 | 7904544 | 442365 | 769933 | 1128900 |

## A.3.5   Motion of Flow Weighting

**Table A.83:** Compression factors and sizes of compressed data vectors obtained for 'Wind Tunnel I' by using dynamics-based optimization. Smaller weights were assigned to higher velocity magnitudes.

| | Compression factor | | | Orig. size | Compressed size | | |
| --- | --- | --- | --- | --- | --- | --- | --- |
| | 1e-03 | 1e-04 | 1e-05 | | 1e-03 | 1e-04 | 1e-05 |
| $\rho$ | 10789.537 | 717.705 | 170.548 | 302107040 | 28000 | 420935 | 1771389 |
| $P$ | 48.043 | 20.658 | 11.304 | 302107040 | 6288293 | 14624142 | 26726129 |
| $T$ | 106.703 | 41.481 | 20.454 | 302107040 | 2831302 | 7283054 | 14770306 |
| $V_0$ | 21.551 | 11.870 | 7.617 | 302107040 | 14018364 | 25450982 | 39659652 |
| $V_1$ | 25.170 | 13.295 | 8.318 | 302107040 | 12002817 | 22723293 | 36318193 |
| $V_2$ | 22.619 | 12.351 | 7.841 | 302107040 | 13356200 | 24459670 | 38528412 |
| $V_0$ L | 46.639 | 19.680 | 10.409 | 302107040 | 6477588 | 15351133 | 29023700 |
| $V_1$ L | 59.434 | 25.426 | 13.722 | 302107040 | 5083101 | 11881908 | 22016435 |
| $V_2$ L | 44.564 | 19.832 | 11.228 | 302107040 | 6779138 | 15233098 | 26906863 |
| $V_0$ vl | 20.599 | 10.802 | 6.996 | 302107040 | 14665966 | 27967544 | 43185533 |
| $V_1$ vl | 23.889 | 11.287 | 7.241 | 302107040 | 12646289 | 26765918 | 41719777 |
| $V_2$ vl | 44.377 | 19.805 | 11.251 | 302107040 | 6807808 | 15253957 | 26852446 |
| $V_0$ vr | 20.025 | 10.044 | 6.641 | 302107040 | 15086177 | 30077752 | 45488489 |
| $V_1$ vr | 23.880 | 11.285 | 7.241 | 302107040 | 12651150 | 26770335 | 41721749 |
| $V_2$ vr | 44.470 | 19.753 | 11.230 | 302107040 | 6793479 | 15294333 | 26900701 |
| $V_0$ hl | 22.628 | 11.922 | 7.436 | 302107040 | 13350819 | 25341157 | 40630004 |
| $V_1$ hl | 22.948 | 11.099 | 7.187 | 302107040 | 13164724 | 27220168 | 42035569 |
| $V_2$ hl | 44.517 | 19.860 | 11.227 | 302107040 | 6786375 | 15211820 | 26909270 |
| $V_0$ hr | 21.142 | 10.779 | 6.828 | 302107040 | 14289164 | 28027080 | 44244049 |
| $V_1$ hr | 22.971 | 11.102 | 7.188 | 302107040 | 13151660 | 27212713 | 42028773 |
| $V_2$ hr | 22.828 | 12.472 | 7.955 | 302107040 | 13234157 | 24222214 | 37977300 |
| Total | 30.284 | 14.865 | 9.123 | 6344247840 | 209492571 | 426793206 | 695414739 |

**Table A.84:** Compression factors and sizes of compressed data vectors obtained for 'Wind Tunnel II' by using dynamics-based optimization. Smaller weights were assigned to higher velocity magnitudes.

| | Compression factor | | | Orig. size | Compressed size | | |
| --- | --- | --- | --- | --- | --- | --- | --- |
| | 1e-03 | 1e-04 | 1e-05 | | 1e-03 | 1e-04 | 1e-05 |
| $P$ | 33.770 | 15.441 | 9.101 | 151642096 | 4490443 | 9820701 | 16662401 |
| $V_0$ | 24.246 | 12.308 | 7.627 | 151642096 | 6254332 | 12320138 | 19883284 |
| $V_1$ | 31.936 | 15.795 | 9.463 | 151642096 | 4748316 | 9600575 | 16024347 |
| $V_2$ | 28.636 | 14.638 | 9.016 | 151642096 | 5295427 | 10359829 | 16819437 |
| Total | 29.178 | 14.407 | 8.742 | 606568384 | 20788518 | 42101243 | 69389469 |

**Table A.85:** Compression factors and sizes of compressed data vectors obtained for 'Car Venting System' by using dynamics-based optimization. Smaller weights were assigned to higher velocity magnitudes.

| | Compression factor | | | Orig. size | Compressed size | | |
| --- | --- | --- | --- | --- | --- | --- | --- |
| | 1e-03 | 1e-04 | 1e-05 | | 1e-03 | 1e-04 | 1e-05 |
| $\epsilon$ | 13.423 | 7.133 | 4.523 | 1620472 | 120726 | 227182 | 358301 |
| $P$ | 13.895 | 8.662 | 6.156 | 3240944 | 233251 | 374170 | 526456 |
| Pt | 264.610 | 54.208 | 22.755 | 3240944 | 12248 | 59787 | 142428 |
| TKE | 6.912 | 4.227 | 3.007 | 1620472 | 234453 | 383344 | 538975 |
| TVis | 6.176 | 3.797 | 2.724 | 1620472 | 262391 | 426800 | 594808 |
| $V_0$ | 5.598 | 3.619 | 2.632 | 1620472 | 289459 | 447776 | 615576 |
| $V_1$ | 5.640 | 3.612 | 2.632 | 1620472 | 287311 | 448595 | 615664 |
| $V_2$ | 5.365 | 3.490 | 2.567 | 1620472 | 302049 | 464264 | 631168 |
| Total | 9.303 | 5.722 | 4.028 | 16204720 | 1741888 | 2831918 | 4023376 |

**Table A.86:** Compression factors and sizes of compressed data vectors obtained for 'Mixing Chamber I' by using dynamics-based optimization. Smaller weights were assigned to higher velocity magnitudes.

| | Compression factor | | | Orig. size | Compressed size | | |
|---|---|---|---|---|---|---|---|
| | 1e-03 | 1e-04 | 1e-05 | | 1e-03 | 1e-04 | 1e-05 |
| $\rho$ | 35.560 | 16.186 | 9.055 | 7451808 | 209556 | 460393 | 822973 |
| $w_{iso}$ | 17.765 | 9.632 | 6.432 | 7451808 | 419460 | 773672 | 1158469 |
| $w_{pol}$ | 17.932 | 9.637 | 6.433 | 7451808 | 415548 | 773212 | 1158461 |
| $c_{iso}$ | 18.066 | 9.738 | 6.480 | 7451808 | 412475 | 765258 | 1149979 |
| $c_{pol}$ | 18.237 | 9.744 | 6.480 | 7451808 | 408615 | 764750 | 1149963 |
| $P$ | 28.078 | 13.777 | 8.249 | 7451808 | 265401 | 540879 | 903366 |
| $P_s$ | 28.084 | 13.779 | 8.249 | 7451808 | 265341 | 540807 | 903350 |
| TVis | 19.075 | 10.400 | 6.847 | 7451808 | 390668 | 716538 | 1088301 |
| $V_0$ | 13.358 | 7.978 | 5.645 | 7451808 | 557863 | 934075 | 1320106 |
| $V_1$ | 13.223 | 7.945 | 5.630 | 7451808 | 563550 | 937897 | 1323682 |
| $V_2$ | 13.904 | 8.155 | 5.731 | 7451808 | 535943 | 913716 | 1300233 |
| Total | 18.443 | 10.093 | 6.676 | 81969888 | 4444420 | 8121197 | 12278883 |

**Table A.87:** Compression factors and sizes of compressed data vectors obtained for 'Mixing Chamber II' by using dynamics-based optimization. Smaller weights were assigned to higher velocity magnitudes.

| | Compression factor | | | Orig. size | Compressed size | | |
|---|---|---|---|---|---|---|---|
| | 1e-03 | 1e-04 | 1e-05 | | 1e-03 | 1e-04 | 1e-05 |
| $\rho$ | 9.012 | 6.173 | 4.690 | 14328232 | 1589954 | 2321188 | 3055306 |
| $P$ | 45.839 | 19.415 | 10.359 | 14328232 | 312579 | 737993 | 1383131 |
| $V_0$ | 13.119 | 7.908 | 5.611 | 14328232 | 1092143 | 1811933 | 2553549 |
| $V_1$ | 13.616 | 8.065 | 5.688 | 14328232 | 1052317 | 1776677 | 2519181 |
| $V_2$ | 13.736 | 8.134 | 5.721 | 14328232 | 1043106 | 1761614 | 2504613 |
| Total | 14.075 | 8.519 | 5.962 | 71641160 | 5090099 | 8409405 | 12015780 |

**Table A.88:** Compression factors and sizes of compressed data vectors obtained for 'Mixing Pipe' by using dynamics-based optimization. Smaller weights were assigned to higher velocity magnitudes.

| | Compression factor | | | Orig. size | Compressed size | | |
|---|---|---|---|---|---|---|---|
| | 1e-03 | 1e-04 | 1e-05 | | 1e-03 | 1e-04 | 1e-05 |
| $H_s$ | 23.465 | 12.076 | 7.930 | 658712 | 28072 | 54545 | 83067 |
| $\rho$ | 22.848 | 12.228 | 7.948 | 658712 | 28830 | 53868 | 82874 |
| $\epsilon$ | 21.197 | 11.509 | 7.373 | 658712 | 31076 | 57233 | 89339 |
| $H$ | 23.465 | 12.076 | 7.930 | 658712 | 28072 | 54545 | 83067 |
| $P$ | 12.809 | 7.755 | 5.533 | 658712 | 51427 | 84939 | 119055 |
| $T$ | 23.465 | 12.076 | 7.930 | 658712 | 28072 | 54545 | 83067 |
| Pt | 1301.802 | 128.780 | 41.546 | 658712 | 506 | 5115 | 15855 |
| TKE | 15.894 | 9.031 | 6.154 | 658712 | 41445 | 72935 | 107043 |
| TVis | 11.482 | 7.217 | 5.252 | 658712 | 57367 | 91267 | 125423 |
| $V_0$ | 11.156 | 7.089 | 5.178 | 658712 | 59047 | 92923 | 127203 |
| $V_1$ | 13.123 | 7.937 | 5.629 | 658712 | 50194 | 82995 | 117019 |
| $V_2$ | 12.421 | 7.620 | 5.459 | 658712 | 53030 | 86443 | 120675 |
| Total | 17.291 | 9.989 | 6.852 | 7904544 | 457138 | 791353 | 1153687 |

## A.3.6 Motion of Flow Weighting Orthogonal

**Table A.89:** Compression factors and sizes of compressed data vectors obtained for 'Wind Tunnel I' by using dynamics-based optimization. Larger weights were assigned to higher velocity magnitudes.

| | Compression factor | | | Orig. size | Compressed size | | |
| --- | --- | --- | --- | --- | --- | --- | --- |
| | 1e-03 | 1e-04 | 1e-05 | | 1e-03 | 1e-04 | 1e-05 |
| $\rho$ | 10439.804 | 553.036 | 129.021 | 302107040 | 28938 | 546270 | 2341537 |
| $P$ | 57.534 | 23.843 | 12.276 | 302107040 | 5250938 | 12670916 | 24608742 |
| $T$ | 83.172 | 34.550 | 17.778 | 302107040 | 3632332 | 8744126 | 16993431 |
| $V_0$ | 19.029 | 10.999 | 7.302 | 302107040 | 15876518 | 27465834 | 41370938 |
| $V_1$ | 21.796 | 11.493 | 7.337 | 302107040 | 13860733 | 26285411 | 41173396 |
| $V_2$ | 20.779 | 11.164 | 7.172 | 302107040 | 14539053 | 27060553 | 42121460 |
| $V_0$ L | 16.604 | 9.533 | 6.557 | 302107040 | 18195154 | 31690781 | 46075922 |
| $V_1$ L | 30.819 | 13.729 | 8.585 | 302107040 | 9802780 | 22005081 | 35190342 |
| $V_2$ L | 26.350 | 12.892 | 8.272 | 302107040 | 11465161 | 23433267 | 36523021 |
| $V_0$ vl | 22.193 | 11.378 | 7.329 | 302107040 | 13612881 | 26551586 | 41218095 |
| $V_1$ vl | 20.761 | 11.177 | 7.187 | 302107040 | 14551984 | 27029221 | 42034642 |
| $V_2$ vl | 69.348 | 27.188 | 13.852 | 302107040 | 4356378 | 11111661 | 21808904 |
| $V_0$ vr | 21.876 | 11.226 | 7.188 | 302107040 | 13810107 | 26886821 | 42026546 |
| $V_1$ vr | 21.174 | 11.285 | 7.240 | 302107040 | 14267977 | 26770778 | 41728755 |
| $V_2$ vr | 69.748 | 27.333 | 13.930 | 302107040 | 4331384 | 11052652 | 21687425 |
| $V_0$ hl | 22.386 | 11.558 | 7.481 | 302107040 | 13495591 | 26139010 | 40381218 |
| $V_1$ hl | 21.361 | 11.479 | 7.334 | 302107040 | 14142971 | 26317381 | 41190095 |
| $V_2$ hl | 70.215 | 26.613 | 13.703 | 302107040 | 4302574 | 11351785 | 22046498 |
| $V_0$ hr | 22.097 | 11.358 | 7.283 | 302107040 | 13671989 | 26597746 | 41482082 |
| $V_1$ hr | 20.891 | 11.151 | 7.110 | 302107040 | 14460779 | 27091647 | 42489169 |
| $V_2$ hr | 68.017 | 25.649 | 13.218 | 302107040 | 4441648 | 11778533 | 22854976 |
| Total | 28.565 | 14.465 | 8.969 | 6344247840 | 222097870 | 438581060 | 707347194 |

**Table A.90:** Compression factors and sizes of compressed data vectors obtained for 'Wind Tunnel II' by using dynamics-based optimization. Larger weights were assigned to higher velocity magnitudes.

| | Compression factor | | | Orig. size | Compressed size | | |
| --- | --- | --- | --- | --- | --- | --- | --- |
| | 1e-03 | 1e-04 | 1e-05 | | 1e-03 | 1e-04 | 1e-05 |
| $P$ | 32.727 | 15.083 | 8.904 | 151642096 | 4633538 | 10053901 | 17029950 |
| $V_0$ | 24.162 | 12.396 | 7.669 | 151642096 | 6275997 | 12233176 | 19772537 |
| $V_1$ | 33.378 | 16.285 | 9.652 | 151642096 | 4543176 | 9311770 | 15711458 |
| $V_2$ | 30.408 | 15.211 | 9.221 | 151642096 | 4986933 | 9968972 | 16444584 |
| Total | 29.676 | 14.592 | 8.796 | 606568384 | 20439644 | 41567819 | 68958529 |

**Table A.91:** Compression factors and sizes of compressed data vectors obtained for 'Car Venting System' by using dynamics-based optimization. Larger weights were assigned to higher velocity magnitudes.

| | Compression factor | | | Orig. size | Compressed size | | |
| --- | --- | --- | --- | --- | --- | --- | --- |
| | 1e-03 | 1e-04 | 1e-05 | | 1e-03 | 1e-04 | 1e-05 |
| $\epsilon$ | 14.014 | 7.399 | 4.659 | 1620472 | 115632 | 219020 | 347822 |
| $P$ | 13.345 | 8.380 | 6.003 | 3240944 | 242853 | 386741 | 539907 |
| Pt | 222.944 | 52.277 | 22.072 | 3240944 | 14537 | 61996 | 146832 |
| TKE | 7.227 | 4.395 | 3.106 | 1620472 | 224225 | 368711 | 521661 |
| TVis | 6.752 | 4.014 | 2.833 | 1620472 | 239996 | 403668 | 571992 |
| $V_0$ | 5.766 | 3.730 | 2.695 | 1620472 | 281056 | 434417 | 601352 |
| $V_1$ | 5.529 | 3.565 | 2.607 | 1620472 | 293069 | 454598 | 621488 |
| $V_2$ | 5.508 | 3.561 | 2.605 | 1620472 | 294180 | 455020 | 621952 |
| Total | 9.501 | 5.820 | 4.079 | 16204720 | 1705548 | 2784171 | 3973006 |

**Table A.92:** Compression factors and sizes of compressed data vectors obtained for 'Mixing Chamber I' by using dynamics-based optimization. Larger weights were assigned to higher velocity magnitudes.

| | Compression factor | | | Orig. size | Compressed size | | |
|---|---|---|---|---|---|---|---|
| | 1e-03 | 1e-04 | 1e-05 | | 1e-03 | 1e-04 | 1e-05 |
| $\rho$ | 36.936 | 16.603 | 9.175 | 7451808 | 201750 | 448826 | 812151 |
| $w_{iso}$ | 18.255 | 9.770 | 6.493 | 7451808 | 408196 | 762728 | 1147649 |
| $w_{pol}$ | 18.404 | 9.780 | 6.494 | 7451808 | 404904 | 761936 | 1147561 |
| $c_{iso}$ | 18.564 | 9.878 | 6.542 | 7451808 | 401403 | 754408 | 1139094 |
| $c_{pol}$ | 18.722 | 9.889 | 6.542 | 7451808 | 398019 | 753524 | 1139006 |
| $P$ | 26.872 | 13.195 | 7.971 | 7451808 | 277305 | 564765 | 934874 |
| $P_s$ | 26.880 | 13.196 | 7.971 | 7451808 | 277230 | 564685 | 934850 |
| TVis | 19.110 | 10.432 | 6.882 | 7451808 | 389947 | 714330 | 1082732 |
| $V_0$ | 13.684 | 8.141 | 5.729 | 7451808 | 544572 | 915361 | 1300762 |
| $V_1$ | 13.584 | 8.091 | 5.703 | 7451808 | 548587 | 920982 | 1306682 |
| $V_2$ | 14.447 | 8.394 | 5.852 | 7451808 | 515820 | 887718 | 1273457 |
| Total | 18.767 | 10.184 | 6.708 | 81969888 | 4367733 | 8049263 | 12218818 |

**Table A.93:** Compression factors and sizes of compressed data vectors obtained for 'Mixing Chamber II' by using dynamics-based optimization. Larger weights were assigned to higher velocity magnitudes.

| | Compression factor | | | Orig. size | Compressed size | | |
|---|---|---|---|---|---|---|---|
| | 1e-03 | 1e-04 | 1e-05 | | 1e-03 | 1e-04 | 1e-05 |
| $\rho$ | 9.543 | 6.426 | 4.836 | 14328232 | 1501481 | 2229679 | 2962881 |
| $P$ | 43.708 | 18.791 | 10.044 | 14328232 | 327818 | 762488 | 1426547 |
| $V_0$ | 13.864 | 8.201 | 5.759 | 14328232 | 1033498 | 1747177 | 2488117 |
| $V_1$ | 14.312 | 8.337 | 5.822 | 14328232 | 1001116 | 1718677 | 2460941 |
| $V_2$ | 14.556 | 8.449 | 5.878 | 14328232 | 984339 | 1695825 | 2437617 |
| Total | 14.777 | 8.786 | 6.084 | 71641160 | 4848252 | 8153846 | 11776103 |

**Table A.94:** Compression factors and sizes of compressed data vectors obtained for 'Mixing Pipe' by using dynamics-based optimization. Larger weights were assigned to higher velocity magnitudes.

| | Compression factor | | | Orig. size | Compressed size | | |
|---|---|---|---|---|---|---|---|
| | 1e-03 | 1e-04 | 1e-05 | | 1e-03 | 1e-04 | 1e-05 |
| $H_s$ | 22.901 | 12.030 | 7.919 | 658712 | 28764 | 54754 | 83177 |
| $\rho$ | 23.521 | 12.162 | 7.909 | 658712 | 28005 | 54162 | 83287 |
| $\epsilon$ | 23.543 | 12.108 | 7.593 | 658712 | 27979 | 54404 | 86755 |
| $H$ | 22.901 | 12.030 | 7.919 | 658712 | 28764 | 54754 | 83177 |
| $P$ | 11.368 | 7.204 | 5.247 | 658712 | 57943 | 91443 | 125543 |
| $T$ | 22.901 | 12.030 | 7.919 | 658712 | 28764 | 54754 | 83177 |
| Pt | 763.282 | 104.641 | 34.919 | 658712 | 863 | 6295 | 18864 |
| TKE | 17.076 | 9.443 | 6.350 | 658712 | 38575 | 69759 | 103735 |
| TVis | 12.256 | 7.515 | 5.407 | 658712 | 53747 | 87651 | 121831 |
| $V_0$ | 11.420 | 7.195 | 5.237 | 658712 | 57683 | 91551 | 125783 |
| $V_1$ | 11.316 | 7.214 | 5.258 | 658712 | 58210 | 91307 | 125271 |
| $V_2$ | 10.590 | 6.886 | 5.070 | 658712 | 62202 | 95663 | 129915 |
| Total | 16.765 | 9.801 | 6.753 | 7904544 | 471499 | 806497 | 1170515 |

## A.4 Compression Factors Wavelet Compression

### A.4.1 Graph Laplace Operator

*Wind Tunnel I*

**Table A.95:** Compression factors obtained for the data sets of 'Wind Tunnel I' by applying the wavelet compression. The graph Laplace operator was used in combination with a coarsening threshold of 0.125. Sizes of the un-/compressed data sets are also listed.

| | Compression factor | | | Orig. size | Compressed size | | |
| | 1e-03 | 1e-04 | 1e-05 | | 1e-03 | 1e-04 | 1e-05 |
|---|---|---|---|---|---|---|---|
| $\rho$ | 33.838 | 84.834 | 31.702 | 302107040 | 8928022 | 3561139 | 9529546 |
| $P$ | 29.891 | 19.807 | 12.879 | 302107040 | 10106997 | 15252225 | 23457922 |
| $T$ | 31.815 | 28.699 | 15.868 | 302107040 | 9495722 | 10526781 | 19038670 |
| $V_0$ | 18.030 | 11.426 | 8.001 | 302107040 | 16755780 | 26440251 | 37759862 |
| $V_1$ | 19.933 | 12.883 | 8.720 | 302107040 | 15155766 | 23450222 | 34644081 |
| $V_2$ | 18.763 | 12.310 | 8.415 | 302107040 | 16101356 | 24541108 | 35900351 |
| $V_0$ L | 17.155 | 10.579 | 7.333 | 302107040 | 17610809 | 28557746 | 41199607 |
| $V_1$ L | 25.420 | 16.156 | 10.172 | 302107040 | 11884812 | 18698909 | 29700741 |
| $V_2$ L | 22.972 | 14.097 | 9.085 | 302107040 | 13151010 | 21430898 | 33254336 |
| $V_0$ vl | 24.169 | 13.847 | 8.945 | 302107040 | 12499645 | 21817534 | 33773056 |
| $V_1$ vl | 19.240 | 12.589 | 8.448 | 302107040 | 15701808 | 23997309 | 35760272 |
| $V_2$ vl | 26.839 | 17.434 | 10.826 | 302107040 | 11256222 | 17328385 | 27905241 |
| $V_0$ vr | 23.784 | 13.788 | 8.943 | 302107040 | 12701914 | 21911496 | 33780648 |
| $V_1$ vr | 18.942 | 12.425 | 8.317 | 302107040 | 15948866 | 24314122 | 36322835 |
| $V_2$ vr | 26.839 | 17.437 | 10.821 | 302107040 | 11256186 | 17325244 | 27919150 |
| $V_0$ hl | 24.336 | 13.934 | 8.956 | 302107040 | 12413823 | 21680781 | 33732093 |
| $V_1$ hl | 19.657 | 12.805 | 8.622 | 302107040 | 15368567 | 23592045 | 35037690 |
| $V_2$ hl | 27.446 | 16.994 | 10.574 | 302107040 | 11007381 | 17777384 | 28569561 |
| $V_0$ hr | 24.060 | 13.872 | 8.944 | 302107040 | 12556581 | 21778376 | 33779084 |
| $V_1$ hr | 19.201 | 12.579 | 8.426 | 302107040 | 15734042 | 24017131 | 35854781 |
| $V_2$ hr | 27.411 | 16.987 | 10.592 | 302107040 | 11021415 | 17784392 | 28522781 |
| Total | 22.932 | 14.900 | 9.679 | 6344247840 | 276656724 | 425783478 | 655442308 |

**Table A.96:** Compression factors obtained for the data sets of 'Wind Tunnel I' by applying the wavelet compression. The graph Laplace operator was used in combination with a coarsening threshold of 0.25. Sizes of the un-/compressed data sets are also listed.

| | Compression factor | | | Orig. size | Compressed size | | |
| | 1e-03 | 1e-04 | 1e-05 | | 1e-03 | 1e-04 | 1e-05 |
|---|---|---|---|---|---|---|---|
| $\rho$ | 34.123 | 87.329 | 31.867 | 302107040 | 8853533 | 3459423 | 9480195 |
| $P$ | 29.715 | 19.750 | 12.917 | 302107040 | 10166883 | 15296330 | 23388251 |
| $T$ | 32.023 | 28.675 | 15.860 | 302107040 | 9433929 | 10535737 | 19047906 |
| $V_0$ | 18.026 | 11.455 | 8.037 | 302107040 | 16759801 | 26374122 | 37591415 |
| $V_1$ | 19.862 | 12.917 | 8.784 | 302107040 | 15210404 | 23389055 | 34394384 |
| $V_2$ | 18.687 | 12.334 | 8.474 | 302107040 | 16166573 | 24493581 | 35649227 |
| $V_0$ L | 17.223 | 10.710 | 7.441 | 302107040 | 17540816 | 28207039 | 40602343 |
| $V_1$ L | 25.546 | 16.527 | 10.471 | 302107040 | 11826170 | 18279233 | 28850524 |
| $V_2$ L | 23.119 | 14.411 | 9.321 | 302107040 | 13067577 | 20963609 | 32410266 |
| $V_0$ vl | 24.193 | 14.106 | 9.166 | 302107040 | 12487160 | 21416859 | 32959013 |
| $V_1$ vl | 19.181 | 12.659 | 8.542 | 302107040 | 15750469 | 23865641 | 35366051 |
| $V_2$ vl | 26.841 | 17.733 | 11.120 | 302107040 | 11255249 | 17036872 | 27168141 |
| $V_0$ vr | 23.798 | 14.038 | 9.159 | 302107040 | 12694535 | 21520381 | 32985657 |
| $V_1$ vr | 18.890 | 12.503 | 8.422 | 302107040 | 15993224 | 24162153 | 35871247 |
| $V_2$ vr | 26.846 | 17.736 | 11.113 | 302107040 | 11253386 | 17033879 | 27184375 |
| $V_0$ hl | 24.352 | 14.194 | 9.179 | 302107040 | 12405624 | 21283440 | 32911415 |
| $V_1$ hl | 19.602 | 12.852 | 8.699 | 302107040 | 15411815 | 23507449 | 34728321 |
| $V_2$ hl | 27.627 | 17.295 | 10.854 | 302107040 | 10935394 | 17467386 | 27832998 |
| $V_0$ hr | 24.077 | 14.133 | 9.163 | 302107040 | 12547524 | 21375389 | 32970700 |
| $V_1$ hr | 19.143 | 12.636 | 8.517 | 302107040 | 15781796 | 23908239 | 35469116 |
| $V_2$ hr | 27.586 | 17.285 | 10.870 | 302107040 | 10951659 | 17478287 | 27792969 |
| Total | 22.945 | 15.068 | 9.841 | 6344247840 | 276493521 | 421054104 | 644654514 |

**Table A.97:** Compression factors obtained for the data sets of 'Wind Tunnel I' by applying the wavelet compression. The graph Laplace operator was used in combination with a coarsening threshold of 0.375. Sizes of the un-/compressed data sets are also listed.

| | Compression factor | | | Orig. size | Compressed size | | |
| | 1e-03 | 1e-04 | 1e-05 | | 1e-03 | 1e-04 | 1e-05 |
|---|---|---|---|---|---|---|---|
| $\rho$ | 34.142 | 87.208 | 31.905 | 302107040 | 8848598 | 3464223 | 9468933 |
| $P$ | 29.682 | 19.687 | 12.899 | 302107040 | 10178210 | 15345742 | 23420262 |
| $T$ | 32.092 | 28.572 | 15.784 | 302107040 | 9413831 | 10573516 | 19140619 |
| $V_0$ | 17.950 | 11.415 | 8.021 | 302107040 | 16830084 | 26465800 | 37664780 |
| $V_1$ | 19.812 | 12.869 | 8.766 | 302107040 | 15248874 | 23476442 | 34463829 |
| $V_2$ | 18.655 | 12.303 | 8.458 | 302107040 | 16194818 | 24556509 | 35718607 |
| $V_0$ L | 17.075 | 10.650 | 7.413 | 302107040 | 17693126 | 28367839 | 40752145 |
| $V_1$ L | 25.286 | 16.283 | 10.362 | 302107040 | 11947809 | 18553766 | 29154460 |
| $V_2$ L | 22.892 | 14.264 | 9.273 | 302107040 | 13196830 | 21180086 | 32579121 |
| $V_0$ vl | 24.006 | 13.935 | 9.080 | 302107040 | 12584909 | 21679730 | 33273348 |
| $V_1$ vl | 19.109 | 12.591 | 8.508 | 302107040 | 15809263 | 23993383 | 35509776 |
| $V_2$ vl | 26.785 | 17.603 | 11.057 | 302107040 | 11279106 | 17162644 | 27322379 |
| $V_0$ vr | 23.634 | 13.878 | 9.078 | 302107040 | 12782673 | 21768634 | 33279957 |
| $V_1$ vr | 18.836 | 12.451 | 8.397 | 302107040 | 16038903 | 24262938 | 35979167 |
| $V_2$ vr | 26.787 | 17.607 | 11.051 | 302107040 | 11277980 | 17158570 | 27336659 |
| $V_0$ hl | 24.165 | 14.018 | 9.092 | 302107040 | 12501664 | 21550769 | 33228177 |
| $V_1$ hl | 19.545 | 12.795 | 8.674 | 302107040 | 15456663 | 23611760 | 34828789 |
| $V_2$ hl | 27.556 | 17.166 | 10.800 | 302107040 | 10963199 | 17599199 | 27973598 |
| $V_0$ hr | 23.908 | 13.963 | 9.079 | 302107040 | 12636142 | 21636421 | 33276548 |
| $V_1$ hr | 19.085 | 12.584 | 8.491 | 302107040 | 15829239 | 24007453 | 35580000 |
| $V_2$ hr | 27.523 | 17.155 | 10.817 | 302107040 | 10976507 | 17610639 | 27928203 |
| Total | 22.847 | 14.962 | 9.792 | 6344247840 | 277688428 | 424026063 | 647879357 |

**Table A.98:** Compression factors obtained for the data sets of 'Wind Tunnel I' by applying the wavelet compression. The graph Laplace operator was used in combination with a coarsening threshold of 0.5. Sizes of the un-/compressed data sets are also listed.

| | Compression factor | | | Orig. size | Compressed size | | |
| | 1e-03 | 1e-04 | 1e-05 | | 1e-03 | 1e-04 | 1e-05 |
|---|---|---|---|---|---|---|---|
| $\rho$ | 34.329 | 87.230 | 31.942 | 302107040 | 8800462 | 3463319 | 9457841 |
| $P$ | 29.542 | 19.774 | 13.276 | 302107040 | 10226447 | 15277941 | 22755712 |
| $T$ | 32.085 | 28.591 | 15.825 | 302107040 | 9415782 | 10566455 | 19090648 |
| $V_0$ | 18.042 | 11.593 | 8.262 | 302107040 | 16744660 | 26059310 | 36564685 |
| $V_1$ | 19.831 | 13.094 | 9.098 | 302107040 | 15233761 | 23071595 | 33205816 |
| $V_2$ | 18.667 | 12.521 | 8.781 | 302107040 | 16184326 | 24127945 | 34405426 |
| $V_0$ L | 17.509 | 11.220 | 7.941 | 302107040 | 17254139 | 26924792 | 38044010 |
| $V_1$ L | 25.777 | 17.539 | 11.568 | 302107040 | 11720193 | 17225056 | 26116622 |
| $V_2$ L | 23.693 | 15.489 | 10.320 | 302107040 | 12751089 | 19504444 | 29273500 |
| $V_0$ vl | 24.338 | 14.748 | 9.902 | 302107040 | 12412951 | 20485148 | 30510991 |
| $V_1$ vl | 19.107 | 12.898 | 8.927 | 302107040 | 15811182 | 23423312 | 33840162 |
| $V_2$ vl | 27.008 | 18.435 | 12.073 | 302107040 | 11185714 | 16387879 | 25023308 |
| $V_0$ vr | 23.933 | 14.668 | 9.893 | 302107040 | 12623192 | 20595975 | 30538430 |
| $V_1$ vr | 18.832 | 12.755 | 8.838 | 302107040 | 16042553 | 23685403 | 34181814 |
| $V_2$ vr | 27.010 | 18.439 | 12.065 | 302107040 | 11184844 | 16383811 | 25040563 |
| $V_0$ hl | 24.497 | 14.812 | 9.916 | 302107040 | 12332380 | 20395657 | 30465345 |
| $V_1$ hl | 19.538 | 13.036 | 9.033 | 302107040 | 15462331 | 23175670 | 33444319 |
| $V_2$ hl | 28.469 | 17.988 | 11.800 | 302107040 | 10611807 | 16794670 | 25602320 |
| $V_0$ hr | 24.223 | 14.790 | 9.895 | 302107040 | 12472101 | 20426532 | 30532676 |
| $V_1$ hr | 19.111 | 12.873 | 8.926 | 302107040 | 15808093 | 23467704 | 33845781 |
| $V_2$ hr | 28.404 | 17.980 | 11.819 | 302107040 | 10636189 | 16802162 | 25561061 |
| Total | 23.077 | 15.540 | 10.443 | 6344247840 | 274914196 | 408244780 | 607501030 |

**Table A.99:** Compression factors obtained for the data sets of 'Wind Tunnel I' by applying the wavelet compression. The graph Laplace operator was used in combination with a coarsening threshold of 0.625. Sizes of the un-/compressed data sets are also listed.

| | Compression factor | | | Orig. size | Compressed size | | |
| | 1e-03 | 1e-04 | 1e-05 | | 1e-03 | 1e-04 | 1e-05 |
|---|---|---|---|---|---|---|---|
| $\rho$ | 34.387 | 87.412 | 31.976 | 302107040 | 8785525 | 3456127 | 9447962 |
| $P$ | 28.997 | 19.567 | 13.209 | 302107040 | 10418660 | 15439408 | 22871812 |
| $T$ | 31.749 | 28.540 | 15.759 | 302107040 | 9515551 | 10585364 | 19170657 |
| $V_0$ | 17.944 | 11.558 | 8.250 | 302107040 | 16836064 | 26138108 | 36617346 |
| $V_1$ | 19.591 | 12.986 | 9.061 | 302107040 | 15420667 | 23264899 | 33341785 |
| $V_2$ | 18.497 | 12.442 | 8.761 | 302107040 | 16332632 | 24280755 | 34485043 |
| $V_0$ L | 17.499 | 11.238 | 7.982 | 302107040 | 17264706 | 26882368 | 37846372 |
| $V_1$ L | 26.009 | 17.661 | 11.734 | 302107040 | 11615658 | 17105673 | 25746415 |
| $V_2$ L | 23.745 | 15.568 | 10.419 | 302107040 | 12723114 | 19405740 | 28994399 |
| $V_0$ vl | 23.968 | 14.721 | 9.968 | 302107040 | 12604582 | 20521944 | 30307578 |
| $V_1$ vl | 19.038 | 12.857 | 8.934 | 302107040 | 15868529 | 23498076 | 33813604 |
| $V_2$ vl | 27.335 | 18.697 | 12.329 | 302107040 | 11052206 | 16158453 | 24504276 |
| $V_0$ vr | 23.585 | 14.654 | 9.953 | 302107040 | 12809523 | 20616547 | 30354024 |
| $V_1$ vr | 18.602 | 12.702 | 8.865 | 302107040 | 16240608 | 23784970 | 34079124 |
| $V_2$ vr | 27.346 | 18.706 | 12.322 | 302107040 | 11047480 | 16150147 | 24517281 |
| $V_0$ hl | 24.129 | 14.795 | 9.987 | 302107040 | 12520736 | 20419648 | 30249777 |
| $V_1$ hl | 19.371 | 12.958 | 9.017 | 302107040 | 15595500 | 23313888 | 33504185 |
| $V_2$ hl | 28.546 | 18.235 | 12.046 | 302107040 | 10583138 | 16567197 | 25080047 |
| $V_0$ hr | 23.862 | 14.762 | 9.960 | 302107040 | 12660437 | 20465428 | 30330899 |
| $V_1$ hr | 18.897 | 12.799 | 8.935 | 302107040 | 15987022 | 23604159 | 33811641 |
| $V_2$ hr | 28.426 | 18.202 | 12.056 | 302107040 | 10627770 | 16597791 | 25058293 |
| Total | 22.944 | 15.540 | 10.501 | 6344247840 | 276510108 | 408256690 | 604132520 |

**Table A.100:** Compression factors obtained for the data sets of 'Wind Tunnel I' by applying the wavelet compression. The graph Laplace operator was used in combination with a coarsening threshold of 0.75. Sizes of the un-/compressed data sets are also listed.

| | Compression factor | | | Orig. size | Compressed size | | |
| | 1e-03 | 1e-04 | 1e-05 | | 1e-03 | 1e-04 | 1e-05 |
|---|---|---|---|---|---|---|---|
| $\rho$ | 33.048 | 79.185 | 30.876 | 302107040 | 9141422 | 3815218 | 9784393 |
| $P$ | 28.880 | 19.441 | 13.067 | 302107040 | 10460765 | 15540012 | 23119728 |
| $T$ | 30.713 | 27.704 | 15.571 | 302107040 | 9836491 | 10904917 | 19402108 |
| $V_0$ | 17.714 | 11.465 | 8.177 | 302107040 | 17054990 | 26350120 | 36946469 |
| $V_1$ | 19.473 | 12.881 | 8.980 | 302107040 | 15514098 | 23453756 | 33643209 |
| $V_2$ | 18.376 | 12.348 | 8.669 | 302107040 | 16440139 | 24465331 | 34850898 |
| $V_0$ L | 17.272 | 11.093 | 7.879 | 302107040 | 17490712 | 27234634 | 38342415 |
| $V_1$ L | 25.647 | 17.258 | 11.478 | 302107040 | 11779294 | 17505171 | 26320425 |
| $V_2$ L | 23.414 | 15.269 | 10.227 | 302107040 | 12902836 | 19785035 | 29540720 |
| $V_0$ vl | 23.749 | 14.462 | 9.789 | 302107040 | 12720623 | 20889842 | 30861423 |
| $V_1$ vl | 18.912 | 12.724 | 8.833 | 302107040 | 15974657 | 23743622 | 34202452 |
| $V_2$ vl | 27.023 | 18.279 | 12.033 | 302107040 | 11179715 | 16527955 | 25106049 |
| $V_0$ vr | 23.365 | 14.396 | 9.775 | 302107040 | 12929807 | 20986171 | 30904557 |
| $V_1$ vr | 18.503 | 12.564 | 8.758 | 302107040 | 16327674 | 24045277 | 34494768 |
| $V_2$ vr | 27.031 | 18.280 | 12.022 | 302107040 | 11176176 | 16526824 | 25129454 |
| $V_0$ hl | 23.909 | 14.534 | 9.804 | 302107040 | 12635739 | 20786702 | 30813252 |
| $V_1$ hl | 19.248 | 12.843 | 8.926 | 302107040 | 15695320 | 23523889 | 33845243 |
| $V_2$ hl | 27.986 | 17.834 | 11.757 | 302107040 | 10794777 | 16940261 | 25695022 |
| $V_0$ hr | 23.648 | 14.501 | 9.782 | 302107040 | 12775273 | 20833543 | 30884584 |
| $V_1$ hr | 18.784 | 12.665 | 8.833 | 302107040 | 16083502 | 23853012 | 34203881 |
| $V_2$ hr | 27.887 | 17.805 | 11.770 | 302107040 | 10833240 | 16967687 | 25667572 |
| Total | 22.678 | 15.299 | 10.337 | 6344247840 | 279747250 | 414678979 | 613758622 |

## Wind Tunnel II

**Table A.101:** Compression factors obtained for the data sets of 'Wind Tunnel II' by applying the wavelet compression. The graph Laplace operator was used in combination with a coarsening threshold of 0.125. Sizes of the un-/compressed data sets are also listed.

| | Compression factor | | | Orig. size | Compressed size | | |
| | 1e-03 | 1e-04 | 1e-05 | | 1e-03 | 1e-04 | 1e-05 |
|---|---|---|---|---|---|---|---|
| $P$ | 25.741 | 18.154 | 11.667 | 151642096 | 5891097 | 8353068 | 12997585 |
| $V_0$ | 17.270 | 10.754 | 7.338 | 151642096 | 8780873 | 14101045 | 20664104 |
| $V_1$ | 25.045 | 15.461 | 9.680 | 151642096 | 6054788 | 9808170 | 15665986 |
| $V_2$ | 23.860 | 14.638 | 9.326 | 151642096 | 6355396 | 10359621 | 16259990 |
| Total | 22.397 | 14.231 | 9.248 | 606568384 | 27082154 | 42621904 | 65587665 |

**Table A.102:** Compression factors obtained for the data sets of 'Wind Tunnel II' by applying the wavelet compression. The graph Laplace operator was used in combination with a coarsening threshold of 0.25. Sizes of the un-/compressed data sets are also listed.

| | Compression factor | | | Orig. size | Compressed size | | |
| | 1e-03 | 1e-04 | 1e-05 | | 1e-03 | 1e-04 | 1e-05 |
|---|---|---|---|---|---|---|---|
| $P$ | 25.724 | 18.128 | 11.684 | 151642096 | 5894926 | 8364976 | 12978108 |
| $V_0$ | 17.311 | 10.801 | 7.370 | 151642096 | 8759747 | 14040065 | 20574358 |
| $V_1$ | 24.976 | 15.483 | 9.708 | 151642096 | 6071602 | 9793876 | 15620348 |
| $V_2$ | 23.811 | 14.664 | 9.357 | 151642096 | 6368563 | 10340876 | 16207041 |
| Total | 22.387 | 14.259 | 9.278 | 606568384 | 27094838 | 42539793 | 65379855 |

**Table A.103:** Compression factors obtained for the data sets of 'Wind Tunnel II' by applying the wavelet compression. The Laplace operator was used in combination with a coarsening threshold of 0.375. Sizes of the un-/compressed data sets are also listed.

| | Compression factor | | | Orig. size | Compressed size | | |
| | 1e-03 | 1e-04 | 1e-05 | | 1e-03 | 1e-04 | 1e-05 |
|---|---|---|---|---|---|---|---|
| $P$ | 25.683 | 17.974 | 11.554 | 151642096 | 5904315 | 8436804 | 13124909 |
| $V_0$ | 17.173 | 10.698 | 7.305 | 151642096 | 8830246 | 14174537 | 20758303 |
| $V_1$ | 24.809 | 15.322 | 9.611 | 151642096 | 6112501 | 9896811 | 15777172 |
| $V_2$ | 23.673 | 14.499 | 9.253 | 151642096 | 6405649 | 10458645 | 16387957 |
| Total | 22.257 | 14.117 | 9.184 | 606568384 | 27252711 | 42966797 | 66048341 |

**Table A.104:** Compression factors obtained for the data sets of 'Wind Tunnel II' by applying the wavelet compression. The Laplace operator was used in combination with a coarsening threshold of 0.5. Sizes of the un-/compressed data sets are also listed.

| | Compression factor | | | Orig. size | Compressed size | | |
| | 1e-03 | 1e-04 | 1e-05 | | 1e-03 | 1e-04 | 1e-05 |
|---|---|---|---|---|---|---|---|
| $P$ | 25.782 | 18.504 | 12.156 | 151642096 | 5881789 | 8195147 | 12474926 |
| $V_0$ | 17.638 | 11.051 | 7.540 | 151642096 | 8597368 | 13721527 | 20110865 |
| $V_1$ | 25.214 | 15.884 | 9.987 | 151642096 | 6014264 | 9547063 | 15183317 |
| $V_2$ | 24.100 | 15.027 | 9.609 | 151642096 | 6292124 | 10091226 | 15781403 |
| Total | 22.645 | 14.597 | 9.545 | 606568384 | 26785545 | 41554963 | 63550511 |

**Table A.105:** Compression factors obtained for the data sets of 'Wind Tunnel II' by applying the wavelet compression. The Laplace operator was used in combination with a coarsening threshold of 0.625. Sizes of the un-/compressed data sets are also listed.

| | Compression factor | | | Orig. size | Compressed size | | |
| | 1e-03 | 1e-04 | 1e-05 | | 1e-03 | 1e-04 | 1e-05 |
|---|---|---|---|---|---|---|---|
| $P$ | 25.459 | 18.632 | 12.425 | 151642096 | 5956320 | 8138929 | 12204261 |
| $V_0$ | 17.856 | 11.215 | 7.646 | 151642096 | 8492434 | 13521339 | 19833717 |
| $V_1$ | 25.065 | 16.058 | 10.149 | 151642096 | 6049876 | 9443568 | 14941884 |
| $V_2$ | 24.054 | 15.248 | 9.759 | 151642096 | 6304264 | 9944877 | 15538212 |
| Total | 22.631 | 14.777 | 9.702 | 606568384 | 26802894 | 41048713 | 62518074 |

**Table A.106:** Compression factors obtained for the data sets of 'Wind Tunnel II' by applying the wavelet compression. The Laplace operator was used in combination with a coarsening threshold of 0.75. Sizes of the un-/compressed data sets are also listed.

| | Compression factor | | | Orig. size | Compressed size | | |
| | 1e-03 | 1e-04 | 1e-05 | | 1e-03 | 1e-04 | 1e-05 |
|---|---|---|---|---|---|---|---|
| $P$ | 25.138 | 18.363 | 12.283 | 151642096 | 6032392 | 8257934 | 12345566 |
| $V_0$ | 17.679 | 11.134 | 7.604 | 151642096 | 8577581 | 13620293 | 19943231 |
| $V_1$ | 24.818 | 15.892 | 10.067 | 151642096 | 6110108 | 9542168 | 15063326 |
| $V_2$ | 23.856 | 15.117 | 9.693 | 151642096 | 6356609 | 10031036 | 15644201 |
| Total | 22.402 | 14.633 | 9.629 | 606568384 | 27076690 | 41451431 | 62996324 |

## Car Venting System

**Table A.107:** Compression factors obtained for the data sets of 'Car Venting System' by applying the wavelet compression. The Laplace operator was used in combination with a coarsening threshold of 0.125. Sizes of the un-/compressed data sets are also listed.

| | Compression factor | | | Orig. size | Compressed size | | |
| | 1e-03 | 1e-04 | 1e-05 | | 1e-03 | 1e-04 | 1e-05 |
|---|---|---|---|---|---|---|---|
| $\epsilon$ | 11.896 | 6.928 | 4.472 | 1620472 | 136220 | 233899 | 362357 |
| $P$ | 16.815 | 9.872 | 6.877 | 3240944 | 192742 | 328294 | 471270 |
| Pt | 69.497 | 39.887 | 24.307 | 3240944 | 46634 | 81253 | 133333 |
| TKE | 7.028 | 4.243 | 3.065 | 1620472 | 230565 | 381879 | 528688 |
| TVis | 6.483 | 3.958 | 2.808 | 1620472 | 249946 | 409460 | 577184 |
| $V_0$ | 6.117 | 3.995 | 2.865 | 1620472 | 264897 | 405604 | 565632 |
| $V_1$ | 6.248 | 3.967 | 2.825 | 1620472 | 259343 | 408496 | 573712 |
| $V_2$ | 6.174 | 3.975 | 2.835 | 1620472 | 262472 | 407708 | 571556 |
| Total | 9.864 | 6.100 | 4.283 | 16204720 | 1642819 | 2656593 | 3783732 |

**Table A.108:** Compression factors obtained for the data sets of 'Car Venting System' by applying the wavelet compression. The Laplace operator was used in combination with a coarsening threshold of 0.25. Sizes of the un-/compressed data sets are also listed.

| | Compression factor | | | Orig. size | Compressed size | | |
| | 1e-03 | 1e-04 | 1e-05 | | 1e-03 | 1e-04 | 1e-05 |
|---|---|---|---|---|---|---|---|
| $\epsilon$ | 11.930 | 6.939 | 4.475 | 1620472 | 135833 | 233517 | 362132 |
| $P$ | 16.916 | 9.912 | 6.899 | 3240944 | 191585 | 326976 | 469770 |
| Pt | 68.955 | 39.662 | 24.387 | 3240944 | 47001 | 81714 | 132895 |
| TKE | 7.036 | 4.245 | 3.066 | 1620472 | 230308 | 381738 | 528608 |
| TVis | 6.500 | 3.965 | 2.811 | 1620472 | 249300 | 408740 | 576436 |
| $V_0$ | 6.146 | 4.006 | 2.870 | 1620472 | 263653 | 404520 | 564616 |
| $V_1$ | 6.277 | 3.980 | 2.831 | 1620472 | 258146 | 407152 | 572368 |
| $V_2$ | 6.189 | 3.980 | 2.838 | 1620472 | 261812 | 407160 | 571044 |
| Total | 9.895 | 6.111 | 4.289 | 16204720 | 1637638 | 2651517 | 3777869 |

**Table A.109:** Compression factors obtained for the data sets of 'Car Venting System' by applying the wavelet compression. The Laplace operator was used in combination with a coarsening threshold of 0.375. Sizes of the un-/compressed data sets are also listed.

| | Compression factor | | | Orig. size | Compressed size | | |
| | 1e-03 | 1e-04 | 1e-05 | | 1e-03 | 1e-04 | 1e-05 |
|---|---|---|---|---|---|---|---|
| $\epsilon$ | 11.895 | 6.939 | 4.477 | 1620472 | 136227 | 233525 | 361941 |
| $P$ | 17.012 | 9.972 | 6.930 | 3240944 | 190514 | 324993 | 467638 |
| Pt | 69.094 | 39.539 | 24.347 | 3240944 | 46906 | 81968 | 133115 |
| TKE | 7.040 | 4.249 | 3.067 | 1620472 | 230183 | 381391 | 528336 |
| TVis | 6.507 | 3.967 | 2.812 | 1620472 | 249040 | 408520 | 576228 |
| $V_0$ | 6.173 | 4.019 | 2.876 | 1620472 | 262510 | 403188 | 563364 |
| $V_1$ | 6.301 | 3.990 | 2.836 | 1620472 | 257159 | 406164 | 571380 |
| $V_2$ | 6.220 | 3.992 | 2.844 | 1620472 | 260536 | 405912 | 569788 |
| Total | 9.923 | 6.125 | 4.296 | 16204720 | 1633075 | 2645661 | 3771790 |

**Table A.110:** Compression factors obtained for the data sets of 'Car Venting System' by applying the wavelet compression. The Laplace operator was used in combination with a coarsening threshold of 0.5. Sizes of the un-/compressed data sets are also listed.

| | Compression factor | | | Orig. size | Compressed size | | |
| | 1e-03 | 1e-04 | 1e-05 | | 1e-03 | 1e-04 | 1e-05 |
|---|---|---|---|---|---|---|---|
| $\epsilon$ | 11.856 | 6.912 | 4.468 | 1620472 | 136675 | 234439 | 362698 |
| $P$ | 16.914 | 9.929 | 6.910 | 3240944 | 191611 | 326403 | 468990 |
| Pt | 69.396 | 39.561 | 24.227 | 3240944 | 46702 | 81923 | 133773 |
| TKE | 7.018 | 4.239 | 3.065 | 1620472 | 230907 | 382319 | 528784 |
| TVis | 6.519 | 3.977 | 2.817 | 1620472 | 248573 | 407480 | 575160 |
| $V_0$ | 6.156 | 4.019 | 2.879 | 1620472 | 263229 | 403248 | 562924 |
| $V_1$ | 6.292 | 3.993 | 2.839 | 1620472 | 257550 | 405788 | 570864 |
| $V_2$ | 6.212 | 3.998 | 2.849 | 1620472 | 260880 | 405348 | 568800 |
| Total | 9.904 | 6.122 | 4.296 | 16204720 | 1636127 | 2646948 | 3771993 |

**Table A.111:** Compression factors obtained for the data sets of 'Car Venting System' by applying the wavelet compression. The Laplace operator was used in combination with a coarsening threshold of 0.625. Sizes of the un-/compressed data sets are also listed.

| | Compression factor | | | Orig. size | Compressed size | | |
| | 1e-03 | 1e-04 | 1e-05 | | 1e-03 | 1e-04 | 1e-05 |
|---|---|---|---|---|---|---|---|
| $\epsilon$ | 11.772 | 6.865 | 4.444 | 1620472 | 137654 | 236050 | 364613 |
| $P$ | 16.906 | 9.926 | 6.930 | 3240944 | 191706 | 326495 | 467678 |
| Pt | 67.093 | 39.390 | 24.201 | 3240944 | 48305 | 82278 | 133920 |
| TKE | 6.980 | 4.224 | 3.060 | 1620472 | 232171 | 382737 | 529555 |
| TVis | 6.520 | 3.980 | 2.819 | 1620472 | 248551 | 407124 | 574792 |
| $V_0$ | 6.139 | 4.011 | 2.876 | 1620472 | 263947 | 404008 | 563528 |
| $V_1$ | 6.292 | 4.002 | 2.844 | 1620472 | 257562 | 404952 | 569780 |
| $V_2$ | 6.202 | 4.001 | 2.850 | 1620472 | 261264 | 404996 | 568680 |
| Total | 9.874 | 6.118 | 4.295 | 16204720 | 1641160 | 2648640 | 3772546 |

**Table A.112:** Compression factors obtained for the data sets of 'Car Venting System' by applying the wavelet compression. The Laplace operator was used in combination with a coarsening threshold of 0.75. Sizes of the un-/compressed data sets are also listed.

| | Compression factor | | | Orig. size | Compressed size | | |
| | 1e-03 | 1e-04 | 1e-05 | | 1e-03 | 1e-04 | 1e-05 |
|---|---|---|---|---|---|---|---|
| $\epsilon$ | 11.737 | 6.861 | 4.444 | 1620472 | 138064 | 236196 | 364672 |
| $P$ | 16.878 | 9.910 | 6.912 | 3240944 | 192023 | 327043 | 468902 |
| Pt | 62.547 | 38.193 | 23.847 | 3240944 | 51816 | 84856 | 135904 |
| TKE | 6.969 | 4.224 | 3.058 | 1620472 | 232527 | 383665 | 529987 |
| TVis | 6.512 | 3.977 | 2.818 | 1620472 | 248831 | 407460 | 575076 |
| $V_0$ | 6.124 | 4.007 | 2.875 | 1620472 | 264627 | 404400 | 563580 |
| $V_1$ | 6.256 | 3.983 | 2.835 | 1620472 | 259011 | 406844 | 571560 |
| $V_2$ | 6.178 | 3.991 | 2.848 | 1620472 | 262300 | 406036 | 568888 |
| Total | 9.826 | 6.100 | 4.289 | 16204720 | 1649199 | 2656500 | 3778569 |

## Mixing Chamber I

**Table A.113:** Compression factors obtained for the data sets of 'Mixing Chamber I' by applying the wavelet compression. The Laplace operator was used in combination with a coarsening threshold of 0.125. Sizes of the un-/compressed data sets are also listed.

| | Compression factor | | | Orig. size | Compressed size | | |
| | 1e-03 | 1e-04 | 1e-05 | | 1e-03 | 1e-04 | 1e-05 |
|---|---|---|---|---|---|---|---|
| $\rho$ | 30.348 | 18.186 | 10.177 | 7451808 | 245549 | 409754 | 732217 |
| $w_{iso}$ | 19.586 | 10.875 | 7.001 | 7451808 | 380474 | 685204 | 1064371 |
| $w_{pol}$ | 19.725 | 10.894 | 7.002 | 7451808 | 377781 | 684016 | 1064237 |
| $c_{iso}$ | 19.922 | 11.006 | 7.058 | 7451808 | 374045 | 677079 | 1055867 |
| $c_{pol}$ | 19.991 | 11.019 | 7.059 | 7451808 | 372751 | 676240 | 1055714 |
| $P$ | 26.587 | 15.241 | 9.080 | 7451808 | 280275 | 488921 | 820690 |
| $P_s$ | 26.587 | 15.240 | 9.080 | 7451808 | 280277 | 488949 | 820642 |
| TVis | 19.140 | 10.385 | 6.821 | 7451808 | 389327 | 717553 | 1092551 |
| $V_0$ | 15.170 | 8.824 | 6.064 | 7451808 | 491219 | 844537 | 1228834 |
| $V_1$ | 15.174 | 8.796 | 6.046 | 7451808 | 491093 | 847150 | 1232442 |
| $V_2$ | 15.801 | 9.126 | 6.208 | 7451808 | 471590 | 816573 | 1200390 |
| Total | 19.731 | 11.174 | 7.211 | 81969888 | 4154381 | 7335976 | 11367955 |

**Table A.114:** Compression factors obtained for the data sets of 'Mixing Chamber I' by applying the wavelet compression. The Laplace operator was used in combination with a coarsening threshold of 0.25. Sizes of the un-/compressed data sets are also listed.

| | Compression factor | | | Orig. size | Compressed size | | |
| | 1e-03 | 1e-04 | 1e-05 | | 1e-03 | 1e-04 | 1e-05 |
|---|---|---|---|---|---|---|---|
| $\rho$ | 30.310 | 18.170 | 10.172 | 7451808 | 245853 | 410114 | 732589 |
| $w_{iso}$ | 19.570 | 10.869 | 6.999 | 7451808 | 380770 | 685616 | 1064735 |
| $w_{pol}$ | 19.707 | 10.888 | 7.000 | 7451808 | 378125 | 684384 | 1064605 |
| $c_{iso}$ | 19.907 | 10.999 | 7.055 | 7451808 | 374329 | 677475 | 1056227 |
| $c_{pol}$ | 19.970 | 11.013 | 7.056 | 7451808 | 373143 | 676620 | 1056070 |
| $P$ | 26.552 | 15.227 | 9.073 | 7451808 | 280651 | 489373 | 821318 |
| $P_s$ | 26.553 | 15.226 | 9.074 | 7451808 | 280641 | 489405 | 821262 |
| TVis | 19.134 | 10.384 | 6.820 | 7451808 | 389453 | 717617 | 1092563 |
| $V_0$ | 15.153 | 8.817 | 6.061 | 7451808 | 491783 | 845125 | 1229454 |
| $V_1$ | 15.162 | 8.791 | 6.044 | 7451808 | 491473 | 847646 | 1232978 |
| $V_2$ | 15.789 | 9.121 | 6.205 | 7451808 | 471957 | 816997 | 1200846 |
| Total | 19.713 | 11.167 | 7.208 | 81969888 | 4158178 | 7340372 | 11372647 |

**Table A.115:** Compression factors obtained for the data sets of 'Mixing Chamber I' by applying the wavelet compression. The Laplace operator was used in combination with a coarsening threshold of 0.375. Sizes of the un-/compressed data sets are also listed.

| | Compression factor | | | Orig. size | Compressed size | | |
| | 1e-03 | 1e-04 | 1e-05 | | 1e-03 | 1e-04 | 1e-05 |
|---|---|---|---|---|---|---|---|
| $\rho$ | 30.263 | 18.108 | 10.146 | 7451808 | 246233 | 411526 | 734485 |
| $w_{iso}$ | 19.503 | 10.840 | 6.986 | 7451808 | 382090 | 687444 | 1066679 |
| $w_{pol}$ | 19.636 | 10.859 | 6.987 | 7451808 | 379501 | 686248 | 1066553 |
| $c_{iso}$ | 19.837 | 10.970 | 7.042 | 7451808 | 375661 | 679307 | 1058171 |
| $c_{pol}$ | 19.898 | 10.983 | 7.043 | 7451808 | 374491 | 678476 | 1058010 |
| $P$ | 26.483 | 15.173 | 9.049 | 7451808 | 281379 | 491133 | 823506 |
| $P_s$ | 26.484 | 15.172 | 9.049 | 7451808 | 281365 | 491153 | 823454 |
| TVis | 19.098 | 10.370 | 6.814 | 7451808 | 390198 | 718592 | 1093624 |
| $V_0$ | 15.114 | 8.802 | 6.054 | 7451808 | 493047 | 846585 | 1230914 |
| $V_1$ | 15.117 | 8.774 | 6.036 | 7451808 | 492949 | 849294 | 1234614 |
| $V_2$ | 15.738 | 9.101 | 6.196 | 7451808 | 473503 | 818781 | 1202602 |
| Total | 19.655 | 11.139 | 7.195 | 81969888 | 4170417 | 7358539 | 11392612 |

**Table A.116:** Compression factors obtained for the data sets of 'Mixing Chamber I' by applying the wavelet compression. The Laplace operator was used in combination with a coarsening threshold of 0.5. Sizes of the un-/compressed data sets are also listed.

| | Compression factor | | | Orig. size | Compressed size | | |
| | 1e-03 | 1e-04 | 1e-05 | | 1e-03 | 1e-04 | 1e-05 |
|---|---|---|---|---|---|---|---|
| $\rho$ | 30.205 | 18.039 | 10.119 | 7451808 | 246709 | 413086 | 736453 |
| $w_{iso}$ | 19.432 | 10.809 | 6.973 | 7451808 | 383478 | 689436 | 1068691 |
| $w_{pol}$ | 19.571 | 10.828 | 6.974 | 7451808 | 380757 | 688220 | 1068553 |
| $c_{iso}$ | 19.764 | 10.938 | 7.029 | 7451808 | 377045 | 681267 | 1060159 |
| $c_{pol}$ | 19.834 | 10.951 | 7.030 | 7451808 | 375711 | 680444 | 1060006 |
| $P$ | 26.402 | 15.118 | 9.024 | 7451808 | 282247 | 492917 | 825786 |
| $P_s$ | 26.402 | 15.116 | 9.024 | 7451808 | 282241 | 492965 | 825734 |
| TVis | 19.043 | 10.350 | 6.805 | 7451808 | 391315 | 720014 | 1095117 |
| $V_0$ | 15.057 | 8.780 | 6.043 | 7451808 | 494904 | 848753 | 1233094 |
| $V_1$ | 15.057 | 8.752 | 6.025 | 7451808 | 494897 | 851442 | 1236750 |
| $V_2$ | 15.686 | 9.081 | 6.187 | 7451808 | 475062 | 820637 | 1204494 |
| Total | 19.590 | 11.108 | 7.181 | 81969888 | 4184366 | 7379181 | 11414837 |

**Table A.117:** Compression factors obtained for the data sets of 'Mixing Chamber I' by applying the wavelet compression. The Laplace operator was used in combination with a coarsening threshold of 0.625. Sizes of the un-/compressed data sets are also listed.

| | Compression factor | | | Orig. size | Compressed size | | |
| | 1e-03 | 1e-04 | 1e-05 | | 1e-03 | 1e-04 | 1e-05 |
|---|---|---|---|---|---|---|---|
| $\rho$ | 30.098 | 17.965 | 10.088 | 7451808 | 247581 | 414794 | 738677 |
| $w_{iso}$ | 19.351 | 10.774 | 6.958 | 7451808 | 385082 | 691628 | 1070923 |
| $w_{pol}$ | 19.483 | 10.793 | 6.959 | 7451808 | 382469 | 690452 | 1070805 |
| $c_{iso}$ | 19.679 | 10.903 | 7.014 | 7451808 | 378673 | 683471 | 1062419 |
| $c_{pol}$ | 19.744 | 10.916 | 7.015 | 7451808 | 377415 | 682676 | 1062266 |
| $P$ | 26.293 | 15.045 | 8.993 | 7451808 | 283419 | 495285 | 828582 |
| $P_s$ | 26.295 | 15.044 | 8.994 | 7451808 | 283389 | 495321 | 828522 |
| TVis | 19.005 | 10.332 | 6.796 | 7451808 | 392099 | 721236 | 1096432 |
| $V_0$ | 14.994 | 8.755 | 6.032 | 7451808 | 496983 | 851109 | 1235466 |
| $V_1$ | 14.999 | 8.730 | 6.015 | 7451808 | 496817 | 853618 | 1238950 |
| $V_2$ | 15.614 | 9.053 | 6.174 | 7451808 | 477254 | 823149 | 1207030 |
| Total | 19.511 | 11.073 | 7.165 | 81969888 | 4201181 | 7402739 | 11440072 |

**Table A.118:** Compression factors obtained for the data sets of 'Mixing Chamber I' by applying the wavelet compression. The Laplace operator was used in combination with a coarsening threshold of 0.75. Sizes of the un-/compressed data sets are also listed.

| | Compression factor | | | Orig. size | Compressed size | | |
| | 1e-03 | 1e-04 | 1e-05 | | 1e-03 | 1e-04 | 1e-05 |
|---|---|---|---|---|---|---|---|
| $\rho$ | 30.021 | 17.886 | 10.058 | 7451808 | 248221 | 416618 | 740885 |
| $w_{iso}$ | 19.269 | 10.740 | 6.944 | 7451808 | 386718 | 693824 | 1073119 |
| $w_{pol}$ | 19.396 | 10.758 | 6.945 | 7451808 | 384185 | 692660 | 1072997 |
| $c_{iso}$ | 19.596 | 10.868 | 7.000 | 7451808 | 380273 | 685671 | 1064619 |
| $c_{pol}$ | 19.659 | 10.880 | 7.001 | 7451808 | 379055 | 684888 | 1064466 |
| $P$ | 26.181 | 14.976 | 8.963 | 7451808 | 284627 | 497597 | 831382 |
| $P_s$ | 26.184 | 14.975 | 8.964 | 7451808 | 284597 | 497633 | 831330 |
| TVis | 18.937 | 10.306 | 6.785 | 7451808 | 393512 | 723081 | 1098333 |
| $V_0$ | 14.928 | 8.731 | 6.020 | 7451808 | 499168 | 853477 | 1237862 |
| $V_1$ | 14.930 | 8.704 | 6.002 | 7451808 | 499113 | 856094 | 1241466 |
| $V_2$ | 15.541 | 9.025 | 6.161 | 7451808 | 479508 | 825689 | 1209594 |
| Total | 19.429 | 11.036 | 7.149 | 81969888 | 4218977 | 7427232 | 11466053 |

## Mixing Chamber II

**Table A.119:** Compression factors obtained for the data sets of 'Mixing Chamber II' by applying the wavelet compression. The Laplace operator was used in combination with a coarsening threshold of 0.125. Sizes of the un-/compressed data sets are also listed.

| | Compression factor | | | Orig. size | Compressed size | | |
| | 1e-03 | 1e-04 | 1e-05 | | 1e-03 | 1e-04 | 1e-05 |
|---|---|---|---|---|---|---|---|
| $\rho$ | 9.339 | 6.339 | 4.786 | 14328232 | 1534270 | 2260192 | 2994037 |
| $P$ | 32.334 | 20.349 | 11.880 | 14328232 | 443131 | 704130 | 1206072 |
| $V_0$ | 16.122 | 9.317 | 6.292 | 14328232 | 888715 | 1537897 | 2277385 |
| $V_1$ | 16.422 | 9.486 | 6.378 | 14328232 | 872485 | 1510513 | 2246469 |
| $V_2$ | 16.532 | 9.617 | 6.447 | 14328232 | 866705 | 1489905 | 2222469 |
| Total | 15.556 | 9.549 | 6.545 | 71641160 | 4605306 | 7502637 | 10946432 |

**Table A.120:** Compression factors obtained for the data sets of 'Mixing Chamber II' by applying the wavelet compression. The Laplace operator was used in combination with a coarsening threshold of 0.25. Sizes of the un-/compressed data sets are also listed.

| | Compression factor | | | Orig. size | Compressed size | | |
| | 1e-03 | 1e-04 | 1e-05 | | 1e-03 | 1e-04 | 1e-05 |
|---|---|---|---|---|---|---|---|
| $\rho$ | 9.338 | 6.339 | 4.785 | 14328232 | 1534424 | 2260372 | 2994153 |
| $P$ | 32.416 | 20.306 | 11.831 | 14328232 | 442015 | 705606 | 1211072 |
| $V_0$ | 16.010 | 9.273 | 6.271 | 14328232 | 894963 | 1545197 | 2284669 |
| $V_1$ | 16.342 | 9.444 | 6.359 | 14328232 | 876781 | 1517169 | 2253301 |
| $V_2$ | 16.435 | 9.575 | 6.428 | 14328232 | 871809 | 1496401 | 2229089 |
| Total | 15.507 | 9.521 | 6.529 | 71641160 | 4619992 | 7524745 | 10972284 |

**Table A.121:** Compression factors obtained for the data sets of 'Mixing Chamber II' by applying the wavelet compression. The Laplace operator was used in combination with a coarsening threshold of 0.375. Sizes of the un-/compressed data sets are also listed.

| | Compression factor | | | Orig. size | Compressed size | | |
| | 1e-03 | 1e-04 | 1e-05 | | 1e-03 | 1e-04 | 1e-05 |
|---|---|---|---|---|---|---|---|
| $\rho$ | 9.331 | 6.336 | 4.783 | 14328232 | 1535492 | 2261564 | 2995464 |
| $P$ | 32.305 | 20.247 | 11.804 | 14328232 | 443532 | 707674 | 1213800 |
| $V_0$ | 15.976 | 9.260 | 6.266 | 14328232 | 896851 | 1547289 | 2286769 |
| $V_1$ | 16.296 | 9.431 | 6.353 | 14328232 | 879241 | 1519233 | 2255301 |
| $V_2$ | 16.397 | 9.561 | 6.422 | 14328232 | 873853 | 1498561 | 2231277 |
| Total | 15.477 | 9.509 | 6.523 | 71641160 | 4628969 | 7534321 | 10982611 |

**Table A.122:** Compression factors obtained for the data sets of 'Mixing Chamber II' by applying the wavelet compression. The Laplace operator was used in combination with a coarsening threshold of 0.5. Sizes of the un-/compressed data sets are also listed.

| | Compression factor | | | Orig. size | Compressed size | | |
| | 1e-03 | 1e-04 | 1e-05 | | 1e-03 | 1e-04 | 1e-05 |
|---|---|---|---|---|---|---|---|
| $\rho$ | 9.323 | 6.331 | 4.781 | 14328232 | 1536944 | 2263069 | 2996954 |
| $P$ | 32.174 | 20.162 | 11.769 | 14328232 | 445337 | 710642 | 1217444 |
| $V_0$ | 15.920 | 9.240 | 6.256 | 14328232 | 900011 | 1550717 | 2290229 |
| $V_1$ | 16.239 | 9.412 | 6.345 | 14328232 | 882321 | 1522257 | 2258357 |
| $V_2$ | 16.339 | 9.540 | 6.412 | 14328232 | 876916 | 1501989 | 2234737 |
| Total | 15.435 | 9.491 | 6.514 | 71641160 | 4641529 | 7548674 | 10997721 |

**Table A.123:** Compression factors obtained for the data sets of 'Mixing Chamber II' by applying the wavelet compression. The Laplace operator was used in combination with a coarsening threshold of 0.625. Sizes of the un-/compressed data sets are also listed.

| | Compression factor | | | Orig. size | Compressed size | | |
| | 1e-03 | 1e-04 | 1e-05 | | 1e-03 | 1e-04 | 1e-05 |
|---|---|---|---|---|---|---|---|
| $\rho$ | 9.313 | 6.327 | 4.778 | 14328232 | 1538588 | 2264775 | 2998759 |
| $P$ | 32.010 | 20.076 | 11.727 | 14328232 | 447616 | 713710 | 1221848 |
| $V_0$ | 15.861 | 9.217 | 6.246 | 14328232 | 903363 | 1554513 | 2294069 |
| $V_1$ | 16.169 | 9.387 | 6.333 | 14328232 | 886169 | 1526357 | 2262425 |
| $V_2$ | 16.278 | 9.516 | 6.401 | 14328232 | 880197 | 1505773 | 2238505 |
| Total | 15.387 | 9.470 | 6.504 | 71641160 | 4655933 | 7565128 | 11015606 |

**Table A.124:** Compression factors obtained for the data sets of 'Mixing Chamber II' by applying the wavelet compression. The Laplace operator was used in combination with a coarsening threshold of 0.75. Sizes of the un-/compressed data sets are also listed.

| | Compression factor | | | Orig. size | Compressed size | | |
| | 1e-03 | 1e-04 | 1e-05 | | 1e-03 | 1e-04 | 1e-05 |
|---|---|---|---|---|---|---|---|
| $\rho$ | 9.304 | 6.323 | 4.776 | 14328232 | 1539960 | 2266176 | 3000197 |
| $P$ | 31.858 | 19.976 | 11.684 | 14328232 | 449755 | 717258 | 1226356 |
| $V_0$ | 15.786 | 9.190 | 6.233 | 14328232 | 907679 | 1559181 | 2298769 |
| $V_1$ | 16.100 | 9.360 | 6.321 | 14328232 | 889973 | 1530713 | 2266869 |
| $V_2$ | 16.201 | 9.484 | 6.386 | 14328232 | 884425 | 1510781 | 2243609 |
| Total | 15.335 | 9.446 | 6.492 | 71641160 | 4671792 | 7584109 | 11035800 |

## Mixing Pipe

**Table A.125:** Compression factors obtained for the data sets of 'Mixing Pipe' by applying the wavelet compression. The Laplace operator was used in combination with a coarsening threshold of 0.125. Sizes of the un-/compressed data sets are also listed.

| | Compression factor | | | Orig. size | Compressed size | | |
| | 1e-03 | 1e-04 | 1e-05 | | 1e-03 | 1e-04 | 1e-05 |
|---|---|---|---|---|---|---|---|
| $H_s$ | 14.915 | 9.188 | 6.578 | 658712 | 44163 | 71692 | 100138 |
| $\rho$ | 15.098 | 9.238 | 6.655 | 658712 | 43629 | 71308 | 98986 |
| $\epsilon$ | 12.427 | 7.823 | 5.583 | 658712 | 53005 | 84203 | 117995 |
| $H$ | 14.915 | 9.188 | 6.578 | 658712 | 44163 | 71692 | 100138 |
| $P$ | 11.148 | 7.215 | 5.257 | 658712 | 59087 | 91299 | 125311 |
| $T$ | 14.915 | 9.188 | 6.578 | 658712 | 44163 | 71692 | 100138 |
| Pt | 34.044 | 36.967 | 24.430 | 658712 | 19349 | 17819 | 26963 |
| TKE | 10.514 | 6.857 | 5.054 | 658712 | 62651 | 96067 | 130327 |
| TVis | 9.005 | 6.142 | 4.657 | 658712 | 73151 | 107255 | 141459 |
| $V_0$ | 9.836 | 6.522 | 4.872 | 658712 | 66967 | 100995 | 135199 |
| $V_1$ | 11.023 | 7.159 | 5.233 | 658712 | 59757 | 92011 | 125883 |
| $V_2$ | 10.663 | 6.981 | 5.129 | 658712 | 61775 | 94363 | 128419 |
| Total | 12.510 | 8.146 | 5.939 | 7904544 | 631860 | 970396 | 1330956 |

**Table A.126:** Compression factors obtained for the data sets of 'Mixing Pipe' by applying the wavelet compression. The Laplace operator was used in combination with a coarsening threshold of 0.25. Sizes of the un-/compressed data sets are also listed.

| | Compression factor | | | Orig. size | Compressed size | | |
| | 1e-03 | 1e-04 | 1e-05 | | 1e-03 | 1e-04 | 1e-05 |
|---|---|---|---|---|---|---|---|
| $H_s$ | 14.832 | 9.159 | 6.568 | 658712 | 44413 | 71916 | 100292 |
| $\rho$ | 15.028 | 9.207 | 6.642 | 658712 | 43831 | 71543 | 99169 |
| $\epsilon$ | 12.346 | 7.789 | 5.565 | 658712 | 53356 | 84567 | 118359 |
| $H$ | 14.832 | 9.159 | 6.568 | 658712 | 44413 | 71916 | 100292 |
| $P$ | 11.090 | 7.190 | 5.244 | 658712 | 59399 | 91619 | 125603 |
| $T$ | 14.832 | 9.159 | 6.568 | 658712 | 44413 | 71916 | 100292 |
| Pt | 34.075 | 36.571 | 24.225 | 658712 | 19331 | 18012 | 27191 |
| TKE | 10.459 | 6.834 | 5.043 | 658712 | 62983 | 96391 | 130627 |
| TVis | 8.974 | 6.128 | 4.649 | 658712 | 73399 | 107499 | 141691 |
| $V_0$ | 9.795 | 6.502 | 4.861 | 658712 | 67251 | 101303 | 135519 |
| $V_1$ | 10.963 | 7.135 | 5.219 | 658712 | 60085 | 92323 | 126203 |
| $V_2$ | 10.637 | 6.971 | 5.123 | 658712 | 61927 | 94495 | 128575 |
| Total | 12.452 | 8.120 | 5.926 | 7904544 | 634801 | 973500 | 1333813 |

**Table A.127:** Compression factors obtained for the data sets of 'Mixing Pipe' by applying the wavelet compression. The Laplace operator was used in combination with a coarsening threshold of 0.375. Sizes of the un-/compressed data sets are also listed.

| | Compression factor | | | Orig. size | Compressed size | | |
| | 1e-03 | 1e-04 | 1e-05 | | 1e-03 | 1e-04 | 1e-05 |
|---|---|---|---|---|---|---|---|
| $H_s$ | 14.641 | 9.087 | 6.527 | 658712 | 44992 | 72488 | 100917 |
| $\rho$ | 14.840 | 9.137 | 6.603 | 658712 | 44388 | 72089 | 99763 |
| $\epsilon$ | 12.251 | 7.744 | 5.543 | 658712 | 53767 | 85063 | 118839 |
| $H$ | 14.641 | 9.087 | 6.527 | 658712 | 44992 | 72488 | 100917 |
| $P$ | 10.988 | 7.145 | 5.220 | 658712 | 59947 | 92191 | 126195 |
| $T$ | 14.641 | 9.087 | 6.527 | 658712 | 44992 | 72488 | 100917 |
| Pt | 33.872 | 36.349 | 24.012 | 658712 | 19447 | 18122 | 27433 |
| TKE | 10.376 | 6.798 | 5.023 | 658712 | 63487 | 96899 | 131147 |
| TVis | 8.934 | 6.109 | 4.638 | 658712 | 73727 | 107823 | 142023 |
| $V_0$ | 9.725 | 6.472 | 4.844 | 658712 | 67731 | 101779 | 135975 |
| $V_1$ | 10.865 | 7.090 | 5.196 | 658712 | 60629 | 92903 | 126767 |
| $V_2$ | 10.548 | 6.930 | 5.103 | 658712 | 62447 | 95055 | 129095 |
| Total | 12.340 | 8.071 | 5.899 | 7904544 | 640546 | 979388 | 1339988 |

**Table A.128:** Compression factors obtained for the data sets of 'Mixing Pipe' by applying the wavelet compression. The Laplace operator was used in combination with a coarsening threshold of 0.5. Sizes of the un-/compressed data sets are also listed.

| | Compression factor | | | Orig. size | Compressed size | | |
|---|---|---|---|---|---|---|---|
| | 1e-03 | 1e-04 | 1e-05 | | 1e-03 | 1e-04 | 1e-05 |
| $H_s$ | 14.557 | 9.043 | 6.503 | 658712 | 45251 | 72840 | 101295 |
| $\rho$ | 14.748 | 9.090 | 6.576 | 658712 | 44665 | 72468 | 100170 |
| $\epsilon$ | 12.221 | 7.733 | 5.537 | 658712 | 53900 | 85183 | 118955 |
| $H$ | 14.557 | 9.043 | 6.503 | 658712 | 45251 | 72840 | 101295 |
| $P$ | 10.926 | 7.116 | 5.203 | 658712 | 60291 | 92571 | 126591 |
| $T$ | 14.557 | 9.043 | 6.503 | 658712 | 45251 | 72840 | 101295 |
| Pt | 33.970 | 36.636 | 24.054 | 658712 | 19391 | 17980 | 27385 |
| TKE | 10.354 | 6.788 | 5.017 | 658712 | 63619 | 97035 | 131291 |
| TVis | 8.912 | 6.098 | 4.632 | 658712 | 73915 | 108015 | 142203 |
| $V_0$ | 9.680 | 6.451 | 4.832 | 658712 | 68051 | 102115 | 136315 |
| $V_1$ | 10.789 | 7.052 | 5.176 | 658712 | 61056 | 93403 | 127259 |
| $V_2$ | 10.489 | 6.902 | 5.087 | 658712 | 62803 | 95435 | 129487 |
| Total | 12.285 | 8.043 | 5.883 | 7904544 | 643444 | 982725 | 1343541 |

**Table A.129:** Compression factors obtained for the data sets of 'Mixing Pipe' by applying the wavelet compression. The Laplace operator was used in combination with a coarsening threshold of 0.625. Sizes of the un-/compressed data sets are also listed.

| | Compression factor | | | Orig. size | Compressed size | | |
|---|---|---|---|---|---|---|---|
| | 1e-03 | 1e-04 | 1e-05 | | 1e-03 | 1e-04 | 1e-05 |
| $H_s$ | 14.428 | 8.996 | 6.479 | 658712 | 45654 | 73224 | 101671 |
| $\rho$ | 14.624 | 9.042 | 6.552 | 658712 | 45044 | 72852 | 100531 |
| $\epsilon$ | 12.123 | 7.694 | 5.517 | 658712 | 54337 | 85611 | 119391 |
| $H$ | 14.428 | 8.996 | 6.479 | 658712 | 45654 | 73224 | 101671 |
| $P$ | 10.825 | 7.073 | 5.181 | 658712 | 60851 | 93127 | 127131 |
| $T$ | 14.428 | 8.996 | 6.479 | 658712 | 45654 | 73224 | 101671 |
| Pt | 33.975 | 36.579 | 23.862 | 658712 | 19388 | 18008 | 27605 |
| TKE | 10.267 | 6.752 | 4.998 | 658712 | 64159 | 97563 | 131803 |
| TVis | 8.856 | 6.072 | 4.617 | 658712 | 74379 | 108479 | 142659 |
| $V_0$ | 9.616 | 6.424 | 4.817 | 658712 | 68499 | 102535 | 136735 |
| $V_1$ | 10.719 | 7.023 | 5.160 | 658712 | 61452 | 93791 | 127651 |
| $V_2$ | 10.433 | 6.877 | 5.073 | 658712 | 63139 | 95787 | 129851 |
| Total | 12.194 | 8.005 | 5.862 | 7904544 | 648210 | 987425 | 1348370 |

**Table A.130:** Compression factors obtained for the data sets of 'Mixing Pipe' by applying the wavelet compression. The Laplace operator was used in combination with a coarsening threshold of 0.75. Sizes of the un-/compressed data sets are also listed.

| | Compression factor | | | Orig. size | Compressed size | | |
|---|---|---|---|---|---|---|---|
| | 1e-03 | 1e-04 | 1e-05 | | 1e-03 | 1e-04 | 1e-05 |
| $H_s$ | 14.303 | 8.946 | 6.453 | 658712 | 46053 | 73635 | 102077 |
| $\rho$ | 14.485 | 8.991 | 6.528 | 658712 | 45474 | 73261 | 100907 |
| $\epsilon$ | 12.042 | 7.657 | 5.498 | 658712 | 54701 | 86027 | 119819 |
| $H$ | 14.303 | 8.946 | 6.453 | 658712 | 46053 | 73635 | 102077 |
| $P$ | 10.758 | 7.043 | 5.165 | 658712 | 61231 | 93531 | 127531 |
| $T$ | 14.303 | 8.946 | 6.453 | 658712 | 46053 | 73635 | 102077 |
| Pt | 34.067 | 36.591 | 23.766 | 658712 | 19336 | 18002 | 27717 |
| TKE | 10.191 | 6.718 | 4.979 | 658712 | 64635 | 98047 | 132299 |
| TVis | 8.812 | 6.051 | 4.605 | 658712 | 74755 | 108855 | 143043 |
| $V_0$ | 9.545 | 6.391 | 4.799 | 658712 | 69011 | 103067 | 137267 |
| $V_1$ | 10.665 | 7.000 | 5.148 | 658712 | 61765 | 94095 | 127951 |
| $V_2$ | 10.375 | 6.849 | 5.057 | 658712 | 63491 | 96183 | 130251 |
| Total | 12.113 | 7.969 | 5.842 | 7904544 | 652558 | 991973 | 1353016 |

## A.4.2 Distance-based Operator

Since most results obtained when employing the distance-based operator were identical to those for the graph Laplace operator. The identical results will not be repeatedly listed. The reader is referred to the previous section.

### Car Venting System

**Table A.131:** Compression factors obtained for the data sets of 'Car Venting System' by applying the wavelet compression. The distance-based operator was used in combination with a coarsening threshold of 0.125. Sizes of the un-/compressed data sets are also listed.

| | Compression factor | | | Orig. size | Compressed size | | |
| | 1e-03 | 1e-04 | 1e-05 | | 1e-03 | 1e-04 | 1e-05 |
|---|---|---|---|---|---|---|---|
| $\epsilon$ | 11.823 | 6.830 | 4.430 | 1620472 | 137056 | 237254 | 365769 |
| $P$ | 17.198 | 10.128 | 7.038 | 3240944 | 188448 | 319998 | 460472 |
| Pt | 30.893 | 29.730 | 21.706 | 3240944 | 104907 | 109011 | 149312 |
| TKE | 6.955 | 4.224 | 3.047 | 1620472 | 232985 | 383628 | 531816 |
| TVis | 6.501 | 4.010 | 2.845 | 1620472 | 249255 | 404100 | 569516 |
| $V_0$ | 6.117 | 3.984 | 2.874 | 1620472 | 264908 | 406724 | 563772 |
| $V_1$ | 6.261 | 3.996 | 2.855 | 1620472 | 258840 | 405508 | 567560 |
| $V_2$ | 6.211 | 3.992 | 2.861 | 1620472 | 260916 | 405952 | 566404 |
| Total | 9,547 | 6,064 | 4,293 | 16204720 | 1697315 | 2672175 | 3774621 |

**Table A.132:** Compression factors obtained for the data sets of 'Car Venting System' by applying the wavelet compression. The distance-based operator was used in combination with a coarsening threshold of 0.25. Sizes of the un-/compressed data sets are also listed.

| | Compression factor | | | Orig. size | Compressed size | | |
| | 1e-03 | 1e-04 | 1e-05 | | 1e-03 | 1e-04 | 1e-05 |
|---|---|---|---|---|---|---|---|
| $\epsilon$ | 11.802 | 6.808 | 4.411 | 1620472 | 137306 | 238034 | 367339 |
| $P$ | 17.153 | 10.105 | 7.027 | 3240944 | 188946 | 320741 | 461204 |
| Pt | 30.920 | 29.617 | 21.626 | 3240944 | 104816 | 109427 | 149864 |
| TKE | 6.915 | 4.205 | 3.033 | 1620472 | 234356 | 385355 | 534212 |
| TVis | 6.482 | 3.984 | 2.825 | 1620472 | 249999 | 406712 | 573536 |
| $V_0$ | 6.087 | 3.958 | 2.856 | 1620472 | 266232 | 409400 | 567340 |
| $V_1$ | 6.254 | 3.988 | 2.844 | 1620472 | 259120 | 406344 | 569776 |
| $V_2$ | 6.187 | 3.970 | 2.842 | 1620472 | 261932 | 408144 | 570176 |
| Total | 9,517 | 6,037 | 4,272 | 16204720 | 1702707 | 2684157 | 3793447 |

**Table A.133:** Compression factors obtained for the data sets of 'Car Venting System' by applying the wavelet compression. The distance-based operator was used in combination with a coarsening threshold of 0.375. Sizes of the un-/compressed data sets are also listed.

| | Compression factor | | | Orig. size | Compressed size | | |
| | 1e-03 | 1e-04 | 1e-05 | | 1e-03 | 1e-04 | 1e-05 |
|---|---|---|---|---|---|---|---|
| $\epsilon$ | 11.642 | 6.725 | 4.364 | 1620472 | 139189 | 240971 | 371311 |
| $P$ | 16.944 | 9.949 | 6.954 | 3240944 | 191278 | 325744 | 466044 |
| Pt | 30.903 | 29.565 | 21.503 | 3240944 | 104876 | 109620 | 150720 |
| TKE | 6.838 | 4.162 | 3.008 | 1620472 | 236970 | 389343 | 538752 |
| TVis | 6.386 | 3.938 | 2.801 | 1620472 | 253737 | 411488 | 578472 |
| $V_0$ | 5.976 | 3.889 | 2.817 | 1620472 | 271164 | 416648 | 575192 |
| $V_1$ | 6.150 | 3.936 | 2.817 | 1620472 | 263512 | 411708 | 575160 |
| $V_2$ | 6.050 | 3.897 | 2.802 | 1620472 | 267852 | 415856 | 578228 |
| Total | 9.375 | 5.955 | 4.227 | 16204720 | 1728578 | 2721378 | 3833879 |

**Table A.134:** Compression factors obtained for the data sets of 'Car Venting System' by applying the wavelet compression. The distance-based operator was used in combination with a coarsening threshold of 0.5. Sizes of the un-/compressed data sets are also listed.

| | Compression factor | | | Orig. size | Compressed size | | |
| | 1e-03 | 1e-04 | 1e-05 | | 1e-03 | 1e-04 | 1e-05 |
|---|---|---|---|---|---|---|---|
| $\epsilon$ | 11.495 | 6.626 | 4.309 | 1620472 | 140973 | 244549 | 376042 |
| $P$ | 16.888 | 9.872 | 6.904 | 3240944 | 191913 | 328294 | 469428 |
| Pt | 30.905 | 29.644 | 21.565 | 3240944 | 104867 | 109330 | 150288 |
| TKE | 6.743 | 4.119 | 2.981 | 1620472 | 240314 | 393388 | 543628 |
| TVis | 6.307 | 3.906 | 2.785 | 1620472 | 256927 | 414872 | 581868 |
| $V_0$ | 5.895 | 3.844 | 2.792 | 1620472 | 274868 | 421584 | 580344 |
| $V_1$ | 6.084 | 3.896 | 2.797 | 1620472 | 266360 | 415912 | 579464 |
| $V_2$ | 5.977 | 3.857 | 2.782 | 1620472 | 271104 | 420160 | 582536 |
| Total | 9.274 | 5.897 | 4.194 | 16204720 | 1747326 | 2748089 | 3863598 |

**Table A.135:** Compression factors obtained for the data sets of 'Car Venting System' by applying the wavelet compression. The distance-based operator was used in combination with a coarsening threshold of 0.625. Sizes of the un-/compressed data sets are also listed.

| | Compression factor | | | Orig. size | Compressed size | | |
| | 1e-03 | 1e-04 | 1e-05 | | 1e-03 | 1e-04 | 1e-05 |
|---|---|---|---|---|---|---|---|
| $\epsilon$ | 11.387 | 6.559 | 4.273 | 1620472 | 142306 | 247075 | 379279 |
| $P$ | 16.745 | 9.804 | 6.867 | 3240944 | 193545 | 330587 | 471936 |
| Pt | 31.103 | 29.855 | 21.510 | 3240944 | 104201 | 108557 | 150672 |
| TKE | 6.651 | 4.080 | 2.958 | 1620472 | 243638 | 397206 | 547900 |
| TVis | 6.225 | 3.871 | 2.768 | 1620472 | 260325 | 418580 | 585396 |
| $V_0$ | 5.800 | 3.790 | 2.759 | 1620472 | 279388 | 427532 | 587428 |
| $V_1$ | 6.018 | 3.852 | 2.771 | 1620472 | 269292 | 420652 | 584720 |
| $V_2$ | 5.891 | 3.803 | 2.750 | 1620472 | 275096 | 426156 | 589232 |
| Total | 9.167 | 5.837 | 4.159 | 16204720 | 1767791 | 2776345 | 3896563 |

**Table A.136:** Compression factors obtained for the data sets of 'Car Venting System' by applying the wavelet compression. The distance-based operator was used in combination with a coarsening threshold of 0.75. Sizes of the un-/compressed data sets are also listed.

| | Compression factor | | | Orig. size | Compressed size | | |
| | 1e-03 | 1e-04 | 1e-05 | | 1e-03 | 1e-04 | 1e-05 |
|---|---|---|---|---|---|---|---|
| $\epsilon$ | 11.175 | 6.435 | 4.221 | 1620472 | 145003 | 251812 | 383894 |
| $P$ | 16.228 | 9.578 | 6.760 | 3240944 | 199717 | 338387 | 479456 |
| Pt | 31.503 | 30.126 | 21.350 | 3240944 | 102877 | 107578 | 151800 |
| TKE | 6.534 | 4.038 | 2.934 | 1620472 | 248025 | 401268 | 552320 |
| TVis | 6.082 | 3.812 | 2.738 | 1620472 | 266421 | 425048 | 591832 |
| $V_0$ | 5.656 | 3.718 | 2.717 | 1620472 | 286492 | 435832 | 596476 |
| $V_1$ | 5.851 | 3.771 | 2.727 | 1620472 | 276960 | 429752 | 594284 |
| $V_2$ | 5.771 | 3.742 | 2.717 | 1620472 | 280792 | 433044 | 596504 |
| Total | 8.971 | 5.741 | 4.106 | 16204720 | 1806287 | 2822721 | 3946566 |

## Mixing Pipe

**Table A.137:** Compression factors obtained for the data sets of 'Mixing Pipe' by applying the wavelet compression. The distance-based operator was used in combination with a coarsening threshold of 0.125. Sizes of the un-/compressed data sets are also listed.

| | Compression factor | | | Orig. size | Compressed size | | |
|---|---|---|---|---|---|---|---|
| | 1e-03 | 1e-04 | 1e-05 | | 1e-03 | 1e-04 | 1e-05 |
| $H_s$ | 14.715 | 9.107 | 6.537 | 658712 | 44764 | 72327 | 100769 |
| $\rho$ | 14.980 | 9.210 | 6.558 | 658712 | 43974 | 71520 | 100446 |
| $\epsilon$ | 12.356 | 7.793 | 5.570 | 658712 | 53313 | 84523 | 118259 |
| $H$ | 14.715 | 9.107 | 6.537 | 658712 | 44764 | 72327 | 100769 |
| $P$ | 11.064 | 7.181 | 5.240 | 658712 | 59535 | 91727 | 125699 |
| $T$ | 14.715 | 9.107 | 6.537 | 658712 | 44764 | 72327 | 100769 |
| Pt | 32.385 | 32.569 | 23.629 | 658712 | 20340 | 20225 | 27877 |
| TKE | 10.449 | 6.837 | 5.043 | 658712 | 63043 | 96339 | 130607 |
| TVis | 8.975 | 6.128 | 4.650 | 658712 | 73395 | 107487 | 141671 |
| $V_0$ | 9.796 | 6.503 | 4.862 | 658712 | 67243 | 101287 | 135483 |
| $V_1$ | 10.974 | 7.140 | 5.223 | 658712 | 60024 | 92259 | 126111 |
| $V_2$ | 10.642 | 6.974 | 5.126 | 658712 | 61895 | 94459 | 128511 |
| Total | 12.408 | 8.092 | 5.912 | 7904544 | 637054 | 976807 | 1336971 |

**Table A.138:** Compression factors obtained for the data sets of 'Mixing Pipe' by applying the wavelet compression. The distance-based operator was used in combination with a coarsening threshold of 0.25. Sizes of the un-/compressed data sets are also listed.

| | Compression factor | | | Orig. size | Compressed size | | |
|---|---|---|---|---|---|---|---|
| | 1e-03 | 1e-04 | 1e-05 | | 1e-03 | 1e-04 | 1e-05 |
| $H_s$ | 14.634 | 9.072 | 6.517 | 658712 | 45012 | 72607 | 101081 |
| $\rho$ | 14.896 | 9.173 | 6.538 | 658712 | 44222 | 71812 | 100758 |
| $\epsilon$ | 12.287 | 7.758 | 5.553 | 658712 | 53609 | 84903 | 118627 |
| $H$ | 14.634 | 9.072 | 6.517 | 658712 | 45012 | 72607 | 101081 |
| $P$ | 11.015 | 7.161 | 5.230 | 658712 | 59799 | 91991 | 125943 |
| $T$ | 14.634 | 9.072 | 6.517 | 658712 | 45012 | 72607 | 101081 |
| Pt | 32.404 | 32.481 | 23.454 | 658712 | 20328 | 20280 | 28085 |
| TKE | 10.397 | 6.814 | 5.031 | 658712 | 63355 | 96667 | 130919 |
| TVis | 8.949 | 6.116 | 4.643 | 658712 | 73607 | 107703 | 141867 |
| $V_0$ | 9.747 | 6.481 | 4.849 | 658712 | 67579 | 101643 | 135831 |
| $V_1$ | 10.930 | 7.120 | 5.214 | 658712 | 60268 | 92515 | 126347 |
| $V_2$ | 10.605 | 6.958 | 5.117 | 658712 | 62111 | 94675 | 128731 |
| Total | 12.353 | 8.066 | 5.897 | 7904544 | 639914 | 980010 | 1340351 |

**Table A.139:** Compression factors obtained for the data sets of 'Mixing Pipe' by applying the wavelet compression. The distance-based operator was used in combination with a coarsening threshold of 0.375. Sizes of the un-/compressed data sets are also listed.

| | Compression factor | | | Orig. size | Compressed size | | |
|---|---|---|---|---|---|---|---|
| | 1e-03 | 1e-04 | 1e-05 | | 1e-03 | 1e-04 | 1e-05 |
| $H_s$ | 14.470 | 9.011 | 6.487 | 658712 | 45524 | 73103 | 101537 |
| $\rho$ | 14.736 | 9.112 | 6.508 | 658712 | 44702 | 72288 | 101214 |
| $\epsilon$ | 12.215 | 7.725 | 5.536 | 658712 | 53925 | 85271 | 118987 |
| $H$ | 14.470 | 9.011 | 6.487 | 658712 | 45524 | 73103 | 101537 |
| $P$ | 10.912 | 7.116 | 5.205 | 658712 | 60367 | 92567 | 126551 |
| $T$ | 14.470 | 9.011 | 6.487 | 658712 | 45524 | 73103 | 101537 |
| Pt | 32.427 | 32.347 | 23.252 | 658712 | 20314 | 20364 | 28329 |
| TKE | 10.329 | 6.786 | 5.016 | 658712 | 63771 | 97067 | 131331 |
| TVis | 8.905 | 6.095 | 4.631 | 658712 | 73971 | 108075 | 142247 |
| $V_0$ | 9.682 | 6.452 | 4.833 | 658712 | 68035 | 102091 | 136291 |
| $V_1$ | 10.841 | 7.080 | 5.191 | 658712 | 60760 | 93035 | 126887 |
| $V_2$ | 10.531 | 6.927 | 5.101 | 658712 | 62551 | 95099 | 129139 |
| Total | 12.256 | 8.024 | 5.874 | 7904544 | 644968 | 985166 | 1345587 |

**Table A.140:** Compression factors obtained for the data sets of 'Mixing Pipe' by applying the wavelet compression. The distance-based operator was used in combination with a coarsening threshold of 0.5. Sizes of the un-/compressed data sets are also listed.

| | Compression factor | | | Orig. size | Compressed size | | |
| | 1e-03 | 1e-04 | 1e-05 | | 1e-03 | 1e-04 | 1e-05 |
|---|---|---|---|---|---|---|---|
| $H_s$ | 14.374 | 8.967 | 6.461 | 658712 | 45828 | 73463 | 101949 |
| $\rho$ | 14.624 | 9.062 | 6.483 | 658712 | 45042 | 72688 | 101610 |
| $\epsilon$ | 12.134 | 7.691 | 5.517 | 658712 | 54286 | 85651 | 119391 |
| $H$ | 14.374 | 8.967 | 6.461 | 658712 | 45828 | 73463 | 101949 |
| $P$ | 10.866 | 7.091 | 5.192 | 658712 | 60619 | 92895 | 126875 |
| $T$ | 14.374 | 8.967 | 6.461 | 658712 | 45828 | 73463 | 101949 |
| Pt | 32.492 | 32.257 | 23.229 | 658712 | 20273 | 20421 | 28357 |
| TKE | 10.269 | 6.759 | 5.000 | 658712 | 64147 | 97463 | 131739 |
| TVis | 8.869 | 6.079 | 4.621 | 658712 | 74271 | 108363 | 142535 |
| $V_0$ | 9.639 | 6.433 | 4.823 | 658712 | 68335 | 102391 | 136583 |
| $V_1$ | 10.766 | 7.046 | 5.173 | 658712 | 61187 | 93483 | 127339 |
| $V_2$ | 10.472 | 6.896 | 5.084 | 658712 | 62903 | 95515 | 129567 |
| Total | 12.188 | 7.990 | 5.856 | 7904544 | 648547 | 989259 | 1349843 |

**Table A.141:** Compression factors obtained for the data sets of 'Mixing Pipe' by applying the wavelet compression. The distance-based operator was used in combination with a coarsening threshold of 0.625. Sizes of the un-/compressed data sets are also listed.

| | Compression factor | | | Orig. size | Compressed size | | |
| | 1e-03 | 1e-04 | 1e-05 | | 1e-03 | 1e-04 | 1e-05 |
|---|---|---|---|---|---|---|---|
| $H_s$ | 14.208 | 8.896 | 6.421 | 658712 | 46362 | 74042 | 102592 |
| $\rho$ | 14.479 | 8.991 | 6.443 | 658712 | 45494 | 73264 | 102239 |
| $\epsilon$ | 12.026 | 7.642 | 5.490 | 658712 | 54772 | 86199 | 119983 |
| $H$ | 14.208 | 8.896 | 6.421 | 658712 | 46362 | 74042 | 102592 |
| $P$ | 10.794 | 7.067 | 5.179 | 658712 | 61027 | 93207 | 127199 |
| $T$ | 14.208 | 8.896 | 6.421 | 658712 | 46362 | 74042 | 102592 |
| Pt | 32.374 | 32.057 | 23.038 | 658712 | 20347 | 20548 | 28593 |
| TKE | 10.182 | 6.718 | 4.979 | 658712 | 64695 | 98055 | 132311 |
| TVis | 8.810 | 6.050 | 4.605 | 658712 | 74767 | 108875 | 143047 |
| $V_0$ | 9.581 | 6.406 | 4.807 | 658712 | 68755 | 102835 | 137019 |
| $V_1$ | 10.685 | 7.012 | 5.155 | 658712 | 61646 | 93935 | 127779 |
| $V_2$ | 10.409 | 6.870 | 5.070 | 658712 | 63283 | 95883 | 129927 |
| Total | 12.089 | 7.945 | 5.830 | 7904544 | 653872 | 994927 | 1355873 |

**Table A.142:** Compression factors obtained for the data sets of 'Mixing Pipe' by applying the wavelet compression. The distance-based operator was used in combination with a coarsening threshold of 0.75. Sizes of the un-/compressed data sets are also listed.

| | Compression factor | | | Orig. size | Compressed size | | |
| | 1e-03 | 1e-04 | 1e-05 | | 1e-03 | 1e-04 | 1e-05 |
|---|---|---|---|---|---|---|---|
| $H_s$ | 14.582 | 9.026 | 6.480 | 658712 | 45172 | 72982 | 101655 |
| $\rho$ | 14.709 | 9.124 | 6.506 | 658712 | 44783 | 72192 | 101251 |
| $\epsilon$ | 11.822 | 7.535 | 5.427 | 658712 | 55718 | 87423 | 121387 |
| $H$ | 14.582 | 9.026 | 6.480 | 658712 | 45172 | 72982 | 101655 |
| $P$ | 11.207 | 7.253 | 5.280 | 658712 | 58779 | 90815 | 124751 |
| $T$ | 14.582 | 9.026 | 6.480 | 658712 | 45172 | 72982 | 101655 |
| Pt | 32.457 | 32.376 | 24.209 | 658712 | 20295 | 20346 | 27209 |
| TKE | 10.093 | 6.668 | 4.949 | 658712 | 65263 | 98787 | 133103 |
| TVis | 8.894 | 6.091 | 4.628 | 658712 | 74063 | 108151 | 142323 |
| $V_0$ | 9.702 | 6.460 | 4.838 | 658712 | 67891 | 101967 | 136167 |
| $V_1$ | 10.836 | 7.086 | 5.195 | 658712 | 60788 | 92963 | 126787 |
| $V_2$ | 10.588 | 6.953 | 5.114 | 658712 | 62211 | 94735 | 128795 |
| Total | 12.249 | 8.014 | 5.869 | 7904544 | 645307 | 986325 | 1346738 |

# Acknowledgements

I would like to express my sincere gratitude to my doctoral advisor Prof. Dr. Trottenberg for the possibility to write this thesis at the Fraunhofer Institute for Algorithms and Scientific Computing. His personal and encouraging guidance has provided a good basis for completing the present thesis.

Special thanks go to Prof. Lorentz for the expert guidance and constructive suggestions throughout the course of this investigation. I am very appreciative to him for his continuous support and for the intensive discussions during my stays in Qatar. I thank him for having me as a guest.

I want to thank Prof. Dr. Tischendorf for reviewing this thesis and for her commitment to guide the doctoral seminar at the University of Cologne.

I also wish to express my appreciation to Mr. Thole for creating a working environment that let me complete this thesis in his department.

Furthermore, I thank my working group at the Fraunhofer Institute for their valuable comments and suggestions as well as for the recreational time spent together at the foosball table.